M000190413

Mastering Kubernetes

Automating container deployment and management

Gigi Sayfan

BIRMINGHAM - MUMBAI

Mastering Kubernetes

Copyright © 2017 Packt Publishing

All rights reserved. No part of this book may be reproduced, stored in a retrieval system, or transmitted in any form or by any means, without the prior written permission of the publisher, except in the case of brief quotations embedded in critical articles or reviews.

Every effort has been made in the preparation of this book to ensure the accuracy of the information presented. However, the information contained in this book is sold without warranty, either express or implied. Neither the author nor Packt Publishing, and its dealers and distributors will be held liable for any damages caused or alleged to be caused directly or indirectly by this book.

Packt Publishing has endeavored to provide trademark information about all of the companies and products mentioned in this book by the appropriate use of capitals. However, Packt Publishing cannot guarantee the accuracy of this information.

First published: May 2017

Production reference: 1180517

Published by Packt Publishing Ltd.
Livery Place
35 Livery Street
Birmingham B3 2PB, UK.

ISBN 978-1-78646-100-1

www.packtpub.com

Credits

Author
Gigi Sayfan

Reviewer
Jakub Pavlik

Acquisition Editor
Rahul Nair

Content Development Editor
Trusha Shriyan

Technical Editor
Varsha Shivhare

Copy Editor
Safis Editing

Project Coordinator
Kinjal Bari

Proofreader
Safis Editing

Indexer
Tejal Daruwale Soni

Graphics
Kirk D'Penha

Production Coordinator
Aparna Bhagat

Cover Work
Aparna Bhagat

About the Author

Gigi Sayfan is a principal software architect at Helix — a bioinformatics and genomics start-up. Gigi has been developing software professionally for more than 20 years in domains as diverse as instant messaging, morphing, chip fabrication process control, embedded multimedia applications for game consoles, brain-inspired machine learning, custom browser development, web services for 3D distributed game platforms, and most recently IoT sensors and virtual reality.

He has written production code in many programming languages such as Go, Python, C, C++, C#, Python, Java, Delphi, JavaScript, and even Cobol and PowerBuilder for operating systems such as Windows (3.11 through 7), Linux, Mac OSX, Lynx (embedded), and Sony PlayStation. His technical expertise includes databases, low-level networking, distributed systems, unorthodox user interfaces, and general software development life cycle.

About the Reviewer

Jakub Pavlik is a co-founder, former CTO, and chief architect of TCP Cloud (acquired by Mirantis in 2016). Jakub and his team worked for several years on the IaaS Cloud platform based on the OpenStack-salt and OpenContrail projects, which they deployed and operated for global service providers. Leveraging his skills from architecture implementation and operation, his TCP Cloud team was acquired by the no. 1 pure play OpenStack company, Mirantis.

Currently, as director of product engineering, together with other skilled professional teams, he collaborates on a new Mirantis Cloud platform for NFV/SDN, IoT, and big data use cases based on Kubernetes, containerized OpenStack, and OpenContrail. He is also a member of the OpenContrail advisory board.

He is also an enthusiast of Linux OS, ice hockey and films, and loves his wife Hanulka.

www.PacktPub.com

eBooks, discount offers, and more

Did you know that Packt offers eBook versions of every book published, with PDF and ePub files available? You can upgrade to the eBook version at www.PacktPub.com and as a print book customer, you are entitled to a discount on the eBook copy. Get in touch with us at customercare@packtpub.com for more details.

At www.PacktPub.com, you can also read a collection of free technical articles, sign up for a range of free newsletters and receive exclusive discounts and offers on Packt books and eBooks.

https://www.packtpub.com/mapt

Get the most in-demand software skills with Mapt. Mapt gives you full access to all Packt books and video courses, as well as industry-leading tools to help you plan your personal development and advance your career.

Why subscribe?

- Fully searchable across every book published by Packt
- Copy and paste, print, and bookmark content
- On demand and accessible via a web browser

Customer Feedback

Thanks for purchasing this Packt book. At Packt, quality is at the heart of our editorial process. To help us improve, please leave us an honest review on this book's Amazon page at https://www.amazon.com/dp/1786461005.

If you'd like to join our team of regular reviewer, you can e-mail us at customerreviews@packtpub.com. We award our regular reviewer with free eBooks and videos in exchange for their valuable feedback. Help us be relentless in improving our products!

Table of Contents

Preface

Mastering Kubernetes is focused on the design and management of Kubernetes clusters. It covers in detail all the capabilities and services provided by Kubernetes for developers and DevOps engineers and developers who need to collaborate to build and evolve complex distributed systems using container orchestration. The book takes the reader through the steps of creating large-scale systems and deploying them on Kubernetes, considering various environments and use cases. Over the course of this journey, you will gain in-depth knowledge of how Kubernetes is organized, when it is appropriate to use certain resources, and how to implement and configure clusters in the most effective way. Via hands-on tasks and exercises, you will develop a deep understanding of Kubernetes architecture, how to install clusters, operate them, upgrade them, and how to deploy software using best practices.

What this book covers

Chapter 1, Understanding Kubernetes Architecture, briefly introduces the main objectives of this book and container orchestration in distributed systems. It takes the reader through the fundamental guiding principles used to build Kubernetes, and covers the design in detail.

Chapter 2, Creating Kubernetes Clusters, is a hands-on chapter in which the user will create several Kubernetes clusters using different tools that vary from quick test clusters to full-fledged industrial strength clusters.

Chapter 3, Monitoring, Logging, and Troubleshooting, explains approaches to event monitoring, logging events, and metric collection from Kubernetes clusters. This will let the reader identify and analyze patterns in cluster behavior.

Chapter 4, High Availability and Reliability, introduces best practices for highly available architectures. Kubernetes can be configured in a variety of ways for high availability and considers cost/performance tradeoffs, live upgrades, and performance bottlenecks.

Chapter 5, Configuring Kubernetes Security, Limits, and Accounts, gives the reader insight into how to secure Kubernetes for production via SSL API, add-ons, Docker authentication, and so on. It explores various security topics, digging deeper into admission control, interfaces to external authorization systems, and namespaces.

Chapter 6, Using Critical Kubernetes Resources, in this chapter, you will participate in the design of a complex microservice-based system. It will consist of a walkthrough deployment of Kubernetes resources, where each resource will be mapped to its counterpart in the application structure or configuration.

Chapter 7, Handling Kubernetes Storage, in this chapter, the reader will be given an explanation of persistent volumes in Kubernetes. The reader will be taken through different storage types in Kubernetes, mapped to specific use cases.

Chapter 8, Running Stateful Applications with Kubernetes, explains problems users will face when running legacy monolithic stateful applications and services such as databases, message queues, and so on. This chapter also introduces environmental shared variables and DNS records for clustering stateful applications.

Chapter 9, Rolling Updates, Scalability, and Quotas, explains advanced Kubernetes features such as horizontal pod auto scaling, cluster size, and rolling updates. It also covers Kubernetes scaling testing and tooling for stress testing.

Chapter 10, Advanced Kubernetes Networking, explains container network interfaces for third-party SDN plugins. It covers in detail CNI plugins, load balancing, and network security policies.

Chapter 11, Running Kubernetes on Multiple Clouds and Cluster Federation, explains how to deploy Kubernetes clusters in production on several specific platforms (bare metal, AWS, GCE). It also explains the need for cluster federation in real world.

Chapter 12, Customizing Kubernetes - APIs and Plugins, explains how to work with Kubernetes at the API level, as well as use cases and motivation to develop third-party resources. The reader will also be introduced to the types of plugins that Kubernetes supports and how to develop custom plugins.

Chapter 13, Handling the Kubernetes Package Manager, explains how to handle Kubernetes applications as packages. It discusses how to find and install existing Helm packages, as well as how to write your own Helm charts.

Chapter 14, The Future of Kubernetes, peers into the future and presents a roadmap and trends for Kubernetes, as well as its position in the orchestration scene and a comparison with its competitors.

What you need for this book

To follow along with the examples in each chapter, you need a recent version of Docker and Kubernetes installed on your machine, ideally Kubernetes 1.6. If your operating system is Windows 10 Professional, you can enable the hypervisor mode, otherwise you will need to install VirtualBox and use a Linux guest OS.

Who this book is for

The book is for system administrators and developers who have intermediate level knowledge with Kubernetes and are now waiting to master its advanced features. You should also have basic networking knowledge. This advanced-level book provides a pathway to mastering Kubernetes.

Conventions

In this book, you will find a number of text styles that distinguish between different kinds of information. Here are some examples of these styles and an explanation of their meaning.

Code words in text, database table names, folder names, filenames, file extensions, pathnames, dummy URLs, user input, and Twitter handles are shown as follows: "The naming convention is <category>/<metrics name> (except for uptime, which has a single metric)."

A block of code is set as follows:

```
type Runtime interface {
  Type() string

  Version() (Version, error)

  APIVersion() (Version, error)

  Status() error

  GetPods(all bool) ([]*Pod, error)
```

Any command-line input or output is written as follows:

```
GET /api/v1/pods
```

New terms and **important words** are shown in bold. Words that you see on the screen, for example, in menus or dialog boxes, appear in the text like this: "The **Username** and **Password** are `root` and `root` by default."

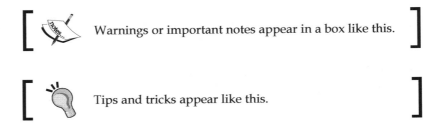

Warnings or important notes appear in a box like this.

Tips and tricks appear like this.

Reader feedback

Feedback from our readers is always welcome. Let us know what you think about this book—what you liked or disliked. Reader feedback is important for us as it helps us develop titles that you will really get the most out of.

To send us general feedback, simply e-mail `feedback@packtpub.com`, and mention the book's title in the subject of your message.

If there is a topic that you have expertise in and you are interested in either writing or contributing to a book, see our author guide at `www.packtpub.com/authors`.

Customer support

Now that you are the proud owner of a Packt book, we have a number of things to help you to get the most from your purchase.

Downloading the color images of this book

We also provide you with a PDF file that has color images of the screenshots/diagrams used in this book. The color images will help you better understand the changes in the output. You can download this file from `http://www.packtpub.com/sites/default/files/downloads/MasteringKubernetes _ColorImages.pdf`.

Errata

Although we have taken every care to ensure the accuracy of our content, mistakes do happen. If you find a mistake in one of our books—maybe a mistake in the text or the code—we would be grateful if you could report this to us. By doing so, you can save other readers from frustration and help us improve subsequent versions of this book. If you find any errata, please report them by visiting http://www.packtpub.com/submit-errata, selecting your book, clicking on the **Errata Submission Form** link, and entering the details of your errata. Once your errata are verified, your submission will be accepted and the errata will be uploaded to our website or added to any list of existing errata under the Errata section of that title.

To view the previously submitted errata, go to https://www.packtpub.com/books/content/support and enter the name of the book in the search field. The required information will appear under the **Errata** section.

Piracy

Piracy of copyrighted material on the Internet is an ongoing problem across all media. At Packt, we take the protection of our copyright and licenses very seriously. If you come across any illegal copies of our works in any form on the Internet, please provide us with the location address or website name immediately so that we can pursue a remedy.

Please contact us at copyright@packtpub.com with a link to the suspected pirated material.

We appreciate your help in protecting our author and our ability to bring you valuable content.

Questions

If you have a problem with any aspect of this book, you can contact us at questions@packtpub.com, and we will do our best to address the problem.

Understanding Kubernetes Architecture

1

Kubernetes is a big open source project with a lot of code and a lot of functionality. You have probably read about Kubernetes, and maybe even dipped your toes in and used it in a side project or maybe even at work. But to understand what Kubernetes is all about, how to use it effectively, and what the best practices are, requires much more. In this chapter, we will build together the foundation necessary to utilize Kubernetes to its full potential. We will start by understanding what container orchestration means. Then we will cover important Kubernetes concepts that will form the vocabulary we will use throughout the book. After that, we will dive into the architecture of Kubernetes proper and look at how it enables all the capabilities Kubernetes provides to its users. Then, we will discuss the various runtimes and container engines that Kubernetes supports (Docker is just one option), and finally, we will discuss the role of Kubernetes in the full continuous integration and deployment pipeline.

At the end of this chapter, you will have a solid understanding of container orchestration, what problems Kubernetes addresses, the rationale for Kubernetes design and architecture, and the different runtime it supports. You'll also be familiar with the overall structure of the open source repository and be ready to jump in and find answers to any question.

Understanding container orchestration

The primary responsibility of Kubernetes is container orchestration. That means making sure that all the containers that execute various workloads are scheduled to run physical or virtual machines. The containers must be packed efficiently following the constraints of the deployment environment and the cluster configuration. In addition, Kubernetes must keep an eye on all running containers and replace dead, unresponsive, or otherwise unhealthy containers. Kubernetes provides many more capabilities that you will learn about in the following chapters. In this section, the focus is on containers and their orchestration.

Physical machines, virtual machines, and containers

It all starts and ends with hardware. In order to run your workloads, you need some real hardware provisioned. That includes actual physical machines, with certain compute capabilities (CPUs or cores), memory, and some local persistent storage (spinning disks or SSDs). In addition, you will need some shared persistent storage and to hook up all these machines using networking so they can find and talk to each other. At this point, you run multiple virtual machines on the physical machines or stay at the bare-metal level (no virtual machines). Kubernetes can be deployed on a bare-metal cluster (real hardware) or on a cluster of virtual machines. Kubernetes in turn can orchestrate the containers it manages directly on bare-metal or on virtual machines. In theory, a Kubernetes cluster can be composed of a mix of bare-metal and virtual machines, but this is not very common.

Containers in the cloud

Containers are ideal to package microservices because, while providing isolation to the microservice, they are very lightweight and you don't incur a lot of overhead when deploying many microservices as you do with virtual machines. That makes containers ideal for cloud deployment, where allocating a whole virtual machine for each microservice would be cost prohibitive.

All major cloud providers, such as AWS, GCE, and Azure, provide container hosting services these days. Some of them, such as Google's GKE, are based on Kubernetes. Others, such as Microsoft Azure's container service, are based on other solutions (Apache Mesos). By the way, AWS has the ECS (the containers service over EC2), which uses their own orchestration solution. The great thing about Kubernetes is that it can be deployed on all those clouds. Kubernetes has a cloud provider interface that allows any cloud provider to implement it and integrate Kubernetes seamlessly.

Cattle versus pets

In the olden days, when systems were small, each server had a name. Developers and users knew exactly what software was running on each machine. I remember that, in many of the companies I worked for, we had multi-day discussions to decide on a naming theme for our servers. For example, composers and Greek mythology characters were popular choices. Everything was very cozy. You treated your servers like beloved pets. When a server died it was a major crisis. Everybody scrambled to try to figure out where to get another server, what was even running on the dead server, and how to get it working on the new server. If the server stored some important data, then hopefully you had an up-to-date backup and maybe you'd even be able to recover it.

Obviously, that approach doesn't scale. When you have a few tens or hundreds of servers, you must start treating them like cattle. You think about the collective and not individuals. You may still have some pets (that is, your build machines), but your web servers are just cattle.

Kubernetes takes the cattle approach to the extreme and takes full responsibility for allocating containers to specific machines. You don't need to interact with individual machines (nodes) most of the time. This works best for stateless workloads. For stateful applications, the situation is a little different, but Kubernetes provides a solution called StatefulSet, which we'll discuss soon.

In this section, we covered the idea of container orchestration and discussed the relationships between hosts (physical or virtual) and containers, as well as the benefits of running containers in the cloud, and finished with a discussion about cattle versus pets. In the following section, we will get to know the world of Kubernetes and learn its concepts and terminology.

Kubernetes concepts

In this section, I'll briefly introduce many important Kubernetes concepts and give you some context as to why they are needed and how they interact with other concepts. The goal is to get familiar with these terms and concepts. Later, we will see how these concepts are woven together to achieve awesomeness. You can consider many of these concepts as building blocks. Some of the concepts, such as node and master, are implemented as a set of Kubernetes components. These components are at a different abstraction level, and I discuss them in detail in a dedicated section, *Kubernetes components*.

Here is the famous Kubernetes architecture diagram:

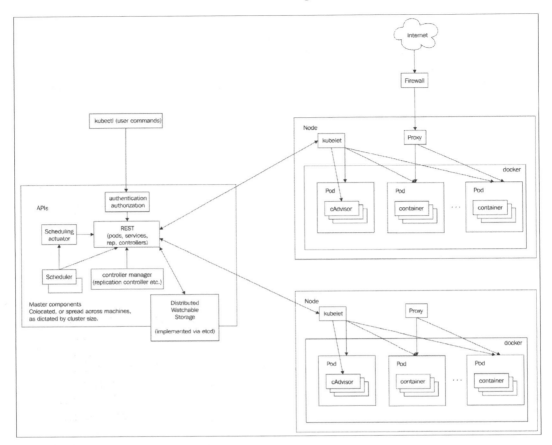

Cluster

A cluster is a collection of hosts storage and networking resources that Kubernetes uses to run the various workloads that comprise your system. Note that your entire system may consist of multiple clusters. We will discuss this advanced use case of federation in detail later.

Node

A node is a single host. It may be a physical or virtual machine. Its job is to run pods. Each Kubernetes node runs several Kubernetes components, such as a kubelet and a kube proxy. Nodes are managed by a Kubernetes master. The nodes are worker bees of Kubernetes and shoulder all the heavy lifting. In the past they were called **minions**. If you read some old documentation or articles, don't get confused. Minions are nodes.

Master

The master is the control plane of Kubernetes. It consists of several components, such as an API server, a scheduler, and a controller manager. The master is responsible for the global, cluster-level scheduling of pods and handling of events. Usually, all the master components are set up on a single host. When considering high-availability scenarios or very large clusters, you will want to have master redundancy. I will discuss highly available clusters in detail in *Chapter 4, High Availability and Scaling*.

Pod

A pod is the unit of work in Kubernetes. Each pod contains one or more containers. Pods are always scheduled together (always run on the same machine). All the containers in a pod have the same IP address and port space; they can communicate using localhost or standard inter-process communication. In addition, all the containers in a pod can have access to shared local storage on the node hosting the pod. The shared storage will be mounted on each container. Pods are important feature of Kubernetes. It is possible to run multiple applications inside a single Docker container by having something like supervisor as the main Docker application that runs multiple processes, but this practice is often frowned upon, for the following reasons:

- **Transparency**: Making the containers within the pod visible to the infrastructure enables the infrastructure to provide services to those containers, such as process management and resource monitoring. This facilitates a number of conveniences for users.

- **Decoupling software dependencies**: The individual containers may be versioned, rebuilt, and redeployed independently. Kubernetes may even support live updates of individual containers someday.

- **Ease of use**: Users don't need to run their own process managers, worry about signal and exit-code propagation, and so on.

- **Efficiency**: Because the infrastructure takes on more responsibility, containers can be more lightweight.

Pods provide a great solution for managing groups of closely related containers that depend on each other and need to co-operate on the same host to accomplish their purpose. It's important to remember that pods are considered ephemeral, throwaway entities that can be discarded and replaced at will. Any pod storage is destroyed with its pod. Each pod gets a unique ID (UID), so you can still distinguish between them if necessary.

Label

Labels are key-value pairs that are used to group together sets of objects, very often pods. This is important for several other concepts, such as replication controller, replica sets, and services that operate on dynamic groups of objects and need to identify the members of the group. There is a NxN relationship between objects and labels. Each object may have multiple labels, and each label may be applied to different objects. There are certain restrictions by design on labels. Each label on an object must have a unique key. The label key must adhere to a strict syntax. It has two parts: prefix and name. The prefix is optional. If it exists then it is separated from the name by a forward slash (/) and it must be a valid DNS sub-domain. The prefix must be 253 characters long at most. The name is mandatory and must be 63 characters long at most. Names must start and end with an alphanumeric character (a-z, A-Z, 0-9) and contain only alphanumeric characters, dots, dashes, and underscores. Values follow the same restrictions as names. Note that labels are dedicated for identifying objects and not for attaching arbitrary metadata to objects. This is what annotations are for (see the following section).

Annotation

Annotations let you associate arbitrary metadata with Kubernetes objects. Kubernetes just stores the annotations and makes their metadata available. Unlike labels, they don't have strict restrictions about allowed characters and size limits. In my experience, you always need such metadata for complicated systems, and it is nice that Kubernetes recognizes this need and provides it out of the box so you don't have to come up with your own separate metadata store and mapping object to their metadata.

We've covered most, if not all, of Kubernetes' concepts; there are a few more I mentioned briefly. In the next section, we will continue our journey into Kubernetes architecture by looking into its design motivations, the internals and implementation, and even pick at the source code.

Label selector

Label selectors are used to select objects based on their labels. Equality-based selectors specify a key name and a value. There are two operators, `=` (or `==`) and `!=`, for equality or inequality based on the value. For example:

```
role = webserver
```

This will select all objects that have that label key and value.

Label selectors can have multiple requirements separated by a comma. For example:

```
role = webserver, application != foo
```

Set-based selectors extend the capabilities and allow selection based on multiple values:

```
role in (webserver, backend)
```

Replication controller and replica set

Replication controllers and replica sets both manage a group of pods identified by a label selector and ensure that a certain number is always up and running. The main difference between them is that replication controllers test for membership by name equality and replica sets can use set-based selection. Replica sets are newer and designated as the next-generation replication controllers. They are still in beta and are not fully supported by all the tools at the time of writing. Hopefully, by the time you read this, they will be full-fledged members.

Kubernetes guarantees that you will always have the same number of pods running as you specified in a replication controller or a replica set. Whenever the number drops due to a problem with the hosting node or the pod itself, Kubernetes will fire up new instances. Note that, if you manually start pods and exceed the specified number, the replication controller will kill some extra pods.

Replication controllers used to be central to many workflows, such as rolling updates and running one-off jobs. As Kubernetes evolved, it introduced direct support for many of these workflows, with dedicated objects such as Deployment, Job, and DaemonSet. We will meet them all later.

Service

Services are used to expose some functionality to users or other services. They usually encompass a group of pods, usually identified by – you guessed it – a label. You can have services that provide access to external resources, or to pods you control directly at the virtual IP level. Native Kubernetes services are exposed through convenient endpoints. Note that services operate at layer 3 (TCP/UDP). Kubernetes 1.2 added the Ingress object, which provides access to HTTP objects. More on that later. Services are published or discovered via one of two mechanisms: DNS, or environment variables. Services can be load-balanced by Kubernetes. But, developers can choose to manage load balancing themselves in case of services that use external resources or require special treatment.

There are many gory details associated with IP addresses, virtual IP addresses, and port spaces. We will discuss them in depth in a future chapter.

Volume

Local storage on the pod is ephemeral and goes away with the pod. Sometimes that's all you need, if the goal is just to exchange data between containers of the node, but sometimes it's important for the data to outlive the pod, or it's necessary to share data between pods. The volume concept supports that need. Note that, while Docker has a volume concept too, it is quite limited (although getting more powerful). Kubernetes uses its own separate volumes. Kubernetes also supports additional container types such as rkt, so it couldn't rely on Docker volumes even in principle.

There are many volume types. Kubernetes currently directly supports each volume type. In the future, another layer of indirection may be added and an abstract volume plugin may be developed. The `emptyDir` volume type mounts a volume on each container that is backed by default by whatever is available on the hosting machine. You can request a memory medium if you want. This storage is deleted when the pod is terminated for any reason. There are many volume types for specific cloud environments, various networked filesystems, and even Git repositories. An interesting volume type is the `persistentDiskClaim`, which abstracts the details a little bit and uses the default persistent storage in your environment (typically in a cloud provider).

StatefulSet

Pods come and go, and if you care about their data then you can use persistent storage. That's all good. But sometimes you want Kubernetes to manage a distributed data store such as Kubernetes or MySQL Galera. These clustered stores keep the data distributed across uniquely identified nodes. You can't model that with regular pods and services. Enter StatefulSet. If you remember earlier, I discussed pets versus cattle and how cattle is the way to go. Well, StatefulSet sits somewhere in the middle. StatefulSet ensures (similar to a replication controller) that a given number of pets with unique identities are running at any given time. Pets have the following properties:

- A stable hostname, available in DNS
- An ordinal index
- Stable storage linked to the ordinal and hostname

StatefulSet can help with peer discovery as well as adding or removing pets.

Secret

Secrets are small objects that contain sensitive info such as credentials and tokens. They are stored as plaintext in etcd, accessible by the Kubernetes API server, and can be mounted as files into pods (using dedicated secret volumes that piggyback on regular data volumes) that need access to them. The same secret can be mounted into multiple pods. Kubernetes itself creates secrets for its components, and you can create your own secrets. Another approach is to use secrets as environment variables. Note that secrets in a pod are always stored in memory (tmpfs in the case of mounted secrets) for better security.

Name

Each object in Kubernetes is identified by a UID and a name. The name is used to refer to the object in API calls. Names should be up to 253 characters long and use lowercase alphanumeric characters, dash (-) and dot (.). If you delete an object, you can create another object with the same name as the deleted object, but the UIDs must be unique across the lifetime of the cluster. The UIDs are generated by Kubernetes, so you don't have to worry about it.

Namespace

A namespace is a virtual cluster. You can have a single physical cluster that contains multiple virtual clusters segregated by namespaces. Each virtual cluster is totally isolated from other virtual clusters, and they can only communicate through public interfaces. Note that Node objects and persistent volumes don't live in a namespace. Kubernetes may schedule pods from different namespaces to run on the same node. Likewise, pods from different namespaces can use the same persistent storage.

When using namespaces, you have to consider network policies and resource quotas to ensure proper access and distribution of the physical cluster resources.

Diving into Kubernetes architecture in depth

Kubernetes has very ambitious goals. It aims to manage and simplify the orchestration, deployment, and management of distributed systems across a wide range of environments and cloud providers. It provides many capabilities and services that should work across all that diversity, while evolving and remaining simple enough for mere mortals to use. This is a tall order. Kubernetes achieves this by following a crystal-clear, high-level design and well-thought-out architecture that promotes extensibility and pluggability. Many parts of Kubernetes are still hard-coded or environment-aware, but the trend is to refactor them into plugins and keep the core generic and abstract. In this section, we will peel Kubernetes like an onion, starting with the various distributed systems design patterns and how Kubernetes supports them, then go over the surface of Kubernetes, which is its set of APIs, and then take a look at the actual components that comprise Kubernetes. Finally, we will take a quick tour of the source-code tree to gain even better insight into the structure of Kubernetes itself.

At the end of this section, you will have a solid understanding of Kubernetes architecture and implementation, and why certain design decisions were made.

Distributed systems design patterns

All happy (working) distributed systems are alike, to paraphrase Tolstoy in Anna Karenina. That means that, to function properly, all well-designed distributed systems must follow some best practices and principles. Kubernetes doesn't want to be just a management system. It wants to support and enable these best practices and provide high-level services to developers and administrators. Let's look at some of those described as design patterns.

Sidecar pattern

The sidecar pattern is about co-locating another container in a pod in addition to the main application container. The application container is unaware of the sidecar container and just goes about its business. A great example is a central logging agent. Your main container can just log to stdout, but the sidecar container will send all logs to a central logging service where they will be aggregated with the logs from the entire system. The benefits of using a sidecar container versus adding central logging to the main application container are enormous. First, applications are not burdened anymore with central logging, which could be a nuisance. If you want to upgrade or change your central logging policy or switch to a totally new provider, you just need to update the sidecar container and deploy it. None of your application containers change, so you can't break them by accident.

Ambassador pattern

The ambassador pattern is about representing a remote service as if it were local and possibly enforcing some policy. A good example of the ambassador pattern is if you have a Redis cluster with one master for writes and many replicas for reads. A local ambassador container can serve as a proxy and expose Redis to the main application container on the localhost. The main application container simply connects to Redis on localhost:6379 (Redis default port), but it connects to the ambassador running in the same pod, which filters the requests, and sends write requests to the real Redis master and read requests randomly to one of the read replicas. Just like with the sidecar pattern, the main application has no idea what's going on. That can help a lot when testing against a real local Redis. Also, if the Redis cluster configuration changes, only the ambassador needs to be modified; the main application remains blissfully unaware.

Adapter pattern

The adapter pattern is about standardizing output from the main application container. Consider the case of a service that is being rolled out incrementally: it may generate reports in a format that doesn't conform to the previous version. Other services and applications that consume that output haven't been upgraded yet. An adapter container can be deployed in the same pod with the new application container and massage their output to match the old version until all consumers have been upgraded. The adapter container shares the filesystem with the main application container, so it can watch the local filesystem, and whenever the new application writes something, it immediately adapts it.

Multi-node patterns

The single-node patterns are all supported directly by Kubernetes via pods. Multi-node patterns such as leader election, work queues, and scatter-gather are not supported directly, but composing pods with standard interfaces to accomplish them is a viable approach with Kubernetes.

The Kubernetes APIs

If you want to understand the capabilities of a system and what it provides, you must pay a lot of attention to its API. The API provides a comprehensive view of what you can do with the system as a user. Kubernetes exposes several sets of REST APIs for different purposes and audiences. Some of the APIs are used primarily by tools and some can be used directly by developers. An important aspect of the APIs is that they are under constant development. The Kubernetes developers keep it manageable by trying to extend (adding new objects and new fields to existing objects) and avoid renaming or dropping existing objects and fields. In addition, all API endpoints are versioned, and often have an alpha or beta notation too. For example:

`/api/v1`

`/api/v2alpha1`

You can access the API through the `kubectl cli`, via client libraries, or directly through REST API calls. There are elaborate authentication and authorization mechanism we will explore in a later chapter. At this point, let's get a glimpse into the surface area of the APIs.

Kubernetes API

This is the main API of Kubernetes. It is huge. All the concepts we discussed before, and many auxiliary concepts, have corresponding API objects and operations. If you have the right permissions you can list, get, create, and update objects. Here is a detailed documentation of one of the most common operations, get a list of all the pods:

`GET /api/v1/pods`

It accepts various query parameters (all optional):

* `pretty`: If `true`, the output is pretty printed
* `labelSelector`: A selector expression to limit the result
* `watch`: If `true`, watch for changes and return a stream of events

- `resourceVersion`: With `watch`, returns only events that occurred after that version
- `timeoutSeconds`: Timeout for the list or watch operation

Autoscaling API

The autoscaling API is very focused and lets you control the horizontal pod `autoscaler`, which manages a group of pods based on CPU utilization and even application-specific metrics. You can list, query, create, update, and destroy `autoscaler` objects using the `/apis/autoscaling/v1` endpoint.

Batch API

The batch API lets you manage jobs. Jobs are pods that perform some activity and terminate. Unlike regular pods managed by a replication controller, they are supposed to terminate when the job is done. The batch API uses the pod template to specify jobs and then allows you, as usual, to list, query, create, and delete jobs through the `/apis/batch/v1` endpoint.

Kubernetes components

A Kubernetes cluster has several master components used to control the cluster, as well as node components that run on each cluster node. Let's get to know all these components and how they work together.

Master components

The master components typically run on one node, but in a highly available or very large cluster, they may be spread across multiple nodes.

API server

The kube API server exposes the Kubernetes REST API. It can easily scale horizontally as it is stateless and stores all the data in the `etcd` cluster. The API server is the embodiment of the Kubernetes control plane.

Etcd

Etcd is a highly reliable distributed data store. Kubernetes uses it to store the entire cluster state. In small, transient cluster a single instance of etcd can run on the same node with all the other master components. But, for more substantial clusters it is typical to have a 3-node or even 5-node etcd cluster for redundancy and high availability.

Controller manager

The controller manager is a collection of various managers rolled up into one binary. It contains the replication controller, the pod controller, the services controller, the endpoints controller, and others. All these managers watch over the state of the cluster via the API and their job is to steer the cluster into the desired state.

Scheduler

The kube-scheduler is responsible for scheduling pods into nodes. This is a very complicated task as it needs to consider multiple interacting factors, such as the following:

- Resource requirements
- Service requirements
- Hardware/software policy constraints
- Affinity and anti-affinity specifications
- Data locality
- Deadlines

DNS

Starting with Kubernetes 1.3, a DNS service is part of the standard Kubernetes cluster. It is scheduled as a regular pod. Every service (except headless services) receives a DNS name. Pods can receive a DNS name too. This is very useful for automatic discovery.

Node components

Nodes in the cluster need a couple of components to interact with the cluster master components, receive workloads to execute, and update the cluster on their status.

Proxy

The kube proxy does low-level network housekeeping on each node. It reflects the Kubernetes services locally and can do TCP and UDP forwarding. It finds cluster IPs via environment variables or DNS.

Kubelet

The kubelet is the Kubernetes representative on the node. It oversees communicating with the master components and manage the running pods. That includes the following:

- Download pod secrets from the API server
- Mount volumes
- Run the pod's container (Docker or Rkt)
- Report the status of the node and each pod
- Run container liveness probes

In this section, we dug into the guts of Kubernetes and explored its architecture from a very high level of vision and supported design patterns, through its APIs and the components used to control and manage the cluster. In the next section, we will take a quick look at the various runtimes that Kubernetes supports.

Kubernetes runtimes

Kubernetes originally only supported Docker as a container runtime engine. But that is no longer the case. Rkt is another supported runtime engine and there are interesting attempts to work with Hyper.sh containers via Hypernetes. A major design policy is that Kubernetes itself should be completely decoupled from specific runtimes. The interaction between Kubernetes and the runtime is through a relatively generic interface that runtime engines must implement. Most of the communication is using the pod and container concepts and the operations that can be performed on a container. Each runtime engine is responsible for implementing the Kubernetes runtime interface to be compatible.

In this section, you'll get a closer look at the runtime interface and get to know the individual runtime engines. At the end of this section, you'll be able to make a well-informed decision about which runtime engine is appropriate for your use case and under what circumstances you may switch or even combine multiple runtimes in the same system.

The runtime interface

The runtime interface for containers is specified in the Kubernetes project on GitHub. Kubernetes is open source, so we can look at it at the following URL:

`https://github.com/kubernetes/kubernetes/blob/master/pkg/kubelet/container/runtime.go`.

I'll present here snippets from this file without the elaborate comments. Even if you're not a full-fledged programmer and know nothing about the Go language, you should be able to grasp the scope and responsibilities of a runtime engine from the viewpoint of Kubernetes:

 A quick note about Go to help you parse the code: The method name comes first, followed by the method's parameters in parentheses. Each parameter is a pair, consisting of a name followed by its type. Finally, the return values are specified. Go allows multiple return types. It is very common to return an `error` object in addition to the actual result. If everything is OK, the `error` object will be nil.

```go
type Runtime interface {
  Type() string

  Version() (Version, error)

  APIVersion() (Version, error)

  Status() error

  GetPods(all bool) ([]*Pod, error)
}
```

The fact that it is an interface means that Kubernetes doesn't provide an implementation. The first group of methods provides general information about the runtime: `Type`, `Version`, `APIVersion`, and `Status`. You can also get all the pods:

```go
SyncPod(pod *api.Pod, apiPodStatus api.PodStatus, podStatus
*PodStatus, pullSecrets []api.Secret, backOff
*flowcontrol.Backoff) PodSyncResult

KillPod(pod *api.Pod, runningPod Pod, gracePeriodOverride *int64)
error
```

```
GetPodStatus(uid types.UID, name, namespace string) (*PodStatus,
error)

GetNetNS(containerID ContainerID) (string, error)

GetPodContainerID(*Pod) (ContainerID, error)

GetContainerLogs(pod *api.Pod, containerID ContainerID, logOptions
*api.PodLogOptions, stdout, stderr io.Writer) (err error)

DeleteContainer(containerID ContainerID) error
```

The next group of methods deal mostly with pods appropriately as this is
the main abstraction in the Kubernetes conceptual model. Then there is the
GetPodContainerID(), which gets you from a container to a pod, and a few more
container-related methods:

- ContainerCommandRunner
- ContainerAttacher
- ImageService

The last three items, ContainerCommandRunner, ContainerAttacher, and
ImageService, are interfaces that the runtime interface inherits. This means that
whoever implements the runtime interface also needs to implement the methods of
these interfaces. The interfaces are defined in the same file. Just the interface names
provide a lot of information about what they do. Kubernetes obviously needs to
run commands in containers, and it needs to attach containers to its pods and pull
container images. I encourage you to pursue this file and get familiar with the code.

Now that you are familiar at the code level with what Kubernetes considers as a
runtime engine, let's look at the individual runtime engines briefly.

Docker

Docker is, of course, the 800 pound gorilla of containers. Kubernetes was originally
designed to manage only Docker containers. The multi-runtime capability was first
introduced in Kubernetes 1.3. Until then, Kubernetes could only manage Docker
containers.

I assume you're very familiar with Docker and what it brings to the table if you are reading this book. Docker enjoys tremendous popularity and growth, but there is also a lot of criticism toward it. Critics often mention the following concerns:

- Security
- Difficulty setting up multi-container applications (in particular, networking)
- Development, monitoring, and logging
- Limitations of Docker containers running one command
- Releasing half-based features too fast

Docker is aware of the criticisms and has addressed some of these concerns. In particular, Docker invested in its Docker swarm product. Docker swarm is a Docker-native orchestration solution that competes with Kubernetes. It is simpler to use than Kubernetes, but it's not as powerful or mature.

 Starting with Docker 1.12, swarm mode is included in the Docker Daemon natively, which upset some people due to bloat and scope creep. That in turn made more people turn to CoreOS rkt as an alternative solution.

Starting with Docker 1.11, released on April 2016, Docker has changed the way it runs containers. The runtime now uses `containerd` and `runC` to run **Open Container Initiative (OCI)** images in containers:

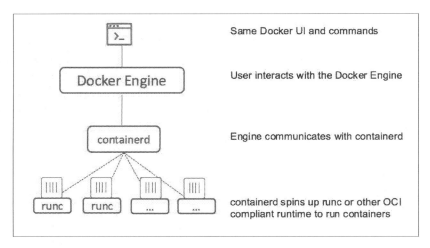

Rkt

Rkt is a new container manager from CoreOS (developers of the CoreOS Linux distro, etcd, flannel, and more). The rkt runtime prides itself on its simplicity and strong emphasis on security and isolation. It doesn't have a Daemon like the Docker engine and relies on the OS init system, such as `systemd`, to launch the rkt executable. Rkt can download images (both **App Container (appc)** images and OCI images), verify them, and run them in containers. Its architecture is much simpler.

App container

CoreOS started a standardization effort in December 2014 called appc. This includes standard image format (ACI), runtime, signing, and discovery. A few months later, Docker started its own standardization effort with OCI. At this point it seems these efforts will converge. This is a great thing as tools, images, and runtime will be able to interoperate freely. We're not there yet.

Rktnetes

Rktnetes is Kubernetes plus rkt as the runtime engine. Kubernetes is still in the process of abstracting away the runtime engine. Rktnetes is not really a separate product. From the outside, all it takes is running the kubelet on each node with a couple of command-line switches. But, since there are fundamental differences between Docker and rkt, you may run into a variety of issues.

Is rkt ready for production usage?

The integration between rkt and Kubernetes is not totally seamless; there are still some rough spots. My recommendation at this stage (late 2016) is to prefer Docker unless you have a very specific reason to use rkt. If you decide that it's important for your use case to use rkt then you should base your cluster on CoreOS. It is most likely that you will find the best integration with the CoreOS cluster, as well as the best documentation and online support.

Hyper containers

Hyper containers are another option. A Hyper container has a lightweight VM (its own guest kernel) and it runs on bare metal. Instead of relying on Linux cgroups for isolation, it relies on a hypervisor. This approach presents an interesting mix compared to standard bare-metal clusters that are difficult to set up and public clouds where containers are deployed on heavyweight VMs.

Hypernetes

Hypernetes is a multi-tenant Kubernetes distribution that uses Hyper containers as well as some OpenStack components for authentication, persistent storage, and networking. Since containers don't share the host kernel, it is safe to run containers of different tenants on the same physical host:

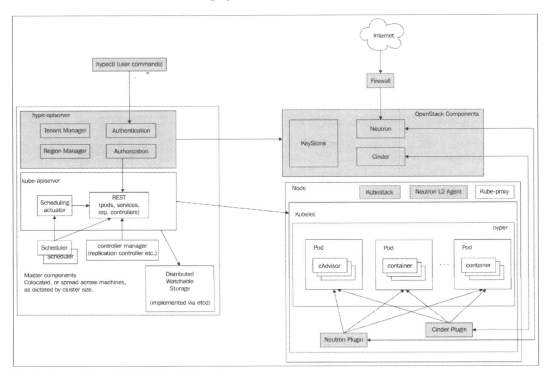

In this section, we've covered the various runtime engines that Kubernetes supports as well as the trend toward standardization and convergence. In the next section, we'll take a step back and look at the big picture, and how Kubernetes fits into the CI/CD pipeline.

Continuous integration and deployment

Kubernetes is a great platform for running your microservice-based applications. But, at the end of the day, it is an implementation detail. Users, and often most developers, may not be aware that the system is deployed on Kubernetes. But Kubernetes can change the game and make things that were too difficult before possible.

In this section, we'll explore the CI/CD pipeline and what Kubernetes brings to the table. At the end of this section you'll be able to design CI/CD pipelines that take advantage of Kubernetes properties such as easy-scaling and development-production parity to improve the productivity and robustness of day-to-day development and deployment.

What is a CI/CD pipeline?

A CI/CD pipeline is a set of steps that a set of changes by developers or operators that modify the code, data or configuration of a system, test them and deploys them to production. Some pipelines are fully automated and some are semi-automated with human checks. In large organizations, there may be test and staging environments where changes are deployed to automatically, but release to production requires manual intervention. The following diagram describes a typical pipeline.

It may be worth mentioning that developers can be completely isolated from production infrastructure. Their interface is just a Git workflow, where a good example is Deis Workflow (PaaS on Kubernetes, similar to Heroku):

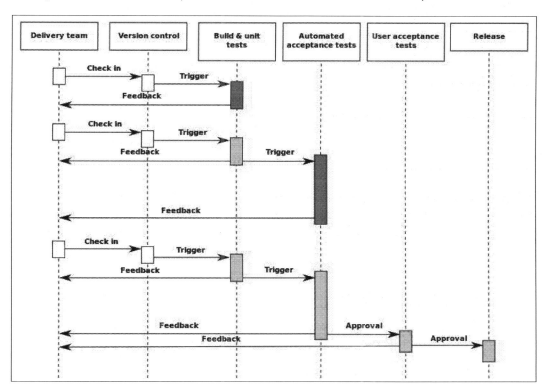

Designing a CI/CD pipeline for Kubernetes

When your deployment target is a Kubernetes cluster, you should rethink some traditional practices. For starters, packaging is different. You need to bake images for your containers. Reverting code changes is super easy and instantaneous by using smart labeling. It gives you a lot of confidence that, if a bad change slips through the testing net, somehow you'll be able to revert to the previous version immediately. But you want to be careful there. Schema changes and data migrations can't be automatically rolled back. Another unique capability of Kubernetes is that developers can run a whole cluster locally. That takes some work when you design your cluster, but since the microservices that comprise your system run in containers, and those containers interact via APIs, it is possible and practical to do. As always, if your system is very data-driven, you will need to accommodate for that and provide data snapshots and synthetic data that your developers can use.

Summary

In this chapter, we covered a lot of ground, and you got to understand the design and architecture of Kubernetes. Kubernetes is an orchestration platform for microservice-based applications running as containers. Kubernetes clusters have master and worker nodes. Containers run within pods. Each pod runs on a single physical or virtual machine. Kubernetes directly supports many concepts, such as services, labels, and persistent storage. You can implement various distributed systems design patterns on Kubernetes. The containers themselves may be Docker, rkt, or Hyper containers.

In *Chapter 2*, *Creating Kubernetes Clusters*, we will explore the various ways to create Kubernetes clusters, discuss when to use different options, and build a multi-node cluster.

2
Creating Kubernetes Clusters

In the previous chapter, we learned what Kubernetes is all about, how it is designed, what concepts it supports, its runtime engines, and how it fits within the CI/CD pipeline.

Creating a Kubernetes cluster is a non-trivial task. There are many options and tools to select from. There are many factors to consider. In this chapter, we'll roll up our sleeves and build Kubernetes clusters. We will also discuss and evaluate tools such as Minikube and kubeadm, and deployment environments such as local, cloud, and bare metal. The topics we will cover are as follows:

- Creating a single-node cluster with Minikube
- Creating multi-node cluster using kubeadm
- Creating clusters in the cloud
- Creating bare-metal clusters from scratch

At the end of this chapter, you will have a solid understanding of the various options to create Kubernetes clusters and knowledge of the best-of-breed tools to support the creation of Kubernetes clusters, and you will also build a couple of clusters, both single-node and multi-node.

Quick single-node cluster with Minikube

In this section, we will create a single-node cluster on Windows. The reason we will target Windows is that Minikube and single-node clusters are most useful for local developer machines. While Kubernetes is typically deployed on Linux in production, many developers work on Windows PCs or Macs. That said, there aren't too many differences if you do want to install Minikube on Linux:

Getting ready

There are some pre-requisites to install before you can create the cluster itself. These include VirtualBox, the kubectl command-line interface to Kubernetes, and of course, Minikube itself. Here is a list of the latest versions at the time of writing:

- **VirtualBox**: http://download.virtualbox.org/virtualbox/5.1.8/ VirtualBox-5.1.8-111374-Win.exe

- **Kubectl**: http://storage.googleapis.com/kubernetes-release/ release/v1.4.0/bin/windows/amd64/kubectl.exe

- **Minikube**: https://storage.googleapis.com/minikube/releases/ v0.12.2/minikube-windows-amd64.exe

With Windows 10 Pro you have the option to use the Hyper-V hypervisor. This is technically a better solution than VirtualBox, but it requires the Pro version of Windows and is completely Windows-specific. By using VirtualBox, these instructions are universal and will be easy to adapt to other versions of Windows, or other operating systems altogether. If you have Hyper-V enabled, you must disable it because VirtualBox can't co-exist with Hyper-V.

Install VirtualBox and make sure kubectl and Minikube are on your path. I personally just throw all command-line programs I use into c:\windows. You may prefer another approach. On Windows, I use the excellent ConEMU to manage multiple consoles, terminals, and SSH sessions. It works with cmd.exe, PowerShell, PuTTY, Cygwin, msys, and Git-Bash. It doesn't get much better than that on Windows.

We'll use PowerShell in administrator mode for the rest of this chapter. I added the following alias and function to my PowerShell profile:

```
Set-Alias -Name k -Value kubectl
function mk
{
minikube-windows-amd64 `
--show-libmachine-logs `
--alsologtostderr      `
@args
}
```

Now I can use k and mk and type less. The flags to Minikube in the mk function provide better logging that way and direct it to the console in addition to files (similar to tee).

Type mk version to verify Minikube is correctly installed and functioning:

```
> mk version
```

```
minikube version: v0.12.2
```

Type k version to verify kubectl is correctly installed and functioning:

```
> k version
```

```
Client Version: version.Info{Major:"1", Minor:"4",
GitVersion:"v1.4.0", GitCommit:"a16c0a7f71a6f93c7e0f222d961f4675c
d97a46b", GitTreeState:"clean", BuildDate:"2016-09-26T18:16:57Z",
GoVersion:"go1.6.3", Compiler:"gc", Platform:"windows/amd64"}
```

```
Unable to connect to the server: dial tcp [::1]:8080: connectex: No
connection could be made because the target machine actively refused it.
```

Don't worry about the error on the last line. There is no cluster running, so kubectl can't connect to anything. That's expected.

You can explore the available commands and flags for both Minikube and kubectl. I will not go over each and every one, only the commands I use.

Creating the cluster

The Minikube tool supports multiple versions of Kubernetes. At the time of writing, this is the list of supported versions:

```
> mk get-k8s-versions
```

The following Kubernetes versions are available:

```
- v1.5.0-alpha.0
- v1.4.3
- v1.4.2
- v1.4.1
- v1.4.0
- v1.3.7
- v1.3.6
- v1.3.5
- v1.3.4
- v1.3.3
- v1.3.0
```

I will go with 1.4.3, the latest stable release. Let's create the cluster by using the start command and specifying v1.4.3 as the version:

```
> mk start --kubernetes-version="v1.4.3"
```

This can take a while as Minikube may need to download an image and then set up the local cluster. Here is the expected output:

```
I1030 01:46:23.841589    12948 notify.go:111] Checking for updates...
Starting local Kubernetes cluster...
Running pre-create checks...
Creating machine...
(minikube) Downloading C:\Users\the_g\.minikube\cache\boot2docker.iso
from file://C:/Users/the_g/.minikube/cache/iso/minikube-0.7.iso...
(minikube) Creating VirtualBox VM...
(minikube) Creating SSH key...
(minikube) Starting the VM...
(minikube) Check network to re-create if needed...
(minikube) Windows might ask for the permission to configure a dhcp
server. Sometimes, such confirmation window is minimized in the taskbar.
(minikube) Waiting for an IP...
Waiting for machine to be running, this may take a few minutes...
Detecting operating system of created instance...
Waiting for SSH to be available...
Detecting the provisioner...
Provisioning with boot2docker...
Copying certs to the local machine directory...
```

```
Copying certs to the remote machine...
Setting Docker configuration on the remote daemon...
Checking connection to Docker...
Docker is up and running!
I1030 01:47:32.517217    12948 cluster.go:273] Setting up certificates for
IP: %s 192.168.99.100
I1030 01:47:33.284815    12948 cluster.go:210] sudo killall localkube ||
true
I1030 01:47:33.394690    12948 cluster.go:212] killall: localkube: no
process killed

I1030 01:47:33.394690    12948 cluster.go:210]
# Run with nohup so it stays up. Redirect logs to useful places.
sudo sh -c 'PATH=/usr/local/sbin:$PATH nohup /usr/local/bin/localkube    \
--generate-certs=false --logtostderr=true --enable-dns=false --node-
ip=192.168.99.100 > /var/lib/localkube/localkube.out 2> /var/lib/
localkube/localkube.err < /dev/null & echo $! > /var/run/localkube.pid &'

I1030 01:47:33.475866    12948 cluster.go:212]
I1030 01:47:33.608029    12948 start.go:166] Using kubeconfig:  C:\Users\
the_g/.kube/config
Kubectl is now configured to use the cluster.
```

Let's review what Minikube did by following the output. You'll need to do a lot of it when creating a cluster from scratch:

- Create a `VirtualBOx` VM
- Set up `boot2docker`
- Create certificates for the local machine and the VM
- Set up networking between the local machine and the VM
- Run the local Kubernetes cluster on the VM

Troubleshooting

If something goes wrong during the process, try to follow the error messages. I ran into several issues (remember this is still experimental on Windows). I initially used Minikube 0.12, which had a bug. I upgraded to 0.12.1, but the failed attempt to create a cluster using 0.12 created a bad VM. You can find all the VMs under `~/.minikube/machines`. I couldn't delete the bad machine due to another process locking it. To keep going, I had to restart my laptop and delete the bad machine. Now, I'm on `v0.12.2`, which works well.

Checking out the cluster

Now that we have a cluster up and running, let's peek inside.

First, let's ssh into the VM:

```
> mk ssh
                        ##         .
                  ## ## ##        ==
               ## ## ## ## ##    ===
           /"""""""""""""""""\___/ ===
      ~~~ {~~ ~~~~ ~~~ ~~~~ ~~~ ~ /  ===- ~~~
           _____ o           __/
             \    \         __/
              _____/


  | |_     __     __   | |_|__ \  _| |  __    __| | ____ _ __
  | '_ \ / _ \ / _ \|  _|  _) / _` |/ _ \ / __| | / / _ \ '__|
  | |_) | (_) | (_) | | |_ / __/ (_| | (_) | (__|   < __/ |
  |_.__/ \___/ \___/ \__|_____,_|\___/ \___|_|\_\__|_|
Boot2Docker version 1.11.1, build master : 901340f - Fri Jul  1 22:52:19
UTC 2016
Docker version 1.11.1, build 5604cbe
docker@minikube:~$ uname -a
Linux minikube 4.4.14-boot2docker #1 SMP Fri Jul 1 21:46:36 UTC 2016
x86_64 GNU/Linux
docker@minikube:~$
```

Great. That works. Now, let's start using kubectl, because it is the Swiss Army Knife of Kubernetes and will be useful for all clusters (including federated clusters).

We will cover many of the kubectl commands in our journey. First, let's check the cluster status using cluster-info:

```
> k cluster-info
Kubernetes master is running at https://192.168.99.100:8443
KubeDNS is running at https://192.168.99.100:8443/api/v1/proxy/
namespaces/kube-system/services/kube-dns
kubernetes-dashboard is running at https://192.168.99.100:8443/api/v1/
proxy/namespaces/kube-system/services/kubernetes-dashboard
```

You can see that the master is running properly and that Minikube was nice enough to provision a DNS service for us, and a dashboard too.

Next, let's check out the nodes in the cluster using `get nodes`:

```
> k get nodes
NAME        STATUS    AGE
minikube    Ready     7h
```

So, we have one node called minikube. To get a lot of information about it, type `k describe node minikube`. The output is verbose; I'll let you try it yourself.

Doing work

We have a nice empty cluster up and running (well, not completely empty as the DNS service and dashboard run as pods in the kube-system namespace). It's time to run some pods. Let's use `echo` server from the Minikube getting started guide:

```
K run echo --image=gcr.io/google_containers/echoserver:1.4 --port=8080
deployment "echo" created
```

Kubernetes created a deployment and we have a pod running. Note the `echo` prefix:

```
k get pods
NAME                    READY    STATUS    RESTARTS    AGE
echo-3580479493-cnfn1   1/1      Running   0           1m
```

To `expose` our pod as a service, type the following:

```
k expose deployment echo --type=NodePort
```

Exposing the service as type `NodePort` means that it is exposed to the host on some port. But it is not the `8080` port we ran the pod on. Ports get mapped in the cluster. To access the service, we need the cluster IP and exposed port:

```
> mk ip
192.168.99.100
> k get service echo --output='jsonpath="{.spec.ports[0].NodePort}"'
32041
```

Now we can access the `echo` service, which returns a lot of information:

```
> curl http://192.168.99.100:32041/hi
```

Congratulations! You just created a local Kubernetes cluster and deployed a service.

Examining the cluster with the dashboard

Kubernetes has a very nice web interface, which is deployed, of course, as a service in a pod. The dashboard is well designed and provides a high-level overview of your cluster as well as drilling down into individual resources, viewing logs, editing resource files, and more. It is the perfect weapon when you want to check out your cluster manually. To launch it, type `minikube dashboard`.

Minikube will open a browser window with the dashboard UI. Note that Microsoft Edge can't display the dashboard. I had to run it myself on a different browser.

Here is the workloads view, which displays deployments, replica sets, replication controllers, and pods. It can also display DaemonSets, pet sets, and jobs, but we don't have any in this cluster.

In this section, we created a local single-node Kubernetes cluster on Windows, explored it a little bit using kubectl, deployed a service, and played with the web UI. In the next section, we'll move to a multi-node cluster.

Creating a multi-node cluster using kubeadm

In this section, I'll introduce you to kubeadm, the recommended tool for creating Kubernetes clusters on all environments. It is still relatively new and has some limitations, but it is the way to go. We will also deploy a custom service with a backing store in two separate pods.

Getting ready

Kubeadm operates on pre-provisioned hardware (physical or virtual). Before we create the Kubernetes cluster, we need to prepare a few VMs and install basic software such as `docker`, `kubelet`, `kubeadm` and `kubectl` (needed only on the master).

Preparing a cluster of vagrant VMs

The following vagrant file will create a cluster of four VMs called n1, n2, n3, and n4. It is based on Bento/Ubuntu-16.04 and not Ubuntu/xenial, which suffers from various issues:

```
# -*- mode: ruby -*-
# vi: set ft=ruby :
hosts = {
```

```
  "n1" => "192.168.77.10",
  "n2" => "192.168.77.11",
  "n3" => "192.168.77.12",
  "n4" => "192.168.77.13"
}
Vagrant.configure("2") do |config|
  # always use Vagrants insecure key
  config.ssh.insert_key = false
  # forward ssh agent to easily ssh into the different machines
  config.ssh.forward_agent = true

  check_guest_additions = false
  functional_vboxsf     = false

  config.vm.box = "bento/ubuntu-16.04"
 hosts.each do |name, ip|
    config.vm.define name do |machine|
      machine.vm.network :private_network, ip: ip
      machine.vm.provider "virtualbox" do |v|
        v.name = name
      end
    end
  end
end
```

Installing the required software

I like Ansible a lot for configuration management. I installed it on the n4 VM (running Ubuntu 16.04) because Ansible doesn't run on Windows (although it can manage Windows servers). From now on I'll use n4 as my control machine, which means we're operating in a Linux environment now:

```
> vagrant ssh v4
Welcome to Ubuntu 16.04.1 LTS (GNU/Linux 4.4.0-38-generic x86_64)

  * Documentation:  https://help.ubuntu.com
  * Management:     https://landscape.canonical.com
  * Support:        https://ubuntu.com/advantage

0 packages can be updated.
0 updates are security updates.
```

I had to install `pip` first, and then Ansible itself via `pip`:

```
vagrant@vagrant:~$ sudo apt-get install python-pip
vagrant@vagrant:~$ sudo pip install ansible
```

I use version `2.1.2.0`:

```
vagrant@vagrant:~/ansible$ ansible --version
ansible 2.1.2.0
```

I created a directory called `ansible` and put three files in it: `hosts`, `vars.yml`, and `playbook.yml`.

The hosts file → inventory.x.

This is the inventory file that tells the `ansible` directory what hosts to operate on. The hosts must be SSH-accessible from the controller machine. I put here the three VMs that the cluster will be installed on:

```
[all]
192.168.77.10
192.168.77.11
192.1680.77.12
```

The vars.yml file

The `vars.yml` file just keeps a list of the packages I want to install on each node. `vim`, `htop`, and `tmux` are my favorite packages to install on each machine I need to manage. The others are required by Kubernetes:

```
---
PACKAGES:
    - vim
    - htop
    - tmux
    - docker.io
    - kubelet
    - kubeadm
    - kubectl
    - kubernetes-cni
```

The playbook.yml file

The `playbook.yml` file is the file you run to install the packages on all hosts:

```
---
- hosts: all
  become: true
```

```
vars_files:
  - vars.yml
strategy: free

tasks:
  - name: Add the Google signing key
    apt_key: url=https://packages.cloud.google.com/apt/doc/apt-key.gpg
    state=present

  - name: Add the k8s APT repo
    apt_repository: repo='deb http://apt.kubernetes.io/ kubernetes-
    xenial main' state=present

  - name: Install packages
    apt: name={{ item }} state=installed update_cache=true force=yes
    with_items: "{{ PACKAGES }}"
```

Since some of the packages are from the Kubernetes APT repo, I need to add it along with the Google signing key.

Run the playbook as follows:

```
ansible-playbook -i hosts playbook.yml
```

 If you run into connection failures, try again. The Kubernetes APT repo is sometimes slow to respond. You need to do this just once (per node).

Creating the cluster

It's time to create the cluster itself. We'll initialize the master on the first VM, then set up networking and add the rest of the VMs as nodes.

Initializing the master

Let's initialize the master on n1 (192.168.77.10). It is critical to use the -api-advertise-addresses flag in case of a vagrant VM-based cloud:

```
vagrant@vagrant:~$ sudo kubeadm init --api-advertise-addresses
192.168.77.10
<master/tokens> generated token: "ccalf6.e87ed55d46d00d91"
<master/pki> created keys and certificates in "/etc/kubernetes/pki"
```

```
<util/kubeconfig> created "/etc/kubernetes/kubelet.conf"

<util/kubeconfig> created "/etc/kubernetes/admin.conf"

<master/apiclient> created API client configuration

<master/apiclient> created API client, waiting for the control plane to
become ready

<master/apiclient> all control plane components are healthy after
34.066056 seconds

<master/apiclient> waiting for at least one node to register and become
ready

<master/apiclient> first node is ready after 6.838296 seconds

<master/discovery> created essential addon: kube-discovery, waiting for
it to become ready

<master/discovery> kube-discovery is ready after 14.503696 seconds

<master/addons> created essential addon: kube-proxy

<master/addons> created essential addon: kube-dns
```

```
Kubernetes master initialised successfully!
```

You can now join any number of machines by running the following on each node:

```
kubeadm join --token cca1f6.e87ed55d46d00d91 192.168.77.10
```

That was easy. Note the last line; we'll need it later to add nodes to the cluster.

Setting up the pod network

This is the big-ticket item. The pods need to be able to talk to each other. That requires a pod network add-on. There are several options. Clusters generated by kubeadm require a CNI-based add-on. I chose to use the Weave Net add-on, which supports the Network Policy resource. Your mileage may vary.

Run the following command on the master VM:

```
vagrant@vagrant:~$ kubectl create -f https://git.io/weave-kube
```

You should see the following:

```
vagrant@vagrant:~$ daemonset "weave-net" created
```

To verify:

```
vagrant@vagrant:~$ kubectl get po --all-namespaces
NAMESPACE       NAME                                    READY       STATUS
RESTARTS    AGE
```

kube-system 40m	etcd-vagrant	1/1	Running	0
kube-system 41m	kube-apiserver-vagrant	1/1	Running	0
kube-system 41m	kube-controller-manager-vagrant	1/1	Running	0
kube-system 41m	kube-discovery-982812725-wfie6	1/1	Running	0
kube-system 40m	kube-dns-2247936740-mwpyo	3/3	Running	0
kube-system 40m	kube-proxy-amd64-tunqf	1/1	Running	0
kube-system 40m	kube-scheduler-vagrant	1/1	Running	0
kube-system 3m	weave-net-vi25g	2/2	Running	0

The last pod is our `weave-net-vi25g`, which is what we're looking for as well as the kube-dns pod. Both are running. All is well.

Adding the worker nodes

Now we can add worker nodes to the cluster using the token we got earlier. On each node, run the following command (don't forget `sudo`):

```
sudo kubeadm join --token cca1f6.e87ed55d46d00d91 192.168.77.10
```

You should see the following:

```
<util/tokens> validating provided token
<node/discovery> created cluster info discovery client, requesting info
from "http://192.168.77.10:9898/cluster-info/v1/?token-id=cca1f6"
<node/discovery> cluster info object received, verifying signature using
given token
<node/discovery> cluster info signature and contents are valid, will use
API endpoints [https://192.168.77.10:443]
<node/csr> created API client to obtain unique certificate for this node,
generating keys and certificate signing request
<node/csr> received signed certificate from the API server, generating
kubelet configuration
<util/kubeconfig> created "/etc/kubernetes/kubelet.conf"
Node join complete:
* Certificate signing request sent to master and response
  received.
* Kubelet informed of new secure connection details.

Run 'kubectl get nodes' on the master to see this machine join.
```

Creating clusters in the cloud (GCP, AWS, Azure)

Creating clusters locally is fun, and important during development and when trying to troubleshoot problems locally. But, in the end, Kubernetes is designed for cloud-native applications (applications that run in the cloud). Kubernetes doesn't want to be aware of individual cloud environments because that doesn't scale. Instead, Kubernetes has the concept of a cloud-provider interface. Every cloud provider can implement this interface and then host Kubernetes. Note that, as of version 1.5, Kubernetes still maintains implementations for many cloud providers in its tree, but in the future, they will be refactored out.

The cloud-provider interface

The cloud-provider interface is a collection of Go data types and interfaces. It is defined in a file called cloud.go, available at http://bit.ly/2fq4NbW. Here is the main interface:

```
type Interface interface {
  LoadBalancer() (LoadBalancer, bool)
  Instances() (Instances, bool)
  Zones() (Zones, bool)
  Clusters() (Clusters, bool)
  Routes() (Routes, bool)
  ProviderName() string
  ScrubDNS(nameservers, searches []string) (nsOut, srchOut []string)
}
```

This is very clear. Kubernetes operates in terms of instances, Zones, Clusters, and Routes, and also requires access to a load balancer and provider name. The ScrubDNS() is the only *low-level* method. All the main methods return yet other interfaces.

For example, the Clusters interface is very simple:

```
type Clusters interface {
  ListClusters() ([]string, error)
  Master(clusterName string) (string, error)
}
```

The ListClusters() method returns cluster names. The Master() method returns the IP address or DNS name of the master node.

The other interfaces are not much more complicated. The entire file is 167 lines long including lots of comments. The take-home point is that it is not too complicated to implement a Kubernetes provider if your cloud utilizes those basic concepts.

GCP

The **Google Cloud Platform** (GCP) is the only cloud provider that supports Kubernetes out of the box. The so-called **Google Kubernetes Engine** (GKE) is a container management solution built on Kubernetes. You don't need to install Kubernetes on GCP, and you can use the Google cloud API to create Kubernetes clusters and provision them. The fact that Kubernetes is a built-in part of the GCP means it will always be well integrated and well tested, and you don't have to worry about changes in the underlying platform breaking the cloud-provider interface.

All in all, if you plan to base your system on Kubernetes and you don't have any existing code on other cloud platforms, then GCP is a solid choice.

AWS

AWS has its own container management service called ECS, but it is not based on Kubernetes. You can run Kubernetes on AWS very well. It is a supported provider and there is a lot of documentation on how to set it up. While you could provision some VMs yourself and use kubeadm, I recommend using the kops (Kubernetes Operations) project. Kops is a Kubernetes project available on GitHub (http://bit.ly/2ft5KA5). It is not part of Kubernetes itself, but it is developed and maintained by the Kubernetes developers.

It supports the following features:

- Automated Kubernetes cluster CRUD for the cloud (AWS)
- **Highly Available (HA)** Kubernetes clusters
- Uses a state-sync model for dry-run and automatic idempotency
- Custom support for kubectl add-ons
- Kops can generate Terraform configuration
- Based on a simple meta-model defined in a directory tree
- Easy command-line syntax
- Community support

To create a cluster, you need to do some minimal DNS configuration via route53, set up a S3 bucket to store the cluster configuration, and then run a single command:

```
kops create cluster --cloud=aws --zones=us-east-1c ${NAME}
```

The complete instructions are here: http://bit.ly/2f7r6EK.

Azure

Azure also has its own container management service. You can use the Mesos-based DC/OS or Docker Swarm to manage them. But you can also use Kubernetes, of course. You can provision the cluster yourself (for example, using Azure's desired state configuration) then create the Kubernetes cluster using kubeadm. But, the recommended approach is to use yet another non-core Kubernetes project, called **kubernetes-anywhere** (http://bit.ly/2eCS7Ps). The goal of kubernetes-anywhere is to provide a cross-platform way to create clusters in a cloud environment (at least GCP, AWS, and Azure).

The process is pretty painless. You need to have Docker, make, and kubectl installed, and of course, your Azure subscription ID. Then, you clone the kubernetes-anywhere repository, run a couple of make commands, and your cluster is good to go.

The complete instructions to create an Azure cluster are at http://bit.ly/2d56WdA.

In this section, we covered the cloud-provider interface and looked at the various recommended ways to create Kubernetes clusters on various cloud providers. The scene is still young and the tools evolve quickly. I believe convergence will happen soon. Tools and projects such as kubeadm, kops, Kargo, and kubernetes-anywhere will eventually merge and provide a uniform and easy way to bootstrap Kubernetes clusters.

Creating a bare-metal cluster from scratch

In the previous section, we looked at running Kubernetes on cloud providers. This is the dominant deployment story for Kubernetes. But there are strong uses cases for running Kubernetes on bare metal. I don't focus here on hosted versus on-premises. This is yet another dimension. If you already manage a lot of servers on-premises, you are in the best position to decide.

Use cases for bare-metal

Bare-metal clusters are a bear, especially if you manage them yourself. There are companies that provide commercial support for bare-metal Kubernetes clusters, such as Platform 9, but the offerings are not mature yet. A solid open-source option is Kargo from Kubespray, which can deploy industrial-strength Kubernetes clusters on bare metal, AWS, GCE, and OpenStack.

Here are some use cases where it makes sense:

- Price: If you already manage large-scale bare clusters, it may be much cheaper to run Kubernetes clusters on your physical infrastructure
- Low network latency: If you must have low latency between your nodes, then the VM overhead might be too much
- Regulatory requirements: If you must comply with regulations, you may not be allowed to use cloud providers
- You want total control over hardware: Cloud providers give you many options, but you may have special needs

When should you consider creating a bare-metal cluster?

The complexities of creating a cluster from scratch are significant. A Kubernetes cluster is not a trivial beast. There is a lot of documentation on the Web on how to set up bare-metal clusters, but as the whole ecosystem moves forward, many of these guides get out of date quickly.

You should consider going down this route if you have the operational capability to trouble to debug problems at every level of the stack. Most of the problems will probably be networking-related, but filesystems and storage drivers can bite you too, as well as general incompatibilities and version mismatches between components such as Kubernetes itself, Docker (or Rkt, if you brave it), Docker images, your OS, your OS kernel, and the various add-ons and tools you use.

The process

There is a lot to do. Here is a list of some of the concerns you'll have to address:

- Implementing your own cloud-provider interface or sidestepping it
- Choosing a networking model and how to implement it (CNI plugin, direct compile)

- Whether or not to use network policy
- Select images for system components
- Security model and SSL certificates
- Admin credentials
- Templates for components such as API Server, replication controller, and scheduler
- Cluster services: DNS, logging, monitoring, and GUI

I recommend the following guide from the Kubernetes site to get a deeper understanding of what it takes to create a cluster from scratch: `http://bit.ly/1ToR9EC`.

Using virtual private cloud infrastructure

If your use case falls under the bare-metal use cases but you don't have the necessary skilled manpower or the inclination to deal with the infrastructure challenges of bare metal, you have the option to use a private cloud such as OpenStack. If you want to aim a little higher in the abstraction ladder, then Mirantis offers a cloud platform built on top of OpenStack and Kubernetes.

In this section, we considered the option to build a bare-metal cluster Kubernetes cluster. We looked into the use cases that require it and highlighted the challenges and difficulties.

Summary

In this chapter, we got into some hands-on cluster creation. We created a single-node cluster using Minikube and a multi-node cluster using kubeadm. Then we looked at the many options to create Kubernetes clusters on cloud providers. Finally, we touched on the complexities of creating Kubernetes clusters on bare metal. The current state of affairs is very dynamic. The basic components are changing rapidly, the tooling is still young, and there are different options for each environment. It's not completely trivial to stand up a Kubernetes cluster, but with some effort and attention to detail you can get it done quickly.

In *Chapter 3*, we will explore the important topics of *Monitoring, Logging, and Troubleshooting*. Once your cluster is up and running and you start deploying workloads, you need you make sure it runs properly and satisfies requirements. This requires ongoing attention and responding to various failures that happen in the real world.

3
Monitoring, Logging, and Troubleshooting

In *Chapter 2, Creating Kubernetes Clusters*, we learned how to create Kubernetes clusters in different environments, experimented with different tools, and created a couple of clusters.

Creating a Kubernetes cluster is just the beginning of the story. Once the cluster is up and running, you need to make it sure it is operational, all the necessary components are in place and properly configured, and that enough resources are deployed to satisfy the requirements. Responding to failures, debugging, and troubleshooting is a major part of managing any complicated system, and Kubernetes is no exception.

The topics we will cover include the following:

- Monitoring with Heapster
- Performance analytics with Kubernetes dashboard
- Central logging
- Detecting problems at the node level
- Troubleshooting scenarios

At the end of this chapter you will have a solid understanding of the various options to monitor Kubernetes clusters, how to access logs, and how to analyze them. You will be able to look at a healthy Kubernetes cluster and verify everything is OK. You will also be able to look at an unhealthy Kubernetes cluster and methodically diagnose it, locate the problems, and address them.

Monitoring Kubernetes with Heapster

Heapster is a Kubernetes project that provides a robust monitoring solution for Kubernetes clusters. It runs as a pod (of course), so it can be managed by Kubernetes itself. Heapster supports Kubernetes and CoreOS clusters. It has a very modular and flexible design. Heapster collects both operational metrics and events from every node in the cluster, stores them in a persistent backend (with a well-defined schema) and allows visualization and programmatic access. Heapster can be configured to use different backends (or sinks, in Heapster's parlance) and their corresponding visualization frontends. The most common combination is InfluxDB as backend and Grafana as frontend. The Google Cloud Platform integrates Heapster with the Google monitoring service. There are many other less common backends, such as the following:

- Log
- InfluxDB
- Google Cloud monitoring
- Google Cloud logging
- Hawkular-Metics (metrics only)
- OpenTSDB
- Monasca (metrics only)
- Kafka (metrics only)
- Riemann (metrics only)
- Elasticsearch

You can use multiple backends by specifying sinks on the commandline:

```
--sink=log --sink=influxdb:http://monitoring-influxdb:80/
```

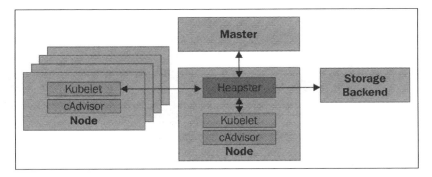

cAdvisor

cAdvisor is part of the kubelet, which runs on every node. It collects information about the CPU/cores usage, memory, network, and filesystems of each container. It provides a basic UI on port 4194, but, most importantly for Heapster, it provides all this information through the kubelet. Heapster records the information collected by cAdvisor on each node and stores it in its backend for analysis and visualization.

The cAdvisor UI is useful if you want to quickly verify that a particular node is set up correctly, for example, while creating a new cluster when Heapster is not hooked up yet.

Here is what it looks like:

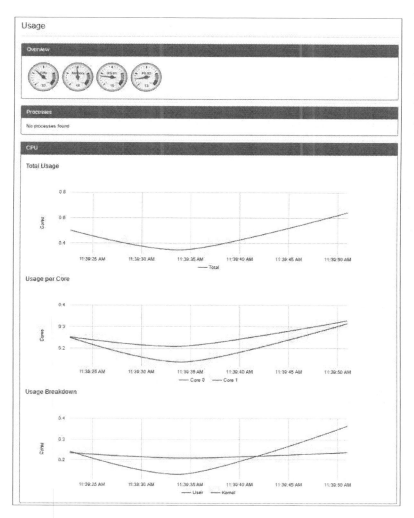

InfluxDB backend

InfluxDB is a modern and robust distributed time-series database. It is very well-suited and used broadly for centralized metrics and logging. It is also the preferred Heapster backend (outside the Google Cloud Platform). The only thing is InfluxDB clustering; high availability is part of enterprise offering.

The storage schema

The InfluxDB storage schema defines the information that Heapster stores in InfluxDB and is available for querying and graphing later. The metrics are divided into multiple categories, called measurements. You can treat and query each metric separately, or you can query a whole category as one measurement and receive the individual metrics as fields. The naming convention is <category>/<metrics name> (except for uptime, which has a single metric). If you have a SQL background you can think of measurements as tables. Each metrics are stored per container. Each metric is labeled with the following information:

- pod_id: Unique ID of a pod
- pod_name: User-provided name of a pod
- pod_namespace: The namespace of a pod
- container_base_image: Base image for the container
- container_name: User-provided name of the container or full cgroup name for system containers
- host_id: Cloud-provider-specified or user-specified identifier of a node
- hostname: Hostname where the container ran
- labels: Comma-separated list of user-provided labels; format is key:value
- namespace_id: UID of the namespace of a pod
- resource_id: A unique identifier used to differentiate multiple metrics of the same type, for example, FS partitions under filesystem/usage

Here are all the metrics grouped by category. As you can see, it is quite extensive.

CPU

- cpu/limit: CPU hard limit in millicores
- cpu/node_capacity: CPU capacity of a node
- cpu/node_allocatable: CPU allocatable of a node

- `cpu/node_reservation`: Share of CPU that is reserved on the node allocatable
- `cpu/node_utilization`: CPU utilization as a share of node allocatable
- `cpu/request`: CPU request (the guaranteed amount of resources) in millicores
- `cpu/usage`: Cumulative CPU usage on all cores
- `cpu/usage_rate`: CPU usage on all cores in millicores

Filesystem

- `filesystem/usage`: Total number of bytes consumed on a filesystem
- `filesystem/limit`: The total size of the filesystem in bytes
- `filesystem/available`: The number of available bytes remaining in the filesystem

Memory

- `memory/limit`: Memory hard limit in bytes
- `memory/major_page_faults`: Number of major page faults
- `memory/major_page_faults_rate`: Number of major page faults per second
- `memory/node_capacity`: Memory capacity of a node
- `memory/node_allocatable`: Memory allocatable of a node
- `memory/node_reservation`: Share of memory that is reserved on the node allocatable
- `memory/node_utilization`: Memory utilization as a share of memory allocatable
- `memory/page_faults`: Number of page faults
- `memory/page_faults_rate`: Number of page faults per second
- `memory/request`: Memory request (the guaranteed amount of resources) in bytes
- `memory/usage`: Total memory usage
- `memory/working_set`: Total working set usage; working set is the memory being used and is not easily dropped by the kernel

Network

- `network/rx`: Cumulative number of bytes received over the network
- `network/rx_errors`: Cumulative number of errors while receiving over the network
- `network/rx_errors_rate`: Number of errors per second while receiving over the network
- `network/rx_rate`: Number of bytes received over the network per second
- `network/tx`: Cumulative number of bytes sent over the network
- `network/tx_errors`: Cumulative number of errors while sending over the network
- `network/tx_errors_rate`: Number of errors while sending over the network
- `network/tx_rate`: Number of bytes sent over the network per second

Uptime

- `uptime`: Number of milliseconds since the container was started

You can work with InfluxDB directly if you're familiar with it. You can either connect to it using its own API or use its web interface. Type the following command to find its port:

```
k describe service monitoring-influxdb --namespace=kube-system | grep
NodePort
```

```
Type:                    NodePort
NodePort:         http    32699/TCP
NodePort:         api     30020/TCP
```

Now you can browse to the InfluxDB web interface using the HTTP port. You'll need to configure it to point to the API port. The **Username** and **Password** are `root` and `root` by default:

Once you're set up you can select what database to use (see the top-right corner). The Kubernetes database is called k8s. You can now query the metrics using the InfluxDB query language.

Grafana visualization

Grafana runs in its own container and serves a sophisticated dashboard that works well with InfluxDB as a data source. To locate the port, type the following command:

```
k describe service monitoring-influxdb --namespace=kube-system | grep
NodePort
```

```
Type:                   NodePort
NodePort:               <unset> 30763/TCP
```

Now you can access the Grafana web interface on that port. The first thing you need to do is set up the data source to point to the InfluxDB backend:

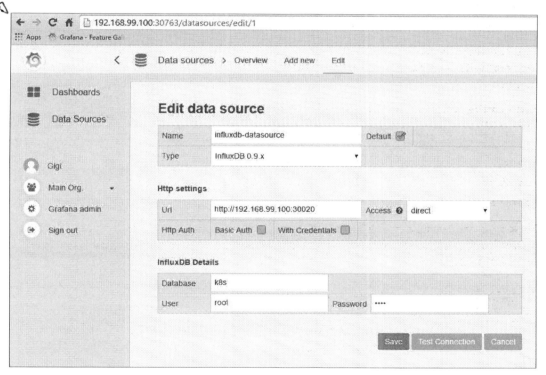

Make sure to test the connection and then go explore the various options in the dashboards. There are several default dashboards, but you should be able to customize it to your preferences. Grafana is designed to let adapt it to your needs.

Performance analysis with the dashboard

My favorite tool by far when I just want to know what's going on in the cluster is the Kubernetes dashboard. There are a couple of reasons for this, as follows:

- It is built-in (always in sync and tested with Kubernetes)
- It's fast
- It provides an intuitive drill-down interface from the cluster level all the way down to individual container
- It doesn't require any customization or configuration

While Heapster, InfluxDB, and Grafana are better for customized and heavy-duty views and queries, the Kubernetes dashboard's pre-defined views can probably answer all your questions 80–90% of the time.

You can also deploy applications and create any Kubernetes resource using the dashboard by uploading the proper YAML or JSON file, but I will not cover this because it is an anti-pattern for manageable infrastructure. It may be useful when playing around with a test cluster, but for actually modifying the state of the cluster, I prefer the commandline. Your mileage may vary.

Let's find the port first:

```
k describe service kubernetes-dashboard --namespace=kube-system | grep
NodePort


Type:               NodePort
NodePort:           <unset> 30000/TCP
```

Top-level view

The dashboard is organized with a hierarchical view on the left (can be hidden by clicking the **hamburger** menu) and dynamic, context-based content on the right. You can drill down the hierarchical view to get deeper into the information that's relevant.

There are several top-level categories:

- **Admin**
- **Workloads**
- **Services and discovery**
- **Storage**
- **Config**

You can also filter everything by a particular namespace or choose all namespaces.

Admin view

The **Admin** view has three sections: **Namespaces**, **Nodes**, and **Persistent Volumes**. It is all about observing the physical resources of the cluster:

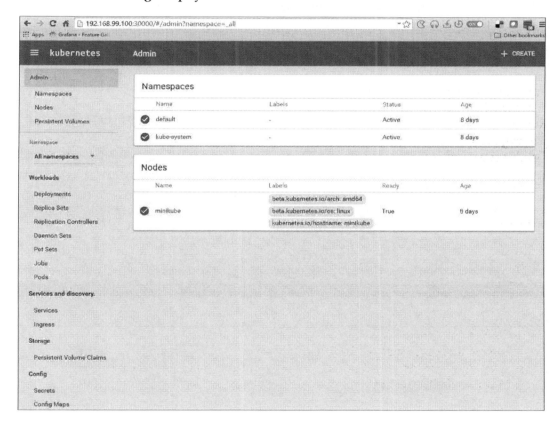

You get, in a glance, a LOT of information: what namespaces are available, their **Status**, and **Age**. For each node, you can see its **Age**, **Labels**, and if it's **Ready** or not.

The cool part is that you can click on **Nodes** under **Admin** and you then get a view with the CPU and memory history of all the nodes in aggregate:

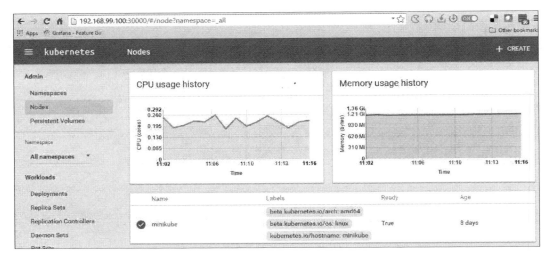

That's not the end, though. Let's click on the **minikube** node itself. We get a detailed screen of information about that node:

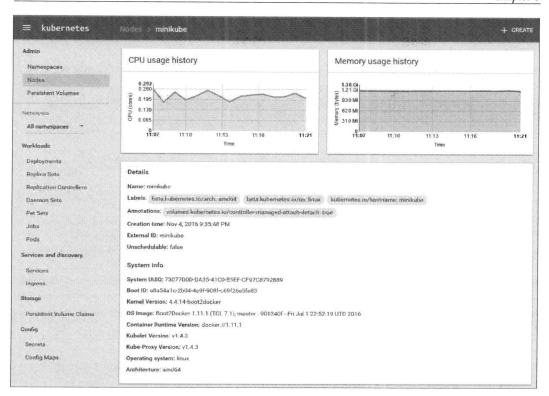

If you scroll down, you'll see even more interesting information. The allocated resources are very important when you deal with performance issues. If a node doesn't have enough resources, then it might not be able to satisfy the needs of its pods. The **Conditions** pane is where it's at.

You get a great, concise view of memory and disk pressure at the individual node level:

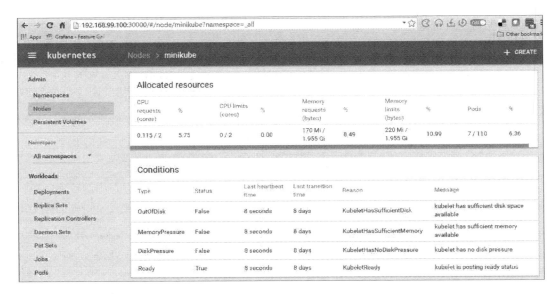

There is also a **Pods** pane, but we'll talk about pods in the next section.

Workloads

The **Workloads** category is the main one. It organizes many types of Kubernetes resources, such as **Deployments**, **Replica Sets**, **Replication Controllers**, **Daemon Sets**, **Pet Sets**, **Jobs**, and of course, **Pods**. You can drill down along any of these dimensions. Here is the top-level **Workloads** view for the default namespace that currently has only the echo service deployed. You can see the **Deployments**, **Replica sets**, and **Pods**:

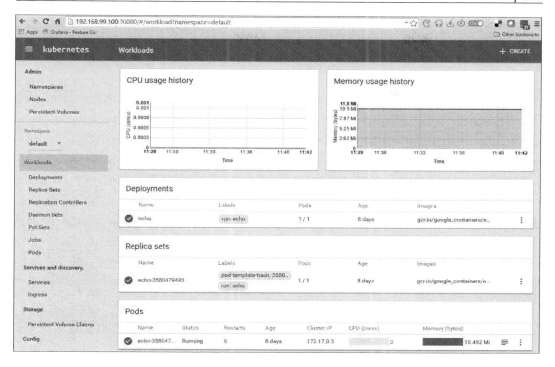

Let's switch to all namespaces and dive into the **Pods** sub-category. This is a very useful view. In each row, you can tell if the pod is running or not, how many times it restarted, its IP, and the CPU and memory usage histories are even embedded as nice little graphs right there:

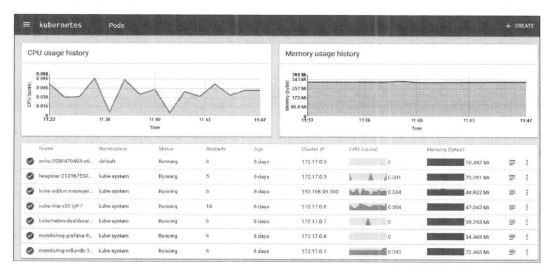

You can also view the **Logs** for any pod right by clicking the **text** symbol (second from the right). Let's check the **Logs** of the InfluxDB pod. Looks like everything is in order and Heapster is successfully writing to it:

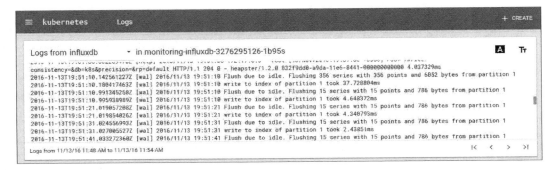

There is one more level of detail we haven't explored yet. We can go down to the container level. Let's click on the **kube-dns** pod. We get the following screen, which shows the individual containers and their run command; we can also view their logs:

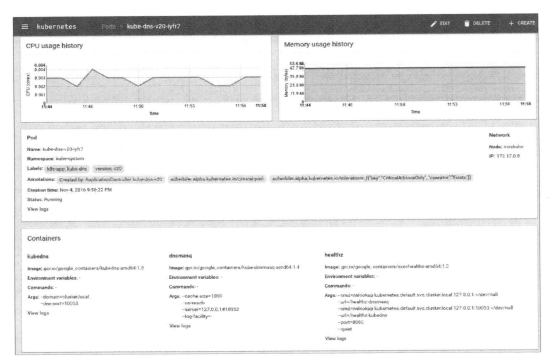

Services and discovery

The **Services and discovery** category is often where you start from. **Services** are the public interface to your Kubernetes cluster. Serious problems will affect your services, which will affect your users:

When you drill down by clicking on a service, you get some information about the service (most important is the label selector) and a pods view.

Adding central logging

Central logging or cluster-level logging is a fundamental requirement for any cluster with more than a couple of nodes, pods, or containers. First, it is impractical to view the logs of each pod or container independently. You can't get a global picture of the system and there will be just too many messages to sift through. You need a solution that aggregates the log messages and lets you slice and dice them easily. The second reason is that containers are ephemeral. Problematic pods will often just die and their replication controller or replica set will just start a new instance, losing all the important log info. By logging to a central logging service, you preserve this critical troubleshooting information.

Planning central logging

Conceptually, central logging is very simple. On each node you run a dedicated agent that intercepts all log messages from all the pods and containers on the node, and sends them, along with enough metadata, to a central repository where they are stored safely.

As usual, if you run on the Google platform, then GKE's got you covered and there is a Google central-logging service integrated nicely. For other platforms, a popular solution is fluentd, Elasticsearch, and Kibana. There is an official add-on to set up the proper services for each component. The fluentd-elasticsearch add-on is here: `http://bit.ly/2f6MF5b`

It is installed as a set of services for Elasticsearch and Kibana, and the fluentd agent is installed on each node.

Fluentd

Fluentd is a unified logging layer that sits between arbitrary data sources and arbitrary data sinks and makes sure that log messages can stream from A to B. Kubernetes comes with an add-on that has a Docker image that deploys the fluentd agent, which knows how to read various logs that are relevant to Kubernetes, such as Docker logs, etcd logs, and kube logs. It also adds labels to each log message to make it easy for users to filter later by label. Here is a snippet from the `td-agent.conf` file:

```
# Example:
# 2016/02/04 06:52:38 filePurge: successfully removed file
/var/etcd/data/member/wal/00000000000006d0-00000000010a23d1.wal
<source>
  type tail
  # Not parsing this, because it doesn't have anything particularly
useful to
  # parse out of it (like severities).
  format none
  path /var/log/etcd.log
  pos_file /var/log/es-etcd.log.pos
  tag etcd
</source>
```

The full configuration file is here:

`http://bit.ly/2fwS6eG`

Elasticsearch

Elasticsearch is a great document store and full-text search engine. It is a favorite in the enterprise because it is very fast, reliable, and scalable. It is used in the Kubernetes central logging add-on as a Docker image and is deployed as a service. Note that a full-fledged production cluster of Elasticsearch (which will be deployed on a Kubernetes cluster) requires its own master, client, and data nodes. For large-scale and highly available Kubernetes clusters, the central logging itself will be clustered. Elasticsearch can use self-discovery.

Here is the `logging.yml` config file:

```
# you can override this using by setting a system property, for
example -Des.logger.level=DEBUG
es.logger.level: INFO
rootLogger: ${es.logger.level}, console
logger:
  # log action execution errors for easier debugging
  action: DEBUG
  # reduce the logging for aws, too much is logged under the default
INFO
  com.amazonaws: WARN


appender:
  console:
    type: console
    layout:
      type: consolePattern
      conversionPattern: "[%d{ISO8601}] [%-5p] [%-25c] %m%n"
```

Kibana

Kibana is Elasticsearch's partner in crime. It is used to visualize and interact with the data stored and indexed by Elasticsearch. It is also installed as a service by the add-on. Here is the Kibana Dockerfile:

```
FROM gcr.io/google_containers/ubuntu-slim:0.4

  MAINTAINER Mik Vyatskov "vmik@google.com"

  ENV DEBIAN_FRONTEND noninteractive
  ENV KIBANA_VERSION 4.6.1
```

```
RUN apt-get update \
   && apt-get install -y curl \
   && apt-get clean

RUN set -x \
   && cd / \
   && mkdir /kibana \
   && curl -O https://download.elastic.co/kibana/kibana/kibana-
$KIBANA_VERSION-linux-x86_64.tar.gz \
   && tar xf kibana-$KIBANA_VERSION-linux-x86_64.tar.gz -C /kibana -
-strip-components=1 \
   && rm kibana-$KIBANA_VERSION-linux-x86_64.tar.gz

COPY run.sh /run.sh

EXPOSE 5601

CMD ["/run.sh"]
```

Detecting node problems

In Kubernetes' conceptual model the unit of work is the pod. But, pods are scheduled on nodes. When it comes to monitoring and reliability, the nodes are what require the most attention because Kubernetes itself (the scheduler and replication controllers) takes care of the pods. Nodes can suffer from a variety of problems that Kubernetes is unaware of. As a result, it will keep scheduling pods to the bad nodes and the pods might fail to function properly. Here are some of the problems that nodes may suffer while still appearing functional:

- Bad CPU
- Bad memory
- Bad disk
- Kernel deadlock
- Corrupt filesystem
- Problems with the Docker Daemon

The kubelet and cAdvisor don't detect these issues. Another solution is needed. Enter the node problem detector.

Node problem detector

The node problem detector is a pod that runs on every node. It needs to solve a difficult problem. It needs to detect various problems across different environments, different hardware, and different OSes. It needs to be reliable enough not to be affected itself (otherwise it can't report the problem), and it needs to have relatively low overhead to avoid spamming the master. In addition, it needs to run on every node. Kubernetes recently received a new capability called DaemonSet that addresses that last concern.

DaemonSet

DaemonSet is a pod for every node. Once you define DaemonSet, every node that's added to the cluster automatically gets a pod. If that pod dies, Kubernetes will start another instance of that pod on that node. Think about it as a fancy replication controller with 1:1 node-pod affinity. Node problem detector is defined as a DaemonSet, which is a perfect match for its requirements.

Problem Daemons

The problem with node problem detector (pun intended) is that there are too many problems it needs to handle. Trying to cram all of them into a single codebase can lead to a complex, bloated, and never-stabilizing codebase. The design of the node problem detector calls for separation of the core functionality of reporting node problems to the master from the specific problem detection. The reporting API is based on generic conditions and events. The problem detection should be done by separate problem Daemons (each in its own container). This way, it is possible to add and evolve new problem detectors without impacting the code node problem detector. In addition, the control plane may have a remedy controller that can resolve some node problems automatically, therefore implementing self-healing:

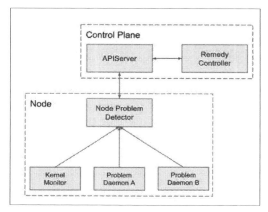

At this stage (Kubernetes 1.4), problem Daemons are baked into the node problem detector binary and execute as Goroutines, so you don't get the benefits of the loosely coupled design just yet.

In this section, we covered the important topic of node problems, which can get in the way to successful scheduling of workloads and how the node problem detector can help. In the next section, we'll talk about various failure scenarios and how to troubleshoot them using Heapster, central logging, the Kubernetes dashboard, and node problem detector.

Troubleshooting scenarios

There are so many things that can go wrong in a large Kubernetes cluster – and they will. This is expected. You can employ best practices and minimize some of them (mostly human errors), by using stricter processes. But, some issues such as hardware failures and networking issues can't be totally avoided. Even human errors should not always be minimized if it means slower development time. In this section, we'll discuss various categories of failures, how to detect them, how to evaluate their impact, and consider the proper response.

Designing robust systems

When you want to design a robust system you first need to understand the possible failure modes, the risk/probability of each failure, and the impact/cost of each failure. Then, you can consider various prevention and mitigation measures, loss-cutting strategies, incident-management strategies, and recovery procedures. Finally, you can come up with a plan that matches risks to mitigation profiles, including cost. A comprehensive design is not trivial and needs to be updated as the system evolves. The higher the stakes the more thorough your plan should be. This process has to be tailored for each organization. A corner of error recovery and robustness is detecting failures and being able to troubleshoot. The following sub-sections describe common failure categories, how to detect them, and where to collect additional information.

Hardware failure

Hardware failures in Kubernetes can be divided into two groups:

* The node is unresponsive
* The node is responsive

When the node is not responsive it can be difficult sometimes to determine if it's a networking issue, a configuration issue or actual hardware failure. You obviously can't utilize any information like logs or run diagnostics on the node itself. What can you do? First, consider if the node was ever responsive. If it's a node that was just added to the cluster it is more likely a configuration issue. If it's a node that was part of the cluster you can look at historical data from the node on Heapster or central logging and see if you detect any errors in the logs or degradation in performance that may indicate failing hardware.

When the node is responsive, it may still suffer from the failure of redundant hardware, such as non-OS disk or some cores. You can detect the hardware failure if the node problem detector is running on the node and raises some event or node condition to the attention of master. Alternatively, you may notice that pods keep getting restarted or jobs take longer to complete. All these may be signs of hardware failure. Another strong hint for hardware failure is if the problems are isolated to a single node and standard maintenance operations such as reboot don't alleviate the symptoms.

If your cluster is deployed in the cloud, replacing a node you suspect as having hardware problems is trivial. It is simple to just manually provision a new VM and remove the bad VM. In some cases, you may want to employ a more automated process and employ a remedy controller as suggested by the node problem detector design. Your remedy controller will listen to problems (or missing health checks) and can automatically replace bad nodes. This approach can work even for private hosting or bare metal if you keep a pool of extra nodes ready to kick in. Large-scale clusters can function just fine, even with reduced capacity most of the time. Either you can tolerate slightly reduced capacity when a small number of nodes are down, or you can over-provision a little bit. This way you have some headway when a node goes down.

Quotas, shares, and limits

Kubernetes is a multi-tenant system. It is designed to utilize resources efficiently, but it schedules pods and allocates resources based on a system of checks and balances between available quotas and limits per namespace, and requests for guaranteed resources from pods and containers. We will dive into the details later in the book. Here, we'll just consider what can go wrong and how to detect it. There are several bad outcomes you can run into:

- **Insufficient resources**: If a pod requires a certain amount of CPU or memory and there is no node with available capacity then the pod can't be scheduled.

- **Under-utilization**: A pod may declare that it requires a certain amount of CPU or memory, and Kubernetes will oblige, but then the pod may only use a small percentage of its requested resources. This is just wasteful.

- **Mismatched node configuration**: A pod that requires a lot of CPU but very little memory may be scheduled to a high-memory node and use all its CPU resources, thereby hogging the node, so no other pod can be scheduled but the unused memory is wasted.

Checking out the dashboard is a great way to look for suspects visually. Nodes and pods that are either over-subscribed or underutilized are candidates for quota and resource request mismatches:

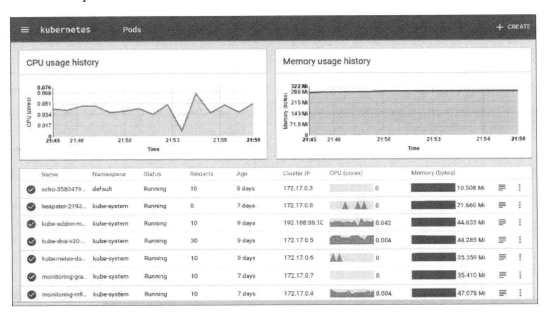

Once you detect a candidate you can dive in using the describe command at the node or pod level. In a large-scale cluster, you should have automated checks that compare the utilization against capacity planning. This is not trivial, because most large systems have some level of fluctuation and a uniform load is not expected. Make sure you understand the demands on your system and that your cluster's capacity is within the normal range or can adjust elastically, as needed.

Bad configuration

Bad configuration is an umbrella term. Your Kubernetes cluster state is configuration; your containers' command-line arguments are configuration; all the environment variables used by Kubernetes, your application services, and any third-party services are configuration; all the configuration files are configuration. In some data-driven systems, configuration is stored in various data stores. Configuration issues are very common because usually, there aren't any established good practices to test them. They often have various fallbacks (for example, search path for configuration files) and defaults, and the production-environment configuration is different than the development or staging environment.

At the Kubernetes cluster level, there are many possible configuration problems, such as the following:

- Incorrect labeling of nodes, pods, or containers
- Scheduling pods without a replication controller
- Incorrect specification of ports for services
- Incorrect ConfigMap

Most of these problems can be addressed by having a proper automated deployment process. But you must have a deep understanding of your cluster architecture and how Kubernetes resources fit together.

Configuration problems typically occur after you change something. It is critical, after each deployment or manual change to the cluster, to verify its state.

Heapster and the dashboard are great options here. I suggest starting from the services and verifying that they are available, responsive, and functional. Then, you can dive deeper and verify that the system also operates within the expected performance parameters.

The logs also provide helpful hints and can pinpoint specific configuration options.

Cost versus performance

Large clusters are not cheap. This is especially true if you run in the cloud. A major part of operating massive-scale systems is keeping track of the expense.

Managing cost on the cloud

One of the greatest benefits of the cloud is that it can satisfy elastic demand that caters for systems that expand and contract automatically by allocating and deallocating resources as needed. Kubernetes fits this model very well and can be extended to provision more nodes as necessary. The risk here is that, if not constrained properly, a denial of service attack (malicious, accidental, or self-inflicted) can lead to arbitrary provisioning of expensive resources. This needs to be monitored carefully so it can be caught early on. Quotas on namespaces can avoid it, but you still need to be able to dive in and pinpoint the core issue. The root cause can be external (a botnet attack), misconfiguration, an internal test gone awry, or a bug in the code that detects or allocate resources.

Managing cost on bare metal

On bare metal, you typically don't have to worry about runaway allocation, but you can easily run into a wall if you need extra capacity and can't provision more resources fast enough. Capacity planning and monitoring your system's performance to detect the need early are primary concerns for ops. Heapster can show historical trends and help identify both peak times and overall growth in demand.

Managing cost on hybrid clusters

Hybrid clusters run on both bare metal and the cloud (and possibly on private hosting services too). The considerations are similar, but you may need to aggregate your analysis. We will discuss hybrid clusters in more detail later.

Summary

In this chapter, we looked at monitoring, logging, and troubleshooting. This is a crucial aspect of operating any system, and in particular a platform such as Kubernetes with so many moving pieces. My greatest worry whenever I'm responsible for something is that something will go wrong and I will have no systematic way to figure out what's wrong and how to fix it. Kubernetes has ample tools and facilities built in, such as Heapster, logging, DaemonSets, and node problem detector. You can also deploy any kind of monitoring solution you prefer.

In the *Chapter 4, High Availability and Reliability*, we will look at highly available and scalable Kubernetes clusters. This is arguably the most important use case for Kubernetes, where it shines compared to other orchestration solutions.

4
High Availability and Reliability

In the previous chapter, we looked at monitoring your Kubernetes cluster, detecting problems at the node level, identifying and rectifying performance problems, and general troubleshooting.

In this chapter, we will dive into the topic of highly available clusters. This is a complicated topic. The Kubernetes project and the community haven't settled on one true way to achieve high availability nirvana. There are many aspects to highly available Kubernetes clusters, such as ensuring that the control plane can keep functioning in the face of failures, protecting the cluster state in etcd, protecting the system's data, and recovering capacity and/or performance quickly. Different systems will have different reliability and availability requirements. How to design and implement a highly available Kubernetes cluster will depend on those requirements.

At the end of this chapter, you will understand the various concepts associated with high availability and be familiar with Kubernetes high availability best practices and when to employ them. You will be able to upgrade live clusters using different strategies and techniques, and you will be able to choose between multiple possible solutions based on trade-offs between performance, cost, and availability.

High-availability concepts

In this section, we will start our journey into high availability by exploring the concepts and building blocks of reliable and highly available systems. The million (trillion?) dollar question is, how do we build reliable and highly available systems from unreliable components? Components will fail; you can take that to the bank. Hardware will fail. Networks will fail; configuration will be wrong; software will have bugs; people will make mistakes. Accepting that, we need to design a system that can be reliable and highly available even when components fail. The idea is to start with redundancy, detect component failure, and replace bad components quickly.

Redundancy

Redundancy is the foundation of reliable and highly available systems at the hardware and data levels. If a critical component fails and you want the system to keep running, you must have another identical component ready to go. Kubernetes itself takes care of your stateless pods via replication controllers and replica sets. But, your cluster state in etcd and the master components themselves need redundancy to function when some components fail. In addition, if your system's tasteful components are not backed up by redundant storage (for example, on a cloud platform) then you need to add redundancy to prevent data loss.

Hot swapping

Hot swapping is the concept of replacing a failed component on the fly without taking the system down, with minimal (ideally, zero) interruption to users. If the component is stateless (or its state is stored in separate redundant storage), then hot swapping a new component to replace it is easy and just involves redirecting all clients to the new component. But, if it stores local state, including in memory, then hot swapping is not trivial. There are two main options:

- Give up on in-flight transactions
- Keep a hot replica in sync

The first solution is much simpler. Most systems are resilient enough to cope with failures. Clients can retry failed requests and the hot-swapped component will service them.

The second solution is more complicated and fragile, and will incur a performance overhead because every interaction must be replicated to both copies (and acknowledged). It may be necessary for some parts of the system.

Leader election

Leader or master election is a common pattern in distributed systems. You often have multiple identical components that collaborate and share the load, but one component is elected as the leader and certain operations are serialized through the leader. You can think of distributed systems with leader election as a combination of redundancy and hot swapping. The components are all redundant and, when the current leader fails or becomes unavailable, a new leader is elected and hot-swapped in.

Smart load balancing

Load balancing is about distributing the workload across multiple components that service incoming requests. When some components the load balancer must first stop sending requests to failed or unreachable components. The second step is to provision new components to restore capacity and update the load balancer. Kubernetes provides great facilities to support this via services, endpoints, and labels.

Idempotency

Many types of failure can be temporary. This is most common with networking issues or with too-stringent timeouts. A component that doesn't respond to a health check will be considered unreachable and another component will take its place. Work that was scheduled to the presumably failed component may be sent for another component. But the original component may still be working and complete the same work. The end result is that the same work may be performed twice. It is very difficult to avoid this situation. To support *exactly once* semantics, you need to pay a heavy price in overhead, performance, latency, and complexity. Thus, most systems opt to support at-least-once semantics, which means it is OK for the same work to be performed multiple times. This property is called **idempotency**. Idempotent systems maintain their state if an operation is performed multiple times.

Self-healing

When component failures occur in dynamic systems, you usually want the system to be able to heal itself. Kubernetes replication controllers and replica sets are great examples of self-healing systems. But failure can extend well beyond pods. In the previous chapter, we discussed resource monitoring and node problem detection. The remedy controller is a great example of the concept of self-healing. Self-healing starts with automated detection of problems followed by automated resolution. Quotas and limits help create checks and balances to ensure an automated self-healing doesn't run amok due to unpredictable circumstances such as DDOS attacks.

In this section, we considered various concepts involved in creating reliable and highly available systems. In the next section, we will apply them and demonstrate best practices for systems deployed on Kubernetes clusters.

High-availability best practices

Building reliable and highly available distributed systems is a non-trivial endeavor. In this section, we will check some of the best practices that enable a Kubernetes-based system to function reliably and be available in the face of various failure categories.

Creating highly available clusters

To create a highly available Kubernetes cluster, the master components must be redundant. That means etcd must be deployed as a cluster (typically across three or five nodes) and the Kubernetes API server must be redundant. Auxiliary cluster-management services such as Heapster's storage may be deployed redundantly too, if necessary. The following diagram depicts a typical reliable and highly available Kubernetes cluster. There are several load-balanced master nodes, each one containing whole master components as well as an etcd component:

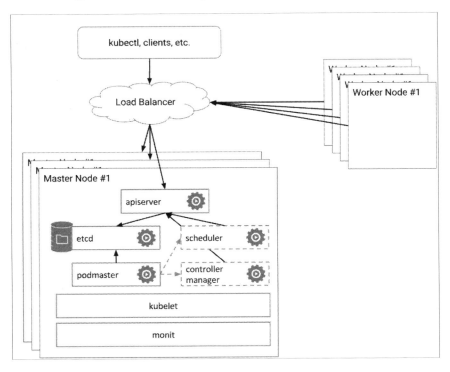

This is not the only way to configure highly available clusters. You may prefer, for example, to deploy a standalone etcd cluster to optimize the machines to their workload or if you require more redundancy for your etcd cluster than the rest of the master nodes.

Making your nodes reliable

Nodes will fail, or some components will fail, but many failures are transient. The basic guarantee is to make sure that the Docker Daemon and kubelet restart automatically in case of a failure.

If you run CoreOS, a modern Debian-based OS (including Ubuntu >= 16.04), or any other OS that uses systemd as its init mechanism, then it's easy to deploy Docker and the kubelet as self-starting Daemons:

```
systemctl enable docker
systemctl enable kublet
```

For other operating systems, the Kubernetes project selected monit for their high-availability example, but you can use any process monitor you prefer.

Protecting your cluster state

The Kubernetes cluster state is stored in etcd. The etcd cluster was designed to be super reliable and distributed across multiple nodes. It's important to take advantage of these capabilities for a reliable and highly available Kubernetes cluster.

Clustering etcd

You should have at least three nodes in your etcd cluster. If you need more reliability and redundancy, you can go five, seven, or any other odd number of nodes. The number of nodes must be odd to have a clear majority in case of a network split.

In order to create a cluster, the etcd nodes should be able to discover each other. There are several methods to accomplish that.

Static discovery

With static discovery, you manage the IP addresses/host names of each etcd directly. This doesn't mean that you manage the etcd cluster outside the Kubernetes cluster or that you're responsible for keeping the etcd cluster healthy. The etcd nodes will run as pods and get restarted automatically if needed.

For example, let's say our `etcd` cluster contains three nodes, as follows:

```
etcd-1 10.0.0.1
etcd-2 10.0.0.2

etcd-2 10.0.0.3
```

Each node will receive this initial cluster information as command-line information:

```
--initial-cluster etcd-1=http://10.0.0.1:2380,etcd-
2=http://10.0.0.2:2380,etcd-3=http://10.0.0.3:2380
--initial-cluster-state new
```

Or, it will receive it as an environment variable:

```
ETCD_INITIAL_CLUSTER="etcd-1=http://10.0.0.1:2380,etcd-
2=http://10.0.0.2:2380,etcd-3=http://10.0.0.3:2380"
ETCD_INITIAL_CLUSTER_STATE=new
```

Etcd discovery

With `etcd` discovery, you use an existing cluster to let the nodes of the new cluster discover each other. This requires, of course, that the new cluster nodes have access to the existing cluster. If you're not worried about the dependency and security implications, you may also use the public `etcd` discovery service at `https://discovery.etcd.io`.

You need to create a `discovery` token. You can specify the cluster `size` if you want; the default is `3`. Here is the command:

```
$ curl https://discovery.etcd.io/new?size=3
```

```
https://discovery.etcd.io/3e86b59982e49066c5d813af1c2e2579cbf573de
```

When working with a `discovery` service, you need to pass the token as a command-line argument:

```
--discovery https://discovery.etcd.io/3e86b59982e49066c5d813af1c2e2579cbf
573de
```

You can also pass it as an environment variable:

```
ETCD_DISCOVERY=https://discovery.etcd.io/3e86b59982e49066c5d813af1c2e2579
cbf573de
```

Note that discovery is relevant for the initial bootstrapping of the initial cluster only. Once the cluster is up and running with the initial nodes, adding and removing nodes from the running cluster is done using a separate protocol, so you don't maintain permanent dependency on the public `etcd` discovery service.

DNS discovery

It is possible to set up discovery using DNS too via SRV records, with and without TLS. The details are outside the scope of this book. You can pursue this route by searching for etcd DNS discovery.

The etcd.yaml file

Depending on the discovery method, the command to start etcd instances on each node will be slightly different in the etcd.yaml pod manifest. The manifest should be copied to each ectd node at /etc/kubernetes/manifests.

Let's look at the different parts of the etcd.yaml manifest file:

```
apiVersion: v1
kind: Pod
metadata:
  name: etcd-server
spec:
  hostNetwork: true
  containers:
  - image: gcr.io/google_containers/etcd:2.0.9
    name: etcd-container
```

The initial section contains the name of the pod, specifies that it uses the host network, and defines a container called etcd-container. Then, the most critical part is the Docker image to use. In this example it is etcd:2.0.9, as in Etcd V2:

```
    command:
    - /usr/local/bin/etcd
    - --name
    - <name>
    - --initial-advertise-peer-urls
    - http://<node ip>:2380
    - --listen-peer-urls
    - http://<node ip>:2380
    - --advertise-client-urls
    - http://<node ip>:4001
    - --listen-client-urls
    - http://127.0.0.1:4001
```

```
- --data-dir
- /var/etcd/data
- --discovery
- <discovery token>
```

The command section lists the command-line arguments etcd requires to operate properly. In this example, the etcd discovery mechanism is used, hence the --discovery flag. The <name>, <node IP>, and <discovery token> should be replaced, for each node, with a unique name (hostname is a good option), the IP address of the node, and the discovery token received earlier (the same token for all nodes):

```
ports:
- containerPort: 2380
  hostPort: 2380
  name: serverport
- containerPort: 4001
  hostPort: 4001
  name: clientport
```

The ports section lists the server (2380) and client (4001) ports, which are mapped to the same ports on the host in this case:

```
volumeMounts:
- mountPath: /var/etcd
  name: varetcd
- mountPath: /etc/ssl
  name: etcssl
  readOnly: true
- mountPath: /usr/share/ssl
  name: usrsharessl
  readOnly: true
- mountPath: /var/ssl
  name: varssl
  readOnly: true
- mountPath: /usr/ssl
  name: usrssl
  readOnly: true
- mountPath: /usr/lib/ssl
```

```
      name: usrlibssl
      readOnly: true
    - mountPath: /usr/local/openssl
      name: usrlocalopenssl
      readOnly: true
    - mountPath: /etc/openssl
      name: etcopenssl
      readOnly: true
    - mountPath: /etc/pki/tls
      name: etcpkitls
      readOnly: true
```

The mounts section lists the varetcd mount at /var/etcd, where etcd writes all its data, and a bunch of SSL and TLS read-only mounts that etcd doesn't modify:

```
volumes:
- hostPath:
    path: /var/etcd/data
  name: varetcd
- hostPath:
    path: /etc/ssl
  name: etcssl
- hostPath:
    path: /usr/share/ssl
  name: usrsharessl
- hostPath:
    path: /var/ssl
  name: varssl
- hostPath:
    path: /usr/ssl
  name: usrssl
- hostPath:
    path: /usr/lib/ssl
  name: usrlibssl
- hostPath:
    path: /usr/local/openssl
  name: usrlocalopenssl
```

```
- hostPath:
    path: /etc/openssl
  name: etcopenssl
- hostPath:
    path: /etc/pki/tls
  name: etcpkitls
```

The `volumes` section provides a volume for each mount mapped to the corresponding host path. While the read-only mounts are probably fine as is, you may want to map the `varetcd` volume to a more robust network storage rather than just depend on the redundancy of the `etcd` nodes themselves.

Verifying the etcd cluster

Once the `etcd` cluster is up and running you can access the `etcdctl` tool to check on the cluster status and health. Kubernetes lets you execute commands directly inside pods or container via the `exec` command (similar to `docker exec`).

Recommended commands are as follows:

- `etcdctl member list`
- `etcdctl cluster-health`
- `etcdctl set test` ("yeah, it works!")
- `etcdctl get test` (should return "yeah, it works!")

etcd 2 versus etcd 3

At the time of writing, Kubernetes 1.4 officially supports etcd v2. etcd v3 is a significant improvement and has many desirable properties, such as the following:

- Double the performance for native clients due to the switch from JSON over REST to protobufs over gRPC
- Improved performance due to support for leases versus verbose key TTLs
- Multiple watches are multiplexed on a single connection using gRPC instead of keeping an open connection for each watch

etcd v3 has been demonstrated to work in Kubernetes, but has not officially become the supported version yet. This is a non-trivial change and work is ongoing. Hopefully, by the time you read this v3 will be the official version. If not, it is possible to migrate etcd v2 to etcd v3.

Protecting your data

Protecting the cluster state and configuration is great, but even more important is protecting your own data. If somehow the cluster state gets corrupted, you can always rebuild the cluster from scratch (although the cluster will not be available during the rebuild). But if your own data is corrupted or lost, you're in deep trouble. The same rules apply; redundancy is king. But while the Kubernetes cluster state is very dynamic, much of your data is maybe less dynamic. For example, a lot of historic data is often important and can be backed up and restored. Live data might be lost, but the overall system may be restored to an earlier snapshot and suffer only temporary damage.

Running redundant API servers

The API servers are stateless, fetching all the necessary data on the fly from `etcd` cluster. This means that you can easily run multiple API servers without needing to coordinate between them. Once you have multiple API servers running you can put a load balancer in front of them to make it transparent to clients.

Running leader election with Kubernetes

Some master components, such as the scheduler and the controller manager, can't have multiple instances active at the same time. This will be chaos, as multiple schedulers try to schedule the same pod into multiple nodes or multiple times into the same node. The correct way to have a highly scalable Kubernetes cluster is to have these components run in leader election mode. This mean that multiple instances are running, but only one is active at a time and if it fails, another one is elected as leader and takes its place.

Kubernetes supports this mode via the `--leader-elect` flag. The scheduler and the controller manager can be deployed as pods by copying their respective manifests to `/etc/kubernetes/manifests`.

Here is a snippet from a scheduler manifest that shows the use of the flag:

```
command:
- /bin/sh
- -c
- /usr/local/bin/kube-scheduler --master=127.0.0.1:8080 --v=2
--leader-elect=true 1>>/var/log/kube-scheduler.log
  2>&1
```

Here is a snippet from a controller manager manifest that shows the use of the flag:

```
- command:
  - /bin/sh
  - -c
  - /usr/local/bin/kube-controller-manager --master=127.0.0.1:8080
--cluster-name=e2e-test-bburns
    --cluster-cidr=10.245.0.0/16 --allocate-node-cidrs=true --cloud-
provider=gce  --service-account-private-key-file=/srv/kubernetes/server.
key
    --v=2 --leader-elect=true 1>>/var/log/kube-controller-manager.log
2>&1
  image: gcr.io/google_containers/kube-controller-manager:fda24638d51a4
8baa13c35337fcd4793
```

Note that it is not possible to have these components restarted automatically by Kubernetes like other pods because these are exactly the Kubernetes components responsible for restarting failed pods, so they can't restart themselves if they fail. There must be a ready-to-go replacement already running.

Leader election for your application

Leader election can be very useful for your application too, but it is notoriously difficult to implement. Luckily, Kubernetes comes to the rescue. There is a documented procedure for supporting leader election for your application via the leader-elector container from Google. The basic concept is to use the Kubernetes endpoints combined with ResourceVersion and Annotations. When you couple this container as a sidecar in your application pod, you get leader-election capabilities in a very streamlined fashion.

Let's run the leader-elector container with three pods and an election called election:

```
> kubectl run leader-elector --image=gcr.io/google_containers/leader-
elector:0.4 --replicas=3 -- --election=election –http=0.0.0.0:4040
```

After a while, you'll see three new pods in your cluster, called leader-elector-xxx:

```
> kubectl get pods
NAME                              READY   STATUS    RESTARTS   AGE
echo-3580479493-n66n4             1/1     Running   12         22d
leader-elector-916043122-10wjj    1/1     Running   0          8m
leader-elector-916043122-6tmn4    1/1     Running   0          8m
leader-elector-916043122-vui6f    1/1     Running   0          8m
```

OK. But who is the master? Let's query the election endpoints:

```
> kubectl get endpoints election -o json
{
    "kind": "Endpoints",
    "apiVersion": "v1",
    "metadata": {
        "name": "election",
        "namespace": "default",
        "selfLink": "/api/v1/namespaces/default/endpoints/election",
        "uid": "48ffc442-b451-11e6-9db1-c2777b74ca9d",
        "resourceVersion": "892261",
        "creationTimestamp": "2016-11-27T03:26:29Z",
        "annotations": {
            "control-plane.alpha.kubernetes.io/leader":
"{\"holderIdentity\":\"leader-elector-916043122-10wjj\",\"leaseDura
tionSeconds\":10,\"acquireTime\":\"2016-11-27T03:26:29Z\",\"renewTi
me\":\"2016-11-27T03:38:02Z\",\"leaderTransitions\":0}"
        }
    },
    "subsets": []
}
```

If you look really hard, you can see it buried in the `metadata.annotations`. To make it easy to detect, I recommend the fantastic `jq` program for slicing and dicing JSON (`https://stedolan.github.io/jq/`). It is very useful to parse the output of the Kubernetes API or `kubectl`:

```
kubectl get endpoints election -o json | jq -r .metadata.annotations[]
| jq .holderIdentity
"leader-elector-916043122-10wjj"
```

To prove that leader election works, let's kill the leader and see if a new leader is elected:

```
kubectl delete pod leader-elector-916043122-10wjj
pod "leader-elector-916043122-10wjj" deleted
```

And we have a new leader:

```
kubectl get endpoints election -o json | jq -r .metadata.annotations[]
| jq .holderIdentity
"leader-elector-916043122-6tmn4"
```

You can also find the leader through HTTP because each `leader-elector` container exposes the leader through a local web server (running on port `4040`):

```
Kubectl proxy
http http://localhost:8001/api/v1/proxy/namespaces/default/pods/
leader-elector-916043122-vui6f:4040/ | jq .name
"leader-elector-916043122-6tmn4"
```

The local web server allows the `leader-elector` container to function as a sidecar container to your main application container within the same pod. Your application container shares the same local network as the `leader-elector` container, so it can access `http://localhost:4040` and get the name of the current leader. Only the application container that shares the pod with the elected leader will run the application; the other application containers in the other pods will be dormant. If they receive requests, they'll forward them to the leader, or some clever load-balancing tricks can be done to automatically send all requests to the current leader.

Making your staging environment highly available

High availability is not trivial to set up. If you go to the trouble of setting up high availability, it means there is a business case for a highly available system. It follows that you want to test your reliable and highly available cluster beforeyou deploy it to production (unless you're Netflix, where you test in production). Also, any change to the cluster may, in theory, break your high availability without disrupting other cluster functions. The essential point is that, just like anything else, if you don't test it, assume it doesn't work.

We've established that you need to test reliability and high availability. The best way to do it is to create a staging environment that replicates your production environment as closely as possible. This can get expensive. There are several ways to manage the cost:

- **Ad hoc HA staging environment**: Create a large HA cluster only for the duration of HA testing

- **Compress time**: Create interesting event streams and scenarios ahead of time, feed the input, and simulate the situations in rapid succession

- **Combine HA testing with performance and stress testing**: At the end of your performance and stress tests, overload the system and see how the reliability and high availability configuration handles the load

Testing high-availability

Testing high-availability takes planning and a deep understanding of your system. The goal of every test is to reveal flaws in the system's design and/or implementation, and to provide good enough coverage that, if the tests pass, you'll be confident that the system behaves as expected.

In the realm of reliability and high-availability, it means you need to figure out ways to break the system and watch it put itself back together.

That requires several pieces, as follows:

- Comprehensive list of possible failures (including reasonable combinations)
- For each possible failure, it should be clear how the system should respond
- A way to induce the failure
- A way to observe how the system reacts

None of the pieces are trivial. The best approach in my experience is to do it incrementally and try to come up with a relatively small number of generic failure categories and generic responses, rather than an exhaustive, ever-changing list of low-level failures.

For example, a generic failure category is node-unresponsive; the generic response could be rebooting the node, the way to induce the failure can be stopping the VM of the node (if it's a VM), and the observation should be that, while the node is down, the system still functions properly based on standard acceptance tests, the node is eventually up, and the system gets back to normal. There may be many other things you want to test, such as whether the problem was logged, whether relevant alerts went out to the right people, and whether various stats and reports were updated.

Note that sometimes, a failure can't be resolved in a single response. For example, in our unresponsive node case, if it's a hardware failure then reboot will not help. In this case, a second line of response gets into play and maybe a new VM is started, configured, and hooked up to the node. In this case, you can't be too generic and you may need to create tests for specific types of pod/role that were on the node (etcd, master, worker, database, monitoring).

If you have high quality requirements, be prepared to spend much more time setting up the proper testing environments and the tests than even the production environment.

One last, important point is to try to be as non-intrusive as possible. That means that, ideally, your production system will not have testing features that allow shutting down parts of it or cause it to be configured to run in reduced capacity for testing. The reason is that it increases the attack surface of your system and it can be triggered by accident by mistakes in configuration. Ideally, you can control your testing environment without resorting to modifying the code or configuration that will be deployed in production. With Kubernetes, it is usually easy to inject pods and containers with custom test functionality that can interact with system components in the staging environment, but will never be deployed in production.

In this section, we looked at what it takes to actually have a reliable and highly available cluster, including etcd, the API server, the scheduler, and the controller manager. We considered best practices for protecting the cluster itself as well as your data, and paid special attention to the issue of starting environments and testing.

Live cluster upgrades

One of the most complicated and risky tasks involved in running a Kubernetes cluster is a live upgrade. The interactions between different parts of the system of different versions are often difficult to predict, but in many situations, it is required. Large clusters with many users can't afford to be offline for maintenance. The best way to attack complexity is to divide and conquer. Microservice architecture helps a lot here. You never upgrade your entire system. You just constantly upgrade several sets of related microservices, and if APIs have changed then you upgrade their clients, too. A properly designed upgrade will preserve backward-compatibility at least until all clients have been upgraded, and then deprecate old APIs across several releases.

In this section, we will discuss how to go about upgrading your cluster using various strategies, such as rolling upgrades and blue-green upgrades. We will also discuss when it's appropriate to introduce breaking upgrades versus backward-compatible upgrades. Then we will get into the critical topic of schema and data migration.

Rolling upgrades

Rolling upgrades are upgrades where you gradually upgrade components from the current version to the next. This means that your cluster will run current and new components at the same time. There are two cases to consider here:

- New components are backward-compatible
- New components are not backward-compatible

If the new components are backward-compatible, then the upgrade should be very easy. In earlier versions of Kubernetes, you had to manage rolling upgrades very carefully with labels and change the number of replicas gradually for both the old and new version (although `kubectl rolling-update` is a convenient shortcut for replication controllers). But, the deployment resource introduced in Kubernetes 1.2 makes it much easier and supports replica sets. It has the following capabilities built-in:

- Running server-side (it keeps going if your machine disconnects)
- Versioning
- Multiple concurrent rollouts
- Updating deployments
- Aggregating status across all pods
- Rollbacks
- Canary deployments
- Multiple upgrade strategies (rolling upgrade is the default)

Here is a sample manifest for a deployment that deploys three `nginx` pods:

```
apiVersion: extensions/v1beta1
kind: Deployment
metadata:
  name: nginx-deployment
spec:
  replicas: 3
  template:
    metadata:
      labels:
        app: nginx
    spec:
      containers:
      - name: nginx
        image: nginx:1.7.9
        ports:
        - containerPort: 80
```

The resource kind is `deployment` and it's got the name `nginx-deployment`, which you can use to refer to this deployment later (for example, for updates or rollbacks). The most important part is, of course, the `spec`, which contains a pod template. The `replicas` determine how many pods will be in the cluster, and the template `spec` has the configuration for each container. In this case, just a single container.

To start the rolling update, you create the `deployment` resource:

```
$ kubectl create -f nginx-deployment.yaml --record
```

You can view the status of the `deployment` later:

```
$ kubectl rollout status deployment/nginx-deployment
```

Complex deployments

The `deployment` resource is great when you just want to upgrade one pod, but you may often need to upgrade multiple pods, and those pods sometimes have version inter-dependencies. In those situations, you sometimes must forego a rolling update or introduce a temporary compatibility layer. For example, suppose service A depends on service B. Service B now has a breaking change. The v1 pods of service A can't interoperate with the pods from service B v2. It is also undesirable from a reliability and change-management point of view to make the v2 pods of service B support the old and new APIs. In this case, the solution may be to introduce an adapter service that implements the v1 API of the B service. This service will sit between A and B, and will translate requests and responses across versions. This adds complexity to the deployment process and require several steps, but the benefit is the A and B services themselves are simple. You can do rolling updates across incompatible versions and all indirection can go away once everybody upgrades to v2 (all A pods and all B pods).

Blue-green upgrades

Rolling updates are great for availability, but sometimes the complexity involved in managing a proper rolling update is considered too high, or it adds a significant amount of work that pushes back more important projects. In these cases, blue-green upgrades provide a great alternative. With a blue-green release, you prepare a full copy of your production environment with the new version. Now you have two copies, old (blue) and new (green). It doesn't matter which one is blue and which one is green. The important thing is that you have two fully independent production environments. Currently, blue is active and services all requests. You can run all your tests on green. Once you're happy, you flip the switch and green becomes active. If something goes wrong, rolling back is just as easy; just switch back from green to blue. I elegantly ignored the storage and in-memory state here. This immediate switch assumes that blue and green are composed of stateless components only and share a common persistence layer.

If there were storage changes or breaking changes to the API accessible to external clients, then additional steps need to be taken. For example, if blue and green have their own storage, then all incoming requests may need to be sent to both blue and green, and green may need to ingest historical data from blue to get in sync before switching:

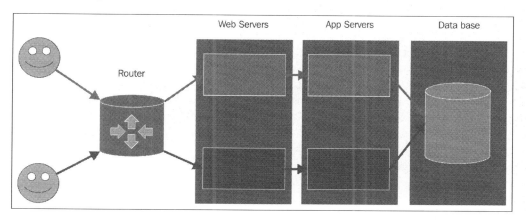

Managing data-contract changes

Data contracts describe how the data is organized. It's an umbrella term for structure metadata. A database schema is the most typical example. The most common example is a relational database schema. Other examples include network payloads, file formats, and even the content of string arguments or responses. If you have a configuration file, then this configuration file has both a file format (JSON, YAML, TOML, XML, INI, custom format) and some internal structure that describes what kind of hierarchy, keys, values, and data types are valid. Sometimes the data contract is explicit and sometimes it's implicit. Either way, you need to manage it carefully, or else you'll get runtime errors when code that's reading, parsing, or validating encounters data with an unfamiliar structure.

Migrating data

Data migration is a big deal. Many systems these days manage measured terabytes, petabytes, or more. The amount of collected and managed data will continue to increase for the foreseeable future. The pace of data collection exceeds the pace of hardware innovation. The essential point is that if you have a lot of data and you need to migrate it, it can take a while. In a previous company, I oversaw a project to migrate close to 100 terabytes of data from one Cassandra cluster of a legacy system to another Cassandra cluster.

The second Cassandra cluster had different schema and was accessed by a Kubernetes cluster 24/7. The project was very complicated, and thus it kept getting pushed back when urgent issues popped up. The legacy system was still in place side-by-side with the next-gen system long after the original estimate.

There were a lot of mechanisms in place to split the data and send it to both clusters, but then we ran into scalability issues with the new system and we had to address those before we could continue. The historical data was important, but it didn't have to be accessed with the same service level as recent hot data. So, we embarked on yet another project to send historical data to cheaper storage. That meant, of course, that client libraries or frontend services had to know how to query both stores and merge the results. When you deal with a lot of data you can't take anything for granted. You run into scalability issues with your tools, your infrastructure, your third-party dependencies, and your processes. Large scale is not just quantity change; it is often qualitative change as well. Don't expect it to go smoothly. It is much more than copying some files from A to B.

Deprecating APIs

API deprecation comes in two flavors: internal and external. **Internal APIs** are APIs used by components that are fully controlled by you and your team or organization. You can be sure that all API users will upgrade to the new API within a short time. **External APIs** are used by users or services outside your direct sphere of influence. There are a few gray-area situations where you work for a huge organization (think Google), and even internal APIs may need to be treated as external APIs. If you're lucky, all your external APIs are used by self-updating applications or through a web interface you control. In those cases, the API is practically hidden and you don't even need to publish it.

If you have a lot of users (or a few very important users) using your API, you should consider deprecation very carefully. Deprecating an API means you force your users to change their application to work with you or stay locked to an earlier version.

There are a few ways you can mitigate the pain:

- Don't deprecate. Extend the existing API or keep the previous API active. It is sometimes pretty simple, although it adds testing burden.

- Provide client libraries in all relevant programming languages to your target audience. This is always a good practice. It allows you to make many changes to the underlying API without disrupting users (as long as you keep the programming language interface stable).

- If you have to deprecate, explain why, allow ample time for users to upgrade, and provide as much support as possible (for example, an upgrade guide with examples). Your users will appreciate it.

Large-cluster performance, cost, and design trade-offs

In the previous section, we looked at live cluster upgrades. We explored various techniques and how Kubernetes supports them. We also discussed difficult problems such as breaking changes, data contract changes, data migration, and API deprecation. In this section, we will consider the various options and configurations of large clusters with different reliability and high-availability properties. When you design your cluster, you need to understand your options and choose wisely based on the needs of your organization.

In this section, we will cover various availability requirements, from best effort all the way to the holy grail of zero downtime, and for each category of availability, we will consider what it means from the perspectives of performance and cost.

Availability requirements

Different systems have very different requirements for reliability and availability. Moreover, different sub-systems have very different requirements. For example, billing systems are always a high priority because if the billing system is down, you can't make money. But, even within the billing system, if the ability to dispute charges is sometimes unavailable, it may be OK from the business point of view.

Best effort

Best effort means, counterintuitively, no guarantee whatsoever. If it works, great! If it doesn't work–oh well. What are you going to do?. This level of reliability and availability may be appropriate for internal components that change often and the effort to make them robust is not worth it. It may also be appropriate for services released in the wild as beta.

Best effort is great for developers. Developers can move fast and break things. They are not worried about the consequences and they don't have to go through a gauntlet of rigorous tests and approvals. The performance of best effort services may be better than more robust services because it can often skip expensive steps such as verifying requests, persisting intermediate results, and replicating data. But, on the other hand, more robust services are often heavily optimized and their supporting hardware is fine-tuned to their workload. The cost of best effort services is usually lower because they don't need to employ redundancy, unless the operators neglect to do basic capacity planning and just over-provision needlessly.

In the context of Kubernetes, the big question is whether all the services provided by the cluster are best effort. If this is the case, then the cluster itself doesn't have to be highly available. You can probably have a single master node with a single instance of etcd, and Heapster or another monitoring solution may not need to be deployed.

Maintenance windows

In a system with maintenance windows, special times are dedicated for performing various maintenance activities, such as applying security patches, upgrading software, pruning log files, and database cleanups. With a maintenance window, the system (or a sub-system) becomes unavailable. This is planned off-time and often, users are notified. The benefit of maintenance windows is that you don't have to worry how your maintenance actions are going to interact with live requests coming into the system. It can drastically simplify operations. System administrators love maintenance windows just as much as developers love best effort systems.

The downside, of course, is that the system is down during maintenance. It may only be acceptable for systems where user activity is limited to certain times (US office hours or week days only).

With Kubernetes, you can do maintenance windows by redirecting all incoming requests via the load balancer to a web page (or JSON response) that notifies users about the maintenance window.

But in most cases, the flexibility of Kubernetes should allow you to do live maintenance. In extreme cases, such as upgrading the Kubernetes version, or the switch from etcd v2 to etcd v3, you may want to resort to a maintenance window. Blue-green deployment is another alternative. But the larger the cluster, the more expansive the blue-green alternative because you must duplicate your entire production cluster, which is both costly and can cause you to run into insufficient quota issues.

Quick recovery

Quick recovery is another important aspect of highly available clusters. Something will go wrong at some point. Your unavailability clock starts running. How quickly can you get back to normal?

Sometimes it's not up to you. For example, if your cloud provider has an outage (and you didn't implement a federated cluster, as we will discuss later) then you just have to sit and wait until they sort it out. But the most likely culprit is a problem with a recent deployment. There are, of course, time-related issues, and even calendar-related issues. Do you remember the leap-year bug that took down Microsoft Azure on February 29, 2012?

The poster boy of quick recovery is, of course, the blue-green deployment–if you keep the previous version running when the problem is discovered.

On the other hand, rolling updates mean that if the problem is discovered early then most of your pods still run the previous version.

Data-related problems can take a long time to reverse, even if your backups are up to date and your restore procedure actually works (definitely test this regularly).

Zero-downtime

Finally, we arrive at the zero-downtime system. There is no such thing as a zero-downtime system. All systems fail and all software systems definitely fail. Sometimes the failure is serious enough that the system or some of its services will be down. Think about zero-downtime as a best effort distributed system design. You design for zero-downtime in the sense that you provide a lot of redundancy and mechanisms to address expected failures without bringing the system down. As always, remember that, even if there is a business case for zero-downtime, it doesn't mean that every component must be.

The plan for zero-downtime is as follows:

- Redundancy at every level: This is a required condition. You can't have a single point of failure in your design because when it fails, your system is down.

- Automated hot swapping of failed components: Redundancy is only as good as the ability of the redundant components to kick into action as soon as the original component has failed. Some components can share the load (for example, stateless web servers), so there is no need for explicit action. In other cases, such as the Kubernetes scheduler and controller manager, you need leader election in place to make sure the cluster keeps humming along.

- Tons of monitoring and alerts to detect problems early: Even with careful design, you may miss something or some implicit assumption might invalidate your design. Often such subtle issues creep up on you and with enough attention, you may discover it before it becomes an all-out system failure. For example, suppose there is a mechanism in place to clean up old log files when disk space is over 90% full, but for some reason, it doesn't work. If you set an alert for when disk space is over 95% full, then you'll catch it and be able
to prevent the system failure.

- Tenacious testing before deployment to production: Comprehensive tests have proven themselves as a reliable way to improve quality. It is hard work to have comprehensive tests for something as complicated as a large Kubernetes cluster running a massive distributed system, but you need it. What should you test? Everything. That's right. For zero-downtime, you need to test both the application and the infrastructure together. Your 100% passing unit tests are a good start, but they don't provide much confidence that when you deploy your application on your production Kubernetes cluster it will still run as expected. The best tests are, of course, on your production cluster after a blue-green deployment or identical cluster. In lieu of a full-fledged identical cluster, consider a staging environment with as much fidelity as possible to your production environment. Here is a list of tests you should run. Each of these tests should be comprehensive because if you leave something untested it might be broken:

  - Unit tests
  - Acceptance tests
  - Performance tests
  - Stress tests
  - Rollback tests
  - Data restore tests
  - Penetration tests

Does that sound crazy? Good. Zero-downtime large-scale systems are hard. There is a reason why Microsoft, Google, Amazon, Facebook, and other big companies have tens of thousands of software engineers (combined) just working on infrastructure, operations, and making sure things are up and running.

- Keep the raw data: For many systems, the data is the most critical asset. If you keep the raw data, you can recover from any data corruption and processed data loss that happens later. This will not really help you with zero-downtime because it can take a while to re-process the raw data, but it will help with zero-data loss, which is often more important. The downside to this approach is that the raw data is often huge compared to the processed data. A good option may be to store the raw data in cheaper storage compared to the processed data.

- Perceived uptime as a last resort: OK. Some part of the system is down. You may still be able to maintain some level of service. In many situations, you may have access to a slightly stale version of the data or can let the user access some other part of the system. It is not a great user experience, but technically the system is still available.

Performance and data consistency

When you develop or operate distributed systems, the CAP theorem should always be in the back of your mind. In this section, we will focus on highly available systems, which means AP. To achieve high availability, we must sacrifice consistency. But that doesn't mean that our system will have corrupt or arbitrary data. The keyword is eventual consistency. Our system may be a little bit behind and provide access to somewhat stale data, but eventually you'll get what you expect. When you start thinking in terms of eventual consistency, it opens the door to potentially significant performance improvements.

For example, if some important value is updated frequently (for example, every second), but you send its value only every minute, you have reduced your network traffic by a factor of 60 and you're on average only 30 seconds behind real-time updates. This is very significant. This is huge. You have just scaled your system to handle 60 times more users or requests.

Summary

In this chapter, we looked at reliable and highly available large-scale Kubernetes clusters. This is arguably the sweet spot for Kubernetes. While it is useful to be able to orchestrate a small cluster running a few containers, it is not necessary, but at scale, you must have an orchestration solution in place you can trust to scale with your system, and provide the tools and the best practices to do that.

You now have a solid understanding of the concepts of reliability and high availability in distributed systems. You delved into the best practices for running reliable and highly available Kubernetes clusters. You explored the nuances of live Kubernetes cluster upgrades and you can make wise design choices regarding levels of reliability and availability, as well as their performance and cost.

In *Chapter 5, Running Kubernetes on Multiple Clouds and Cluster Federation*, we will address the important topic of security in Kubernetes. We will also discuss the challenges of securing Kubernetes and the risks involved. We will learn all about namespaces, service accounts, admission control, authentication, authorization, and encryption.

5

Configuring Kubernetes Security, Limits, and Accounts

In *Chapter 4*, *High Availability and Reliability*, we looked at reliable and highly available Kubernetes clusters, the basic concepts, the best practices, how to do live cluster upgrades, and the many design trade-offs regarding performance and cost.

In this chapter, we will explore the important topic of security. Kubernetes clusters are complicated systems composed of multiple layers of interacting components. Isolation and compartmentalization of different layers is very important when running critical applications. To secure the system and ensure proper access to resources, capabilities, and data, we must first understand the unique challenges facing Kubernetes as a general-purpose orchestration platform that runs unknown workloads. Then we can take advantage of various security, isolation, and access control mechanisms to make sure the cluster, the applications running on it, and the data are all safe. We will discuss various best practices and when it is appropriate to use each mechanism.

At the end of this chapter, you will have a good understanding of Kubernetes security challenges. You will gain practical knowledge of how to harden Kubernetes against various potential attacks, establishing defense in depth, and will even be able to safely run a multi-tenant cluster while providing different users full isolation as well as full control over their part of the cluster.

Understanding Kubernetes security challenges

Kubernetes is a very flexible system that manages very low-level resources in a generic way. Kubernetes itself can be deployed on many operating systems and hardware or virtual-machine solutions on-premises or in the cloud. Kubernetes runs workloads implemented by runtimes it interacts with through a well-defined runtime interface, but without understanding how they are implemented. Kubernetes manipulates critical resources such as networking, DNS, and resource allocation on behalf or in service of applications it knows nothing about. This means that Kubernetes is faced with the difficult task of providing good security mechanisms and capabilities in a way that application administrators can utilize, while protecting itself and the application administrators from common mistakes.

In this section, we will discuss security challenges in several layers or components of a Kubernetes cluster: nodes, network, images, pods, and containers. Defense in depth is an important security concept that requires systems to protect themselves at each level, both to mitigate attacks that penetrated other layers and to limit the scope and damage of a breach. Recognizing the challenges in each layer is the first step toward defense in depth.

Node challenges

The nodes are the hosts of the runtime engines. If an attacker gets access to a node, this is a serious threat. It can control at least the host itself and all the workloads running on it. But it gets worse. The node has a kubelet running that talks to the API server. A sophisticated attacker can replace the kubelet with a modified version and effectively evade detection by communicating normally with the Kubernetes API server, yet running its own workloads instead of the scheduled workloads. The node will have access to shared resources and to secrets that may allow it to infiltrate even deeper. A node breach is very serious, both because of the possible damage and the difficulty of detecting it after the fact.

Nodes can be compromised at the physical level too. This is more relevant on bare-metal machines where you can tell which hardware is assigned to the Kubernetes cluster.

Another attack vector is resource drain. Imagine that your nodes become part of a bot network that, unrelated to your Kubernetes cluster, just runs its own workloads and drains CPU and memory. The danger here is that Kubernetes and your infrastructure may scale automatically and allocate more resources.

Another problem is installation of debugging and troubleshooting tools or modifying configuration outside of automated deployment. Those are typically untested and, if left behind and active, can lead to at least degraded performance, but can also cause more sinister problems.

Where security is concerned, it's a numbers game. You want to understand the attack surface of the system and where you're vulnerable. Let's list all the node challenges:

- Attacker takes control of the host
- Attacker replaces the kubelet
- Attacker takes control over a node that runs master components (API server, scheduler, controller manager)
- Attacker gets physical access to a node
- Attacker drains resources unrelated to the Kubernetes cluster
- Self-inflicted damage through installation of debugging and troubleshooting tools or configuration change

Network challenges

Any non-trivial Kubernetes cluster spans at least one network. There are many challenges related to networking. You need to understand how your system components are connected at a very fine level. Which components are supposed to talk to each other? What network protocols do they use? What ports? What data do they exchange?

There is a complex chain of exposing ports and capabilities or services:

- Container to host
- Host to host within the internal network
- Host to the world

Using overlay networks (which will be discussed more in *Chapter 10, Advanced Kubernetes Networking*) can help with defense in depth where, even if an attacker gains access to a Docker container, they are sandboxed and can't escape to the underlay network infrastructure.

Discovering components is a big challenge too. There are several options here, such as DNS, dedicated discovery services, and load balancers. Each comes with a set of pros and cons that take careful planning and insight to get right for your situation.

Making sure two containers can find each other and exchange information is not trivial.

You need to decide which resources and endpoints should be publicly accessible. Then you need to come up with a proper way to authenticate users and services, and authorize them to operate on resources.

Sensitive data must be encrypted on the way in and out of the cluster and sometimes at rest, too. That means key management and safe key exchange, which is one of the most difficult problems to solve in security.

If your cluster shares networking infrastructure with other Kubernetes clusters or non-Kubernetes processes then you have to be diligent about isolation and separation.

The ingredients are network policies, firewall rules, and **software-defined networking (SDN)**. The recipe is often customized. This is especially challenging with on-premises and bare-metal clusters. Let's recap:

- Come up with a connectivity plan
- Choose components, protocols, and ports
- Figure out dynamic discovery
- Public versus private access
- Authentication and authorization
- Design firewall rules
- Decide on a network policy
- Key management and exchange

There is a constant tension between making it easy for containers, users, and services to find and talk to each other at the network level versus locking down access and preventing attacks through the network or attacks on the network itself.

Many of these challenges are not Kubernetes-specific. However, the fact that Kubernetes is a generic platform that manages key infrastructure and deals with low-level networking makes it necessary to think about dynamic and flexible solutions that can integrate system-specific requirements into Kubernetes.

Image challenges

Kubernetes runs containers that comply with one of its runtime engines. It has no idea what these containers are doing. You can put certain limits on containers via quotas. You can also limit their access to other parts of the network via network policies. But, in the end, containers do need access to host resources, other hosts in the network, distributed storage, and external services. The image determines the behavior of a container. There are two categories of problems with images:

- Malicious images
- Vulnerable images

Malicious images are images that contain code or configuration that was designed by an attacker to do some harm or collect information. Malicious images can be injected into your image preparation pipeline, including any image repositories you use.

Vulnerable images are images you designed that just happen to contain some vulnerability that allows an attacker to take control of the running container or cause some other harm, including injecting their own code later.

It's hard to tell which category is worse. At the extreme, they are equivalent because they allow seizing total control of the container. The other defenses are in place (remember defense in depth?), and the restrictions put on the container will determine how much damage it can do. Minimizing the danger of bad images is very challenging. Fast-moving companies utilizing microservices may generate many images daily. Verifying an image is not an easy task either. Consider, for example, how Docker images are made of layers. The base images that contain the operating system may become vulnerable any time a new variability is discovered. Moreover, if you rely on base images prepared by someone else (very common) then malicious code may find its way into those base images, which you have no control over and you trust implicitly.

To summarize image challenges:

- Kubernetes doesn't know what images are doing
- Kubernetes must provide access to sensitive resources for the designated function
- It's difficult to protect the image preparation and delivery pipeline (including image repositories)
- Speed of development and deployment of new images conflict with careful review changes

- Base images that contain the OS can easily get out of date and become vulnerable
- Base images are often not under your control and might be more prone to injection of malicious code

Configuration and deployment challenges

Kubernetes clusters are administered remotely. Various manifests and policies determine the state of the cluster at each point in time. If an attacker gets access to a machine with administrative control over the cluster, they can wreak havoc, such as collecting information, injecting bad images, weakening security, and tempering with logs. As usual, bugs and mistakes can be just as harmful, by neglecting important security measures and leaving the cluster open for an attack. It is very common these days for employees with administrative access to the cluster work remotely from home or a coffee shop and have their laptops with them, where you are one `kubectl` command from opening the flood gates.

Let's reiterate the challenges:

- Kubernetes is administered remotely
- An attacker with remote administrative access can gain complete control over the cluster
- Configuration and deployment is typically more difficult to test than code
- Remote or out-of-office employees risk extended exposure, allowing an attacker to gain access to their laptops or phones with administrative access

Pod and container challenges

In Kubernetes, pods are the unit of work and contain one or more containers. The pod is just a grouping and deployment construct, but in practice containers that are deployed together in the same pod usually interact through direct mechanisms. The containers all share the same localhost network and often share mounted volumes from the host. This easy integration between containers in the same pod can result in exposing parts of the host to all the containers. This might allow one bad container (either malicious or just vulnerable) to open the way for escalated attack on other containers in the pod and later taking over the node itself. Master add-ons are often collocated with master components and present that kind of danger, especially because many of them are experimental. The same goes for DaemonSets that run pods on every node.

Multi-container pod challenges include the following:

- Same pod containers share the localhost network
- Same pod containers often share a mounted volume on the host filesystem
- Bad containers might easily poison other containers in the pod
- Bad containers have an easier time attacking the node
- Experimental add-ons that are collocated with master components might be experimental and less secure

Organisational, cultural, and process challenges

Security is often at loggerheads with productivity. This is a normal trade-off and nothing to worry about. Traditionally, when developer and operations were separate, this conflict was managed at an organizational level. Developers pushed for more productivity and treated security requirements as the cost of doing business. Operations controlled the production environment and were responsible for access and security procedures. The DevOps movement brought down the wall between developers and operations. Now, speed of development often takes a front seat. Concepts such as continuous deployment deploying multiple times a day without human intervention were unheard of in most organizations. Kubernetes was designed for this new world of DevOps and clouds. But, it was developed based on Google's experience. Google had a lot of time and skilled experts to develop the proper processes and tooling to balance rapid deployments with security. For smaller organizations, this balancing act might be very challenging and security could be compromised.

The challenges facing organizations that adopt Kubernetes are as follows:

- Developers that control operation of Kubernetes might be less security-oriented
- Speed of development might be considered more important
- Continuous deployment might make it difficult to detect certain security problems before they reach production
- Smaller organizations might not have the knowledge and expertise to manage security properly in Kubernetes clusters

In this section, we reviewed the many challenges you face when you try to build a secure Kubernetes cluster. Most of these challenges are not specific to Kubernetes, but using Kubernetes means there is a large part of your system that is generic and is unaware of what the system is doing. This can pose problems when trying to lock down a system. The challenges are spread across different levels:

- Node challenges
- Network challenges
- Image challenges
- Configuration and deployment challenges
- Pod and container challenges
- Organizational and process challenges

In the next section, we will look at the facilities Kubernetes provides to address some of those challenges. Many of the challenges require solutions at the larger system scope. It is important to realize that just utilizing all of Kubernetes security features is not enough.

Hardening Kubernetes

The previous section cataloged and listed the variety of security challenges facing developers and administrators deploying and maintaining Kubernetes clusters. In this section, we will hone in on the design aspects, mechanisms, and features offered by Kubernetes to address some of the challenges. You can get to a pretty good state of security by judicious use of capabilities such as service accounts, network policies, authentication, authorization, AppArmor, and secrets.

Remember that a Kubernetes cluster is one part of a bigger system that includes other software systems, people, and processes. Kubernetes can't solve all problems. You should always keep in mind general security principles, such as defense in depth, need-to-know basis, and principle of least privilege. In addition, log everything you think may be useful in the event of an attack and have alerts for early detection when the system deviates from its state. It may be just a bug or it may be an attack. Either way, you want to know about it and respond.

Understanding service accounts in Kubernetes

Kubernetes has regular users managed outside the cluster for humans connecting to the cluster (for example, via the `kubectl` command), and it has service accounts.

SERVICE ACCOUNT = NAMESPACE

Regular users are global and can access multiple namespaces in the cluster. Service accounts are constrained to one namespace. This is important. It ensures namespace isolation, because whenever the API server receives a request from a pod, its credentials will apply only to its own namespace.

Kubernetes manages service accounts on behalf of the pods. Whenever Kubernetes instantiates a pod it assigns the pod a service account. The service account identifies all the pod processes when they interact with the API server. Each service account has a set of credentials mounted in a secret volume. Each namespace has a default service account called default. When you create a pod, it is automatically assigned the default service account unless you specify a different service account.

You can create additional service accounts. Create a file called `custom-service-account.yaml` with the following content:

```
apiVersion: v1
kind: ServiceAccount
metadata:
  name: custom-service-account
```

Now type the following:

```
kubectl create -f custom-service-account.yaml
```

That will result in the following output:

```
serviceaccount "custom-service-account" created
```

Here is the service account listed alongside the default service account:

```
> kubectl get serviceAccounts
NAME                      SECRETS   AGE
custom-service-account    1         3m
default                   1         29d
```

 Note that a secret was created automatically for your new service account.

To get more detail, type the following:

```
 kubectl get serviceAccounts/custom-service-account
apiVersion: v1
kind: ServiceAccount
```

```
metadata:
  creationTimestamp: 2016-12-04T19:27:59Z
  name: custom-service-account
  namespace: default
  resourceVersion: "1243113"
  selfLink: /api/v1/namespaces/default/serviceaccounts/custom-service-
account
  uid: c3cbec89-ba57-11e6-87e3-428251643d3a
secrets:
- name: custom-service-account-token-pn3lt
```

You can see the secret itself, which includes a `ca.crt` file and a token, by typing the following:

```
kubectl get secrets/custom-service-account-token-pn3lt -o yaml
```

How does Kubernetes manage service accounts?

The API server has a dedicated component called service account admission controller. It is responsible for checking, at pod creation time, if it has a custom service account and, if it does, that the custom service account exists. If there is no service account specified, then it assigns the default service account.

It also ensures the pod has `ImagePullSecrets`, which are necessary when images need to be pulled from a remote image registry. If the pod spec doesn't have any secrets, it uses the service account's `ImagePullSecrets`.

Finally, it adds a volume with an API token for API access and a `volumeSource` mounted at `/var/run/secrets/kubernetes.io/serviceaccount`.

The API token is created and added to the secret by another component called the **Token Controller** whenever a service account is created. The Token Controller also monitors secrets and adds or removes tokens wherever secrets are added or removed to/from a service account.

The service account controller ensures the default service account exists for every namespace.

Accessing the API server

Accessing the API requires a chain of steps that include authentication, authorization, and admission control. At each stage the request may be rejected. Each stage consists of multiple plugins that are chained together. The following diagram illustrates this:

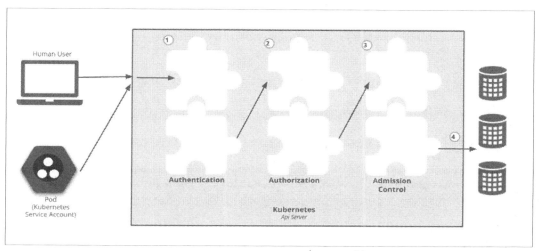

Authenticating users · kube/config

When you first create the cluster, a client certificate and key are created for you. Kubectl uses them to authenticate itself to the API server and vice versa over TLS on port 443 (an encrypted HTTPS connection). You can find your client key and certificate by checking your .kube/config file:

```
> cat C:\Users\the_g\.kube\config | grep client

    client-certificate: C:\Users\the_g\.minikube\apiserver.crt
    client-key: C:\Users\the_g\.minikube\apiserver.key
```

 Note that if multiple users need to access the cluster, the creator should provide the client certificate and key to the other users in a secure manner.

This is just establishing basic trust with the Kubernetes API server itself. You're not authenticated yet. Various authentication modules may look at the request and check for various additional client certificates, password, tokens, and JWT tokens (for service accounts). Most requests require an authenticated user (either a regular user or a service account), although there are some anonymous requests too. If a request fails to authenticate with all the authenticators it will be rejected with a `401` HTTP status code (unauthorized, which is a bit of a misnomer).

The cluster administrator determines what authentication strategies to use by providing various command-line arguments to the API server:

- `--client-ca-file=<filename>` (for x509 client certificates specified in a file)
- `--token-auth-file=<filename>` (for bearer tokens specified in a file)
- `--basic-auth-file=<filename>` (for user/password pairs specified in a file)

Service accounts use an automatically loaded authentication plugin. The administrator may provide two optional flags:

- `--service-account-key-file=<filename>` (PEM encoded key for signing bearer tokens. If unspecified, the API server's TLS private key will be used.)
- `--service-account-lookup` (If enabled, tokens that are deleted from the API will be revoked.)

There are several other methods, such as open ID connect, web hook, keystone (the OpenStack identity service), and authenticating proxy. The main theme is that the authentication stage is extensible and can support any authentication mechanism.

The various authentication plugins will examine the request and, based on the provided credentials, will associate the following attributes: username (user-friendly name), **UID** (**unique identifier** and more consistent than the username), and groups (a set of group names the user belongs to). There may also be extra fields, which are just maps of string keys to string values.

The authenticator has no knowledge whatsoever of what a particular user is allowed to do. They just map a set of credentials to a set of identities. It is the job of the authorizers to figure out if the request is valid for the authenticated user.

Authorizing requests

Once a user is authenticated, authorization commences. Kubernetes has generic authorization semantics. A set of authorization plugins receives the request, which includes information such as the authenticated username and the request's verb (list, get, watch, create, and so on). If any authorization plugin authorizes the request, it may continue. If all authorizers rejected the request, it will be rejected with a 403 HTTP status code (forbidden).

The cluster administrator determines what authorization plugins to use by specifying the ---authorization-mode command-line flag, which is a comma-separated list of plugin names. The following modes are supported:

- --authorization-mode=AlwaysDeny blocks all requests (used in tests).

- --authorization-mode=AlwaysAllow allows all requests; use if you don't need authorization.

- --authorization-mode=ABAC allows for a simple local-file-based, user-configured authorization policy. **ABAC** stands for **Attribute-Based Access Control.**

- --authorization-mode=RBAC is an experimental implementation that allows for authorization to be driven by the Kubernetes API. **RBAC** stands for **Roles-Based Access Control.**

- --authorization-mode=Webhook allows for authorization to be driven by a remote service using REST.

You can add your own custom authorization plugin by implementing the following straightforward Go interface:

```
type Authorizer interface {
  Authorize(a Attributes) (authorized bool, reason string, err error)
}
```

The Attributes input argument is also an interface that provides all the information you need to make an authorization decision:

```
type Attributes interface {
  GetUser() user.Info
  GetVerb() string
  IsReadOnly() bool
  GetNamespace() string
  GetResource() string
  GetSubresource() string
```

```
  GetName() string
  GetAPIGroup() string
  GetAPIVersion() string
  IsResourceRequest() bool
  GetPath() string
}
```

Using admission control plugins

OK. The request was authorized, but there is one more step before it can be executed. The request must go through a gauntlet of admission-control plugins. Unlike the authenticators and the authorizers, if a single admission controller rejects a request, it is denied.

Admission controllers are a neat concept. The idea is that there may be global cluster concerns that could be grounds for rejecting a request. Without admission controllers, all authorizers would have to be aware of these concerns and reject the request. But, with admission controllers, this logic can be performed once. In addition, an admission controller may modify the request. As usual, the cluster administrator decides which admission control plugins run by providing a command-line argument called *admission-control*. The value is a comma-separated and ordered list of plugins.

Let's look at what plugins are available:

- **AlwaysAdmit**: Passthrough (I'm not sure why it's needed)
- **AlwaysDeny**: Reject everything (useful for testing)
- **ImagePolicyWebhook**: This complicated plugin connects to an external backend to decide whether a request should be rejected based on the image
- **ServiceAccount**: Automation for service accounts
- **ResourceQuota**: Reject requests that violate the namespace's resource quota
- **LimitRanger**: Reject requests that violate resource limits
- **InitialResources** (experimental): Assigns compute resources and limit based on historical usage, if not specified
- **NamespaceLifecycle**: Reject requests for creating objects in terminating or non-existing namespaces
- **DefaultStorageClass**: Adds a default storage class to requests for the creation of a **PersistentVolumeClaim** that doesn't specify a storage class

As you can see, the admission control plugins have very diverse functionality. They support namespace-wide policies and enforce validity of requests mostly from a resource management point of view. This frees the authorization plugins to focus on valid operations. The **ImagePolicyWebHook** is the gateway to validating images, which is a big challenge.

The division of responsibility for validating an incoming request through the separate stages of authentication, authorization, and admission, each with its own plugins, makes a complicated process much more manageable to understand and use.

Securing pods

Pod security is a major concern, since Kubernetes schedules the pods and lets them run. There are several independent mechanisms for securing pods and containers. Together these mechanisms support defense in depth, where, even if an attacker (or a mistake) bypasses one mechanism, it will get blocked by another.

Using a private image repository

This approach gives you a lot of confidence that your cluster will only pull images that you have previously vetted, and you can manage upgrades better. You can configure your $HOME/.dockercfg or $HOME/.docker/config.json on each node. But, on many cloud providers, you can't do it because nodes are provisioned automatically for you.

ImagePullSecrets

This approach is recommended for clusters on cloud providers. The idea is that the credentials for the registry will be provided by the pod, so it doesn't matter what node it is scheduled to run on. This circumvents the problem with .dockercfg at the node level.

First, you need to create a secret object for the credentials:

```
> kubectl create secret the-registry-secret
  --docker-server=<docker registry server>
  --docker-username=<username>
  --docker-password=<password>
  --docker-email=<email>
secret "docker-registry-secret" created.
```

You can create secrets for multiple registries (or multiple users for the same registry) if needed. The kubelet will combine all the ImagePullSecrets.

But, since pods can access secrets only in their own namespace, you must create a secret on each namespace where you want the pod to run.

Once the secret is defined, you can add it to the pod spec and run some pods on your cluster. The pod will use the credentials from the secret to pull images from the target image registry:

```
apiVersion: v1
kind: Pod
metadata:
  name: cool-pod
  namespace: the-namespace
spec:
  containers:
    - name: cool-container
      image: cool/app:v1
  imagePullSecrets:
    - name: the-registry-secret
```

Specifying a security context

A security context is a set of operating-system-level security settings such as UID, gid, capabilities, and SELinux role. These settings are applied at the container level as a container security content. You can specify a pod security context that will apply to all the containers in the pod. The pod security context can also apply its security settings (in particular, fsGroup and seLinuxOptions) to volumes.

Here is a sample pod security context:

```
apiVersion: v1
kind: Pod
metadata:
  name: hello-world
spec:
  containers:
    ...
  securityContext:
    fsGroup: 1234
```

```
    supplementalGroups: [5678]
    seLinuxOptions:
      level: "s0:c123,c456"
```

The container security context is applied to each container and it overrides the pod security context. It is embedded in the containers section of the pod manifest. Container context settings can't be applied to volumes, which remain at the pod level.

Here is a sample container security content:

```
apiVersion: v1
kind: Pod
metadata:
  name: hello-world
spec:
  containers:
    - name: hello-world-container
      # The container definition
      # ...
      securityContext:
        privileged: true
        seLinuxOptions:
          level: "s0:c123,c456"
```

Protecting your cluster with AppArmor

AppArmor is a Linux kernel security module. With AppArmor, you can restrict a process running in a container to a limited set of resources such as network access, Linux capabilities, and file permissions. You configure AppArmor though profiles.

Requirements

AppArmor support was added as Beta in Kubernetes 1.4. It is not available for every operating system, so you must choose a supported OS distribution in order to take advantage of it. Ubuntu and SUSE Linux support AppArmor and enable it by default. Other distributions have optional support. To check if AppArmor is enabled, type the following:

```
cat /sys/module/apparmor/parameters/enabled
  Y
```

If the result is Y then it's enabled.

The profile must be loaded into the kernel. Check the following file:

`/sys/kernel/security/apparmor/profiles`

Also, only the Docker runtime supports AppArmor at this time.

Securing a pod with AppArmor

Since AppArmor is still in Beta, you specify the metadata as annotations and not as bonafide fields. When it gets out of Beta that will change.

To apply a profile to a container, add the following annotation:

```
container.apparmor.security.beta.kubernetes.io/<container-name>:
<profile-ref>
```

The profile reference can be either the default profile, `runtime/default`, or a profile file on the host `localhost/<profile-name>`.

Here is a sample profile that prevents writing to files:

```
#include <tunables/global>

profile k8s-apparmor-example-deny-write flags=(attach_disconnected) {
  #include <abstractions/base>

  file,

  # Deny all file writes.
  deny /** w,
}
```

AppArmor is not a Kubernetes resource, so the format is not the YAML or JSON you're familiar with.

To verify the profile was attached correctly, check the attributes of process 1:

`kubectl exec <pod-name> cat /proc/1/attr/current`

Pods can be scheduled on any node in the cluster by default. This means the profile should be loaded into every node. This is a classic use case for DaemonSet.

Writing AppArmor profiles

Writing profiles for AppArmor by hand is not trivial. There are some tools that can help: `aa-genprof` and `aa-logprof` can generate a profile for you and assist in fine-tuning it by running your application with AppArmor in complain mode. The tools keep track of your application's activity and AppArmor warnings, and create a corresponding profile. This approach works, but it feels clunky.

My favorite tool is bane (`https://github.com/jessfraz/bane`), which generates AppArmor profiles from a simpler profile language based on TOML syntax. Bane profiles are very readable and easy to grasp. Here is a snippet from a bane profile:

```
Name = "nginx-sample"
[Filesystem]
# read only paths for the container
ReadOnlyPaths = [
    "/bin/**",
    "/boot/**",
    "/dev/**",
]


# paths where you want to log on write
LogOnWritePaths = [
    "/**"
]



# allowed capabilities
[Capabilities]
Allow = [
    "chown",
    "setuid",
]


[Network]
Raw = false
Packet = false
Protocols = [
```

```
    "tcp",
    "udp",
    "icmp"
]
```

The generated AppArmor profile is pretty gnarly.

Pod security policies

Pod security policy (PSP) is available as Beta in Kubernetes 1.4. It must be enabled, and you must also enable the PSP admission control to use them. A PSP is defined at the cluster-level and defines the security context for pods. There are a couple of differences between using a PSP and directly specifying a security content in the pod manifest as we did earlier:

- Apply the same policy to multiple pods or containers
- Let the administrator control pod creation so users don't create pods with inappropriate security contexts
- Dynamically generate different security content for a pod via the admission controller

PSPs really scale the concept of security contexts. Typically, you'll have a relatively small number of security policies compared to the number of pods (or rather, pod templates). This means that many pod templates and containers will have the same security policy. Without PSP, you have to manage it individually for each pod manifest.

Here is a sample PSP that allows everything:

```
{
  "kind": "PodSecurityPolicy",
  "apiVersion":"extensions/v1beta1",
  "metadata": {
    "name": "permissive"
  },
  "spec": {
      "seLinux": {
          "rule": "RunAsAny"
      },
      "supplementalGroups": {
          "rule": "RunAsAny"
```

```
    },
    "runAsUser": {
        "rule": "RunAsAny"
    },
    "fsGroup": {
        "rule": "RunAsAny"
    },
    "volumes": ["*"]
  }
}
```

Managing network policies

Node, pod, and container security is imperative, but it's not enough. Network segmentation is critical to design a secure Kubernetes clusters that allows multi-tenancy, as well as to minimize the impact of security breaches. Defense in depth mandates that you compartmentalize parts of the system that don't need to talk to each other, as well as carefully managing the direction, protocols, and ports of traffic.

Network policy allows you fine-grained control and proper network segmentation of your cluster. At the core, a network policy is a set of firewall rules applied to a set of namespaces and pods selected by labels. This a very flexible because labels can define virtual network segments and be managed as a Kubernetes resource.

Choosing a supported networking solution

Some networking backends don't support network policies. For example, the popular Flannel can't be used to apply policies.

Here is a list of supported network backends:

- Calico
- WeaveNet
- Canal
- Romana

Defining a network policy

You define a network policy using a standard YAML manifest.

Here is a sample policy:

```
apiVersion: extensions/v1beta1
kind: NetworkPolicy
metadata:
 name: the-network-policy
 namespace: default
spec:
 podSelector:
  matchLabels:
    role: db
 ingress:
  - from:
    - namespaceSelector:
       matchLabels:
        project: cool-project
    - podSelector:
       matchLabels:
        role: frontend
   ports:
    - protocol: tcp
      port: 6379
```

The spec part has two important parts, the podSelector and the ingress. The podSelector governs which pods this network policy applies to. The ingress governs which namespaces and pods can access these pods and which protocols and ports they can use.

In the sample network policy, the pod selector specified the target for the network policy to be all the pods that are labeled role: db. The ingress section has a from sub-section with a namespace selector and a pod selector. All the namespaces in the cluster that are labeled project: cool-project, and within these namespaces, all the pods that are labeled role: frontend, can access the target pods labeled role: db. The ports section defines a list of pairs (protocol and port) that further restrict what protocols and ports are allowed. In this case, the protocol is tcp and the port is 6379 (Redis standard port).

Note that the network policy is cluster-wide, so pods from multiple namespaces in the cluster can access the target namespace. The current namespace is always included, so even if it doesn't have the project: cool label, pods with role: frontend can still have access.

It's important to realize that the network policy operates in whitelist fashion. By default, all access is forbidden, and the network policy can open certain protocols and ports to certain pods that match the labels. This means that, if your networking solution doesn't support network policies, all access will be denied.

Another implication of the whitelist nature is that, if multiple network policies exist, the union of all the rules apply. If one policy gives access to port 1234 and another gives access to port 5678 for the same set of pods, then a pod may access through either 1234 or 5678.

Using secrets

Secrets are paramount in secure systems. They can be credentials such as username and password, access tokens, API keys, or crypto keys. Secrets are typically small. If you have large amounts of data you want to protect, you should encrypt it and keep the encryption/decryption key as secrets.

Storing secrets in Kubernetes

Kubernetes stores secrets in etcd as plaintext. This means that direct access to etcd should be limited and carefully guarded. Secrets are managed at the namespace level. Pods can mount secrets either as files via secret volumes or as environment variables. From a security standpoint, this means that any user or service that can create a pod in a namespace can have access to any secret managed for that namespace. If you want to limit access to a secret, put it in a namespace accessible to a limited set of users or services.

When a secret is mounted to a pod it is never written to disk. It is stored in tmpfs. When the kubelet communicates with the API server it is uses TLS normally, so the secret is protected in transit.

Creating secrets

Secrets must be created before you try to create a pod that requires them. The secret must exist, otherwise the pod creation will fail.

You can create secrets with the following command:

```
kubectl create secret.
```

Here I create a generic secret called hush-hash, which contains two keys, username and password:

```
kubectl create secret generic hush-hush --from-literal=username=tobias
--from-literal=password=cutoffs
```

The resulting secret is opaque:

```
> kubectl describe secrets/hush-hush
Name:           hush-hush
Namespace:      default
Labels:         <none>
Annotations:    <none>


Type:   Opaque


Data
====
password:       7 bytes
username:       6 bytes
```

You can create secrets from files using `--from-file` instead of `--from-literal`, and you can also create secrets manually if you encode the secret value as `base64`.

Key names inside a secret must follow the rules for DNS sub-domains (without the leading dor).

Decoding secrets

To get the content of a secret you can use `kubectl get secret`:

```
> kubectl get secrets/hush-hush -o yaml
apiVersion: v1
data:
  password: Y3V0b2Zmcw==
  username: dG9iaWFz
kind: Secret
metadata:
```

creationTimestamp: 2016-12-06T22:42:54Z

name: hush-hush

namespace: default

resourceVersion: "1450109"

selfLink: /api/v1/namespaces/default/secrets/hush-hush

uid: 537bd4d6-bc05-11e6-927a-26f559225611
type: Opaque

The values are base64-encoded. You need to decode them yourself:

```
> echo "Y3V0b2Zmcw==" | base64 -decode
cutoofs
```

Using secrets in a container

Containers can access secrets as files by mounting volumes from the pod. Another approach is to access the secrets as environment variables. Finally, a container can access the Kubernetes API directly or use kubectl get secret.

To use a secret mounted as a volume, the pod manifest should declare the volume and it should be mounted in the container's spec:

```
{
 "apiVersion": "v1",
 "kind": "Pod",
  "metadata": {
    "name": "pod-with-secret",
    "namespace": "default"
  },
  "spec": {
    "containers": [{
      "name": "the-container",
      "image": "redis",
      "volumeMounts": [{
        "name": "secret-volume",
        "mountPath": "/mnt/secret-volume",
        "readOnly": true
      }]
    }],
```

```
    "volumes": [{
      "name": "secret-volume",
      "secret": {
        "secretName": "hush-hush"
      }
    }]
  }
}
```

The volume name (`secret-volume`) binds the pod volume to the mount in the container. Multiple containers can mount the same volume.

When this pod is running, the username and password are available as files under /etc/secret-volume:

```
> kubectl exec pod-with-secret cat /mnt/secret-volume/username
tobias
```

```
> kubectl exec pod-with-secret cat /mnt/secret-volume/password
cutoffs
```

Running a multi-user cluster

In this section, we will look briefly at the option to use a single cluster to host systems for multiple users or multiple user communities. The idea is that those users are totally isolated and may not even be aware that they share the cluster with other users. Each user community will have its own resources, and there will be no communication between them (except maybe through public endpoints). The Kubernetes namespace concept is the ultimate expression of this idea.

The case for a multi-user cluster

Why should you run a single cluster for multiple isolated users or deployments? Isn't it simpler to just have a dedicated cluster for each user? There are two main reasons: cost and operational complexity. If you have many relatively small deployments and you want to create a dedicated cluster to each one, then you'll have a separate master node and possibly a three-node `etcd` cluster for each one. That can add up. Operational complexity is very important too. Managing tens or hundreds or thousands of independent clusters is no picnic. Every upgrade and every patch needs to be applied to each cluster. Operations might fail and you'll have to manage a fleet of clusters where some of them are in slightly different state than the others. Meta-operations across all clusters may be more difficult. You'll have to aggregate and write your tools to perform operations and collect data from all clusters.

Let's look at some use cases and requirements for multiple isolated communities or deployments:

- A platform or service provider for <Blank>-as-a-service
- Managing separate testing, staging, and production environments
- Delegating responsibility to community/deployment admins
- Enforcing resource quotas and limits on each community
- Users see only resources in their community

Using namespaces for safe multi-tenancy

Kubernetes namespaces are the perfect answer to safe multi-tenant clusters. This is not a surprise as this was one of the design goals of namespaces.

You can easily create namespaces in addition to the built-in kube-system and default. Here is a YAML file that will create a new namespace called custom-namespace. All it has is a metadata item called name. It doesn't get any simpler:

```
apiVersion: v1
kind: Namespace
metadata:
  name: custom-namespace
```

Let's create the namespace:

```
> Kubectl create -f custom-namespace.yaml
namespace "custom-namespace" created


> kubectl get namesapces
NAME                STATUS     AGE
custom-namespace    Active     39s
default             Active     32d
kube-system         Active     32d
```

The status field can be *active* or *terminating*. When you delete a namespace, it will get into the terminating state. When the namespace is in this state you will not be able to create new resources in this namespace. This simplifies the clean-up of namespace resources and ensures the namespace is really deleted. Without it, the replication controller might create new pods when existing pods are deleted.

To work with a namespace, you add the `--namespace` argument to `kubectl` commands:

```
> kubectl create -f some-pod.yaml --namespace=custom-namespace
pod "some-pod" created
```

Listing pods in the custom-namespace returns only the pod we just created:

```
> kubectl get pods --namespace=custom-namespace
NAME          READY      STATUS       RESTARTS     AGE
some-pod      1/1        Running      0            6m
```

Listing pods without the namespace returns the pods in the default namespace:

does not default to all namespaces

```
> Kubectl get pods
NAME                             READY     STATUS      RESTARTS     AGE
echo-3580479493-n66n4            1/1       Running     16           32d
leader-elector-191609294-1t95t   1/1       Running     4            9d
leader-elector-191609294-m6fb6   1/1       Running     4            9d
leader-elector-191609294-piu8p   1/1       Running     4            9d
pod-with-secret                  1/1       Running     1            1h
```

Avoiding namespace pitfalls

Namespaces are great, but they can add some friction. When you use just the default namespace, you can simply omit the namespace. When using multiple namespaces, you must qualify everything with the namespace. This can add some burden, but doesn't present any danger. However, if some users (for example, cluster administrators) can access multiple namespaces, then you're open to accidentally modifying or querying the wrong namespace. The best way to avoid this situation is to hermetically seal the namespace and require different users and credentials for each namespace.

Also, tools that help make clear what namespace you're operating on (for example, shell prompt if working from commandline or listing the namespace prominently in a web interface).

Make sure that users that can operate on a dedicated namespace don't have access to the default namespace. Otherwise, every time they forget to specify a namespace, they'll operate quietly on the default namespace.

Summary

In this chapter, we covered the many security challenges facing developers and administrators building systems and deploying applications on Kubernetes clusters. But we also explored the many security features and the flexible plugin-based security model that provides many ways to limit, control, and manage containers, pods, and nodes. Kubernetes already provides versatile solutions to most security challenges, and it will only get better as capabilities such as AppArmor and PodSecurityPolicy move from Beta status to general availability. Finally, we considered how to use namespaces to support multiple user communities or deployments in the same Kubernetes cluster.

In *Chapter 6, Using Critical Kubernetes Resources*, we will look in detail into many Kubernetes resources and concepts, and how to use them and combine them effectively. The Kubernetes object model is built on top of a solid foundation of a small number of generic concepts such as resources, manifests, and metadata. This empowers an extensible, yet surprisingly consistent, object model to expose a very diverse set of capabilities for developers and administrators.

6
Using Critical Kubernetes Resources

In this chapter, we will design a massive-scale platform that will challenge Kubernetes' capabilities and scalability. The Hue platform is all about creating an omniscient and omnipotent digital assistant. Hue is a digital extension of you. Hue will help you do anything, find anything, and, in many cases will do a lot on your behalf. It will obviously need to store a lot information, integrate with many external services, respond to notifications and events, and be smart about interacting with you.

We will take the opportunity in this chapter to get to know kubectl and related tools a little better and explore in detail familiar resources we've seen before, such as pods, as well as new resources such as Jobs. At the end of this chapter, you will have a clear picture of how impressive Kubernetes is and how it can be used as the foundation for hugely complex systems.

Designing the Hue platform

In this section, we will set the stage and define the scope of the amazing Hue platform. Hue is not Big Brother, Hue is Little Brother! Hue will do whatever you allow it to do. Hue will be able to do a lot, but some people might be concerned, so you get to pick how much or how little Hue can help you with. Get ready for a wild ride!

Defining the scope of Hue

Hue will be manage your digital persona. It will know you better than you know yourself. Here is a list of some of the services Hue can manage and help you with:

- Search and content aggregation
- Medical

- Smart home
- Finance – bank, savings, retirement, investing
- Office
- Social
- Travel
- Wellbeing
- Family
- Smart reminders and notifications

  Let's think of the possibilities. Hue will know you, but also know your friends, the aggregate of other users across all domains. Hue will update its models in real-time. It will not be confused by stale data. It will act on your behalf, present relevant information, and learn your preferences continuously. It can recommend new shows or books that you may like, make restaurant reservations based on your schedule and your family or friends, and control your house automation.

- Security, identity, and privacy

  Hue is your proxy online. The ramifications of someone stealing your Hue identity, or even just eavesdropping on your Hue interaction, are devastating. Potential users may even be reluctant to trust the Hue organization with their identity. Let's devise a non-trust system where users have the power to pull the plug on Hue at any time. Here are a few ideas in the right direction.

- Strong identity via a dedicated device with multi-factor authorization, including multiple biometric reasons:
    - Frequently rotating credentials
    - Quick service pause and identity reverification of all external services (will require original proof of identity to each provider)
    - The Hue backend will interact with all external services via short-lived tokens
    - Architecting Hue as a collection of loosely-coupled microservices

  Hue's architecture will need to support enormous variation and flexibility. It will also need to be very extensible where existing capabilities and external services are constantly upgraded, and new capabilities and external services are integrated into the platform. That level of scale calls for microservices, where each capability or service is totally independent of other services except for well-defined interfaces via standard and/or discoverable APIs.

Hue components

Before embarking on our microservice journey, let's review the types of component we need to construct for Hue.

User profile

The user profile is a major component, with lots of sub-components. It is the essence of the user, their preferences, history across every area, and everything that Hue knows about them.

User graph

The user graph component models networks of interactions between users across multiple domains. Each user participates in multiple networks: social networks such as Facebook and Twitter, professional networks, hobby networks, and volunteering communities. Some of these networks are ad-hoc and Hue will be able to structure them to benefit users. Hue can take advantage of the rich profiles it has of user connections to improve interactions even without exposing private information.

Identity

Identity management is critical, as mentioned previously, so it deserves a separate component. A user may prefer to manage multiple mutually exclusive profiles with separate identities. For example, maybe users are not comfortable with mixing their health profile with their social profile at the risk of inadvertently exposing personal health information to their friends.

Authorizer

The authorizer is a critical component where the user explicitly authorizes Hue to perform certain actions or collect various data on its behalf. This includes access to physical devices, accounts of external services, and level of initiative.

External service

Hue is an aggregator of external services. It is not designed to replace your bank, your health provider, or your social network. It will keep a lot of metadata about your activities, but the content will remain with your external services. Each external service will require a dedicated component to interact with the external service API and policies. When no API is available, Hue emulates the user by automating the browser or native apps.

Generic sensor

A big part of Hue's value proposition is to act on the user's behalf. In order to do that effectively, Hue needs to be aware of various events. For example, if Hue reserved a vacation for you but it senses that a cheaper flight is available, it can either automatically change your flight or ask you for confirmation. There is an infinite number of things to sense. To reign in sensing, a generic sensor is needed. The generic sensor will be extensible, but exposes a generic interface that the other parts of Hue can utilize uniformly even as more and more sensors are added.

Generic actuator

This is the counterpart of the generic sensor. Hue needs to perform actions on your behalf. For example, reserving a flight. To do that, Hue needs a generic actuator that can be extended to support particular functions but can interact with other components, such as the identity manager and the authorizer, in a uniform fashion.

User learner

This is the brain of Hue. It will constantly monitor all your interactions (that you authorize) and update its model of you. This will allow Hue to become more and more useful over time, predict what you need and what will interest you, provide better choices, surface more relevant information at the right time, and avoid being annoying and overbearing.

Hue microservices

The complexity of each of the components is enormous. Some of the components, such as the external service, the generic sensor, and generic actuator, will need to operate across hundreds, thousands, or more external services that constantly change outside the control of Hue. Even the user learner needs to learn the user's preferences across many areas and domains. Microservices address this need by allowing Hue to evolve gradually and grow more isolated capabilities without collapsing under its own complexity. Each microservice interacts with generic Hue infrastructure services through standard interfaces and, optionally, with a few other services through well-defined and versioned interfaces. The surface area of each microservice is manageable and the orchestration between microservices is based on standard best practices.

Plugins

Plugins are the key to extending Hue without a proliferation of interfaces. The thing about plugins is that often, you need plugin chains that cross multiple abstraction layers. For example, if we want to add a new integration for Hue with YouTube, then you can collect a lot of YouTube-specific information – your channels, favorite videos, recommendation, and videos you watched. To display this information to users and allow them to act on it, you need plugins across multiple components and eventually in the user interface as well. Smart design will help by aggregating categories of actions such as recommendations, selections, and delayed notifications to many different services.

The great thing about plugins is that they can be developed by anyone. Initially, the Hue development team will have to develop the plugins, but as Hue becomes more popular, external services will want to integrate with Hue and build Hue plugins to enable their service.

That will lead, of course, to a whole eco system of plugin registration, approval, and curation.

Data stores

Hue will need several types of data store, and multiple instances of each type, to manage its data and metadata:

- Relational database
- Graph database
- Time-series database
- In-memory caching

Due to the scope of Hue, each one of these databases will have to be clustered and distributed.

Stateless microservices

The microservices should be mostly stateless. This will allow specific instances to be started and killed quickly, and migrated across the infrastructure as necessary. The state will be managed by the stores and accessed by the microservices with short-lived access tokens.

Queue-based interactions

All these microservices need to talk to each other. Users will ask Hue to perform tasks on their behalf. External services will notify Hue of various events. Queues coupled with stateless microservices provide the perfect solution. Multiple instances of each microservice will listen to various queues and respond when relevant events or requests are popped from the queue. This arrangement is very robust and easy to scale. Every component can be redundant and highly available. While each component is fallible, the system is very fault-tolerant.

A queue can be used for asynchronous RPC or request-response style interactions too, where the calling instance provides a private queue name and the collie posts the response to the private queue.

Planning workflows

Hue often needs to support workflows. A typical workflow will get a high-level task, such as make a dentist appointment; it will extract the user's dentist details and schedule, match it with the user's schedule, choose between multiple options, potentially confirm with the user, make the appointment, and set up a reminder. We can classify workflows into fully automatic and human workflows where humans are involved. Then there are workflows that involve spending money.

Automatic workflows

Automatic workflows don't require human intervention. Hue has full authority to execute all the steps from start to finish. The more autonomy the user allocates to Hue the more effective it will be. The user should be able to view and audit all workflows, past and present.

Human workflows

Human workflows require interaction with a human. Most often it will be the user itself that needs to make a choice from multiple options or approve an action. But it may involve a person on another service. For example, to make an appointment with a dentist, you may have to get a list of available times from the secretary.

Budget-aware workflows

Some workflows, such as paying bills or purchasing a gift, require spending money. While, in theory, Hue can be granted unlimited access to the user's bank account, most users will probably be more comfortable with setting budgets for different workflows or just making spending a human-approved activity.

Using Kubernetes to build the Hue platform

In this section, we will look at various Kubernetes resources and how they can help us build Hue. First, we'll get to know the versatile kubectl a little better, then we will look at how to run long-running processes in Kubernetes, exposing services internally and externally, using namespaces to limit access, launching ad-hoc jobs, and mixing in non-cluster components. Obviously, Hue is a huge project, so we will demonstrate the ideas on a local Minikube cluster and not actually build a real Hue Kubernetes cluster.

Using Kubectl effectively

Kubectl is your Swiss Army Knife. It can do pretty much anything around the cluster. Under the hood, kubectl connects to your cluster via the API. It reads your `.kube/config` file, which contains information necessary to connect to your cluster or clusters. The commands are divided into multiple categories:

- **Generic commands** – Deal with resources in a generic way: create, get, delete, run, apply, patch, replace, and so on
- **Cluster management commands** – Deal with nodes and the cluster at large: cluster-info, certificate, drain, and so on
- **Troubleshooting commands** – Describe, logs, attach, exec, and so on
- **Deployment commands** – Deal with deployment and scaling: rollout, scale, auto-scale, and so on
- **Settings commands** – Deal with labels and annotations: label, annotate, and so on
- **Misc commands** – Help, config, and version

You can view the configuration with Kubernetes config view.

Here is the configuration for a Minikube cluster: .kube/config

```
apiVersion: v1
clusters:
- cluster:
    certificate-authority: C:\Users\the_g\.minikube\ca.crt
    server: https://192.168.99.100:8443
  name: minikube
contexts:
```

```
    - context:
        cluster: minikube
        user: minikube
      name: minikube
    current-context: minikube
    kind: Config
    preferences: {}
    users:
    - name: minikube
      user:
        client-certificate: C:\Users\the_g\.minikube\apiserver.crt
        client-key: C:\Users\the_g\.minikube\apiserver.key
```

Understanding Kubectl resource configuration files

Many kubectl operations such as create require complicated hierarchical output (since the API requires this output). Kubectl uses YAML or JSON configuration files. Here is a JSON configuration file for creating a pod:

```
apiVersion: v1
kind: Pod
metadata:
  name: ""
  labels:
    name: ""
  namespace: ""
  annotations: []
  generateName: ""
spec:
    ...
```

ApiVersion

This very important Kubernetes API keeps evolving and can support different versions of the same resource via different versions of the API.

Kind

Kind tells Kubernetes what type of resource it is dealing with. In this case, Pod. This is always required.

Metadata

A lot of information that describes the pod and where it operates:

- **Name** – Identifies the pod uniquely within its namespace
- **Labels** – Multiple labels can be applied
- **Namespace** – The namespace the pod belongs to
- **Annotations** – A list of annotations available for query

Spec

Spec is a pod template that contains all the information necessary to launch a pod. It can be quite elaborate, so we'll explore it in multiple parts:

```
"spec": {
  "containers": [
  ],
  "restartPolicy": "",
  "volumes": [
  ]
}
```

Container spec

The pod spec's container is a list of container specs. Each container spec has the following structure:

```
{
  "name": "",
  "image": "",
  "command": [
    ""
  ],
  "args": [
    ""
  ],
```

```
"env": [
  {
    "name": "",
    "value": ""
  }
],
"imagePullPolicy": "",
"ports": [
  {
    "containerPort": 0,
    "name": "",
    "protocol": ""
  }
],
"resources": {
  "cpu": ""
  "memory": ""
}
}
```

Each container has an image, a command that, if specified, replaces the Docker image command. It also has arguments and environment variables. Then, there are of course the image pull policy, ports, and resource limits. We covered those in earlier chapters.

Deploying long-running microservices in pods

Long-running microservices should run in pods and be stateless. Let's look at how to create pods for one of Hue's microservices. Later, we will raise the level of abstraction and use a deployment.

Creating pods

Let's start with a regular pod configuration file for creating a Hue learner internal service. This service doesn't need to be exposed as a public service and it will listen to a queue for notifications and store its insights in some persistent storage.

We need a simple container that the pod will run in. Here is possibly the simplest Docker file ever, which will simulate the Hue learner:

```
FROM busybox
CMD ash -c "echo 'Started...'; while true ; do sleep 10 ; done"
```

It uses the busybox base image, which prints to standard output Started... and then goes into an infinite loop, which is, by all accounts, long-running:

```
I have built two Docker images tagged as "g1g1/hue-learn:v3.0" and "g1g1/
hue-learn:v4.0" and pushed them to the DockerHub registry ("g1g1" is my
user name).
docker build -t . g1g1/hue-learn:v3.0
docker build -t . g1g1/hue-learn:v4.0
docker push g1g1/hue-learn:v3.0
docker push g1g1/hue-learn:v4.0
```

Now these images are available to be pulled into containers inside of Hue's pods.

We'll use YAML here because it's more concise and human-readable. Here are the boilerplate and metadata labels:

```
apiVersion: v1
kind: Pod
metadata:
  name: hue-learner
  labels:
    app: hue
   runtime-environment: production
    tier: internal-service
  annotations:
    version: "3.0"
```

The reason I use an annotation for the version and not a label is that labels are used to identify the set of pods in the deployment. Modifying labels is not allowed.

Next comes the important containers spec, which defines for each container the mandatory name and image:

```
spec:
  containers:
  - name: hue-learner
    image: g1g1/hue-learn:v3.0
```

The resources section tells Kubernetes the resource requirements of the container, which allows for more efficient and compact scheduling and allocations. Here, the container requests `200` milli-cpu units (0.2 core) and 300 MiB (228 bytes):

```
resources:
  requests:
    cpu: 200m
    memory: 256Mi
```

The environment section allows the cluster administrator to provide environment variables that will be available to the container. Here it tells it to discover the queue and the store from `dns`. In a testing environment, it may use a different discovery method:

```
env:
- name: DISCOVER_QUEUE
  value: dns
- name: DISCOVER_STORE
  value: dns
```

Decorating pods with labels

Labeling pods wisely is key for flexible operations. It lets you evolve your cluster live, organize your microservices into groups you can operate on uniformly, and drill down ad-hoc to observe different subsets.

For example, our Hue learner pod has the following labels:

- **runtime-environment**: production
- **tier**: internal-service

The version label can be used to support running multiple versions at the same time. If both version 2 and version 3 need to run at the same time, either to provide backward compatibility or just temporarily during the migration from v2 to v3, then having a version label allows both scaling pods of different versions independently, as well as exposing services independently. The runtime-environment label allows performing global operations on all pods that belong to a certain environment. The "tier" label can be used to query all pods that belong to a particular tier. These are just an example; your imagination is the limit here.

Deploying long- running processes with deployments

In a large-scale system, pods should never be just created and let loose. If a pod dies unexpectedly for whatever reason, you want another one to replace it to maintain overall capacity. You can create replication controllers or replica sets yourself, but that leaves the door open to mistakes, as well as the possibility of partial failure. It makes much more sense to specify how many replicas you want when you launch your pods.

Let's deploy three instances of our Hue learner microservice with a Kubernetes deployment resource. Note that deployment objects are considered Beta at this point. This should not discourage you from using them. It just means they are newer and haven't been tested in the field as much as objects such as pods. But, since your cluster should have multiple monitoring and alerting systems, then even if something goes horribly wrong with deployments, you should be able to detect it. The benefits of using them outweigh the slight risk that, due to their Beta status, they'll break your system:

```
apiVersion: extensions/v1beta1
kind: Deployment
metadata:
  name: hue-learn
spec:
  replicas: 3
  template:
      <pod spec goes here>
```

The pod spec is identical to the spec section from the pod configuration file previously.

Let's create the deployment and check its status:

```
> kubectl create -f .\deployment.yaml
deployment "hue-learn" created
> kubectl get deployment hue-learn
NAME         DESIRED    CURRENT    UP-TO-DATE    AVAILABLE    AGE
hue-learn    3          3          3             3            4m
```

You can get a lot more information about the deployment using the kubectl describe command.

Updating a deployment

The Hue platform is a large and ever-evolving system. You need to upgrade constantly. Deployments can be updated to roll out updates in a painless manner. You change the pod template to trigger a rolling update fully managed by Kubernetes.

Currently, all the pods are running with `version 3.0`:

```
Kubectl get pods -o json | jq .items[0].metadata.annotations.version
"3.0"
```

NAME	READY	STATUS	RESTARTS	AGE
hue-learn-237202748-d770r	1/1	Running	0	2m
hue-learn-237202748-fwv2t	1/1	Running	0	2m
hue-learn-237202748-tpr4s	1/1	Running	0	2m

Let's update the deployment to upgrade to version 4.0. Modify the version in the `deployment.yaml` file. Don't modify labels; it will cause an error. Typically, you modify the image and some related metadata in annotations. Then we can use the apply command to upgrade the version:

```
kubectl apply -f deployment.yaml
deployment "hue-learn" updated
Kubectl get pods -o json | jq .items[0].metadata.annotations.version
"4.0"
```

Separating internal and external services

Internal services are services that are accessed directly only by other services or jobs in the cluster (or administrators that log in and run ad-hoc tools). In some cases, internal services are not accessed at all, and just perform their function and store their results in a persistent store that other services access in a decoupled way.

But some services need to be exposed to users or external programs. Let's look at a fake Hue service that manages a list of reminders for a user. It doesn't do anything, but we'll use it to illustrate how to expose services.

I pushed the dummy Hue-reminders image to DockerHub:

```
docker push g1g1/hue-reminders:v2.2
```

Deploying an internal service

Here is the deployment, which is very similar to the Hue-learner deployment, except that I dropped the `annotations`, `env`, and `resources` sections, kept just one label to save space, and added a `ports` section to the container. That's crucial, because a service must expose a port through which other services can access it:

```
apiVersion: extensions/v1beta1
kind: Deployment
metadata:
  name: hue-reminders
spec:
  replicas: 2
  template:
    metadata:
      name: hue-reminders
      labels:
        app: hue-reminders
    spec:
      containers:
      - name: hue-reminders
        image: g1g1/hue-reminders:v2.2
        ports:
        - containerPort: 80
```

When we run the deployment, two Hue reminders pods are added to the cluster:

```
> kubectl create -f hue-reminders-deployment.yaml
> kubectl get pods
NAME                           READY   STATUS    RESTARTS   AGE
hue-learn-1348235373-4k355     1/1     Running   1          19h
hue-learn-1348235373-f5303     1/1     Running   1          19h
hue-learn-1348235373-r4xl6     1/1     Running   1          19h
hue-reminders-972023352-nw0gt  1/1     Running   0          18s
hue-reminders-972023352-vjtmq  1/1     Running   0          18s
```

OK. The pods are running. In theory, other services can look up or be configured with their internal IP address and just access them directly because they are all in the same network space. But this doesn't scale. Every time a reminders pod dies and is replaced by a new one, or when we just scale up the number of pods, all the services that access these pods must know about it. Services solve this issue by providing a single access point to all the pods. The service is:

```
apiVersion: v1
kind: Service
metadata:
  name: hue-reminders
  labels:
    app: hue-reminders
spec:
  ports:
  - port: 80
    protocol: TCP
  selector:
    app: hue-reminders
```

The service has a selector that selects all the pods that have labels that match it. It also exposes a port, which other services will use to access it (it doesn't have to be the same port as the container's port).

Creating the Hue-reminders service

Let's create the service and explore it a little bit:

```
kubectl create -f .\hue-reminders-service.yaml
service "hue-reminders" created
kubectl describe svc hue-reminders
Name:                hue-reminders
Namespace:           default
Labels:              app=hue-reminders
Selector:            app=hue-reminders
Type:                ClusterIP
IP:                  10.0.0.238
Port:                <unset> 80/TCP
Endpoints:           172.17.0.7:80,172.17.0.8:80
Session Affinity:    None
```

The service is up-and-running. Other pods can find it through environment variables or DNS. The environment variables for all services are set at pod creation time. That means that, if a pod is already running when you create your service, you'll have to kill it and let Kubernetes recreate it with the environment variables (you always have a replication controller or replica set, right?):

```
> kubectl exec hue-learn-3352346070-56cd5 -- printenv | grep HUE_
REMINDERS_SERVICE
```

```
HUE_REMINDERS_SERVICE_PORT=80
HUE_REMINDERS_SERVICE_HOST=10.0.0.238
```

But using DNS is much simpler. Your service DNS name is `<service name>.<namespace>.svc.cluster.local`:

```
> kubectl exec hue-reminders-972023352-nw0gt -- nslookup hue-reminders
Server:    10.0.0.10
Address 1: 10.0.0.10 kube-dns.kube-system.svc.cluster.local
```

```
Name:      hue-reminders
Address 1: 10.0.0.238 hue-reminders.default.svc.cluster.local
```

Exposing a service externally

The service is accessible inside the cluster. If you want to expose it to the world, Kubernetes provides two ways to do it:

- Configure nodePort for direct access
- Configure a Cloud load balancer if you run it in a Cloud environment

Before you configure a service for external access, you should make sure it is secure. The Kubernetes documentation has a good example that covers all the gory details here:

https://github.com/kubernetes/kubernetes/tree/master/examples/https-nginx/.

We've already covered the principles in *Chapter 5, Configuring Kubernetes Security, Limits, and Accounts*.

Here is the spec section of the hue-reminders service when exposed to the world through NodePort:

```
spec:
  type: NodePort
  ports:
  - port: 8080
    targetPort: 80
    protocol: TCP
    name: http
  - port: 443
    protocol: TCP
    name: https
  selector:
    app: hue-reminders
```

Ingress

Ingress is a Kubernetes configuration object that lets you expose a service to the outside world and take care of a lot of details. It can do the following:

- Provide an externally visible URL to your service
- Load-balance traffic
- Terminate SSL
- Provide name-based virtual hosting

To use Ingress, you must have an Ingress controller running in your cluster. Note that Ingress is still in Beta and has many limitations. If you're running your cluster on GKE, you're probably OK. Otherwise, proceed with caution. One of the current limitations of the Ingress controller is that it isn't built for scale. As such, it is not a good option for the Hue platform yet. We'll cover the Ingress controller in greater detail in *Chapter 10, Advanced Kubernetes Networking*.

Here is what an Ingress resource looks like:

```
apiVersion: extensions/v1beta1
kind: Ingress
metadata:
  name: test
spec:
```

```
rules:
- host: foo.bar.com
  http:
    paths:
    - path: /foo
      backend:
        serviceName: fooSvc
        servicePort: 80
- host: bar.baz.com
  http:
    paths:
    - path: /bar
      backend:
        serviceName: barSvc
        servicePort: 80
```

The nginx Ingress controller will interpret this Ingress request and create a corresponding configuration file for the nginx web server:

```
http {
  server {
    listen 80;
    server_name foo.bar.com;

    location /foo {
      proxy_pass http://fooSvc;
    }
  }
  server {
    listen 80;
    server_name bar.baz.com;

    location /bar {
      proxy_pass http://barSvc;
    }
  }
}
```

It is possible to create other controllers.

Using namespace to limit access

The Hue project is moving along nicely, and we have a few hundred microservices and about 100 developers and DevOps engineers working on it. Groups of related microservices emerge, and you notice that many of these groups are pretty autonomous. They are completely oblivious to the other groups. Also, there are some sensitive areas such as health and finance that you want to control access to more effectively. Enter namespaces.

Let's create a new service, Hue-finance, and put it in a new namespace called restricted.

Here is the YAML file for the new restricted namespace:

```
{
  "kind": "Namespace",
  "apiVersion": "v1",
  "metadata": {
    "name": "restricted",
    "labels": {
      "name": "restricted"
    }
  }
}
> kubectl create -f .\namespace.yaml
namespace "restricted" created
```

Once the namespace has been created, we need to configure a context for the namespace. This will allow restricting access just to this namespace:

```
> kubectl config set-context restricted --namespace=restricted
--cluster=minikube --user=minikube
Context "restricted" set.


> kubectl config use-context restricted
Switched to context "restricted".
```

Let's check our cluster configuration:

```
> Kubectl config view
apiVersion: v1
clusters:
```

```
- cluster:
    certificate-authority: C:\Users\the_g\.minikube\ca.crt
    server: https://192.168.99.100:8443
  name: minikube
contexts:
- context:
    cluster: minikube
    user: minikube
  name: minikube
- context:
    cluster: minikube
    namespace: restricted
    user: minikube
  name: restricted
current-context: restricted
kind: Config
preferences: {}
users:
- name: minikube
  user:
    client-certificate: C:\Users\the_g\.minikube\apiserver.crt
    client-key: C:\Users\the_g\.minikube\apiserver.key
```

As you can see, the current context is restricted.

Now, in this empty namespace, we can create our hue-finance service, and it will be on its own:

```
> kubectl create -f .\hue-finance-deployment.yaml
deployment "hue-finance" created


>kubectl get pods
NAME                            READY   STATUS    RESTARTS   AGE
hue-finance-2518532322-0s8s2    1/1     Running   0          6s
hue-finance-2518532322-27sfm    1/1     Running   0          6s
hue-finance-2518532322-s4dtp    1/1     Running   0          6s
```

You don't have to switch contexts. You can also use the --namespace=<namespace> and --all-namespaces command-line switches.

Launching jobs

Hue has a lot of long-running processes deployed as microservices, but it also has a lot of tasks that run, accomplish some goal, and exit. Kubernetes supports this functionality via the Job resource. A Kubernetes job manages one or more pods and ensures that they run until success. If one of the pods managed by the job fails or is deleted, then the job will run a new pod until it succeeds.

Here is a job that runs a Python process to compute the factorial of 5 (hint: it's 120):

```
apiVersion: batch/v1
kind: Job
metadata:
  name: factorial5
spec:
  template:
    metadata:
      name: factorial5
    spec:
      containers:
      - name: factorial5
        image: python:3.5
        command: ["python",
                  "-c",
                  "import math; print(math.factorial(5))"]
      restartPolicy: Never
```

Note that the restartPolicy must be either Never or OnFailure The default Always value is invalid because a job shouldn't restart after a successful completion.

Let's start the job and check its status:

```
> kubectl create -f .\job.yaml
job "factorial5" created


> kubectl get jobs
NAME          DESIRED    SUCCESSFUL    AGE
factorial5    1          1             25s
```

The pods of completed tasks are not displayed by default. You must use the
`--show-all` option:

```
kubectl get pods --show-all
NAME                      READY    STATUS       RESTARTS    AGE
factorial5-v9f80          0/1      Completed    0           1m
hue-finance-25185-0s8s2   1/1      Running      0           4h
hue-finance-25185-27sfm   1/1      Running      0           4h
hue-finance-25185-s4dtp   1/1      Running      0           4h
```

The `factorial5` pod has a status of `"Completed."` Let's check out its
output:

```
> kubectl logs factorial5-v9f80
120
```

Running jobs in parallel

You can also run a job with parallelism. There are two fields in the spec, called
`completions` and `parallelism`. The `completions` are set to 1 by default. If you
want more than one successful completion, then increase this value. Parallelism
determines how many pods to launch. A job will not launch more pods than needed
for successful completions, even if the parallelism number is greater.

Let's run another job that just sleeps for 20 seconds until it has three successful
completions. We'll use a parallelism factor of 6, but only three pods will be launched:

```
apiVersion: batch/v1
kind: Job
metadata:
  name: sleep20
spec:
  completions: 3
  parallelism: 6
  template:
    metadata:
      name: sleep20
    spec:
      containers:
      - name: sleep20
        image: python:3.5
```

```
      command: ["python",
                "-c",
                "import time; print('started...');
                 time.sleep(20); print('done.')"]
    restartPolicy: Never
```

```
> Kubectl get pods
NAME                      READY    STATUS     RESTARTS    AGE
sleep20-1t8sd             1/1      Running    0           10s
sleep20-sdjb4             1/1      Running    0           10s
sleep20-wv4jc             1/1      Running    0           10s
```

Cleaning up completed jobs

When a job completes, it sticks around – and its pods, too. This is by design, so you can look at logs or connect to pods and explore. But normally, when a job has completed successfully, it is not needed anymore. It's your responsibility to clean up completed jobs and their pods. The easiest way is to simply delete the job object, which will delete all the pods too:

```
> kubectl delete jobs/factroial5
job "factorial5" deleted
> kubectl delete jobs/sleep20
job "sleep20" deleted
```

Scheduling cron jobs

Kubernetes cron jobs are jobs that run for a specified time, once or repeatedly. They behave as regular Unix cron jobs specified in the /etc/crontab file.

In Kubernetes 1.4 they were known as a ScheduledJob. But, in Kubernetes 1.5, the name was changed to CronJob You must enable cron jobs by starting the API server with the following:

```
--runtime-config=batch/v2alpha1
```

Here is the configuration to launch a cron job every minute to remind you to stretch. In the schedule, you may replace the * with ?:

```
apiVersion: batch/v2alpha1
kind: CronJob
metadata:
```

```
    name: stretch
spec:
  schedule: "*/1 * * * *"
  jobTemplate:
    spec:
      template:
        metadata:
          labels:
            name: stretch
        spec:
          containers:
          - name: stretch
            image: python
            args:
            - python
            - -c
            - from datetime import datetime; print('[{}] Stretch'.
format(datetime.now()))
            restartPolicy: OnFailure
```

In the pod spec, under the job template, I added a label called name The reason is that cron jobs and their pods are assigned names with a random prefix by Kubernetes. The label allows you to easily discover all the pods of a particular cron job.

Kubectl get pods

See the following command lines:

```
NAME                        READY       STATUS            RESTARTS    AGE
stretch-1482165720-qm5bj    0/1         ImagePullBackOff  0           1m
stretch-1482165780-bkqjd    0/1         ContainerCreating 0           6s
```
Note that each invocation of a cron job launches a new job object with a new pod:
```
> kubectl get jobs
NAME                 DESIRED     SUCCESSFUL     AGE
stretch-1482165300   1           1              11m
stretch-1482165360   1           1              10m
stretch-1482165420   1           1              9m
stretch-1482165480   1           1              8m
```

When a cron job invocation completes, its pod gets into a `Completed` state and will not be visible without the `-show-all` or `-a` flags:

```
> Kubectl get pods --show-all
NAME                        READY    STATUS       RESTARTS    AGE
stretch-1482165300-g5ps6    0/1      Completed    0           15m
stretch-1482165360-cln08    0/1      Completed    0           14m
stretch-1482165420-n8nzd    0/1      Completed    0           13m
stretch-1482165480-0jq31    0/1      Completed    0           12m
```

As usual, you can check the output of the pod of a completed cron job using the `logs` command:

```
> kubectl logs stretch-1482165300-g5ps6
[2016-12-19 16:35:15.325283] Stretch
```

You must also clean up all the individual jobs, otherwise they will stick around forever. Just deleting the cron job is not enough; it will just stop scheduling more jobs.

You can use the designated label (`name=stretch` in this case) to locate all the job objects launched by the cron job.

In summary, the cleanup of a cron job involves the following:

- Deleting the cron job
- Deleting all job objects that match the label

  ```
  > kubectl delete cronjobs/stretch
  cronjob "stretch" deleted

  > kubectl delete jobs -l name=stretch
  job "stretch-1482165300" deleted
  job "stretch-1482165360" deleted
  job "stretch-1482165420" deleted
  job "stretch-1482165480" deleted
  ```

You can also suspend a cron job so it doesn't create more jobs.

Mixing non-cluster components

Most real-time system components in the Kubernetes cluster will communicate with out-of-cluster components. Those could be completely external third-party services accessible through some API, but can also be internal services running in the same local network that, for various reasons, are not part of the Kubernetes cluster.

There are two categories here: inside the cluster network and outside the cluster network. Why is the distinction important?

Outside-the-cluster-network components

These components have no direct access to the cluster. They can only access it through APIs, externally visible URLs, and exposed services. These components are treated just like any external user. Often, cluster components will just use external services, which poses no security issue. For example, in my previous job we had a Kubernetes cluster that reported exceptions to a third-party service (`https://sentry.io/welcome/`). It was one-way communication from the Kubernetes cluster to the third-party service.

Inside-the-cluster-network components

These are components that run inside the network but are not managed by Kubernetes. There are many reasons to run such components. They could be legacy applications that have not be kubernetized yet, or some distributed data store that is not easy to run inside Kubernetes. The reason to run these components inside the network is for performance, and to have isolation from the outside world so traffic between these components and pods can be more secure. Being part of the same network ensures low-latency, and the reduced need for authentication is both convenient and can avoid authentication overhead.

Managing the Hue platform with Kubernetes

In this section, we will look at how Kubernetes can help operate a huge platform such as Hue. Kubernetes itself provides a lot of capabilities to orchestrate pods and manage quotas and limits, detecting and recovering from certain types of generic failures (hardware malfunctions, process crashes, unreachable services). But, in a complicated system such as Hue, pods and services may be up-and-running but in an invalid state or waiting for other dependencies in order to perform their duties. This is tricky because if a service or pod is not ready yet but is already receiving requests, then you need to manage it somehow: fail (puts responsibility on the caller), retry (how many, how long, how often?), and queue for later (who will manage this queue?).

It is often better if the system at large can be aware of the readiness state of different components, or if components are visible only when they are truly ready. Kubernetes doesn't know Hue, but it provides several mechanisms such as liveness probes, readiness probes, and init containers to support application-specific management of your cluster.

Using liveness probes to ensure your containers are alive

kubelet watches over your containers. If a container process crashes, kubelet will take care of it based on the restart policy. But this is not always enough. Your process may not crash, but instead run into an infinite loop or a deadlock. The restart policy might not be nuanced enough. With a liveness probe, you get to decide when a container is considered alive. Here is a pod template for the Hue music service. It has a `livenessProbe` section, which uses the `httpGet` probe. An HTTP probe requires a scheme (http or https, default to http, a host [default to PodIp], a path, and a port). The probe is considered successful if the HTTP status is between 200 and 399. Your container may need some time to initialize, so you can specify an `initialDelayInSeconds`. The Kubelet will not hit the liveness check during this period:

```
apiVersion: v1
kind: Pod
metadata:
  labels:
    app: hue-music
  name: hue-music
spec:
  containers:
    image: the_g1g1/hue-music
    livenessProbe:
      httpGet:
        path: /pulse
        port: 8888
        httpHeaders:
          - name: X-Custom-Header
            value: Awesome
      initialDelaySeconds: 30
      timeoutSeconds: 1
    name: hue-music
```

If a liveness probe fails for any container, then the pod's restart policy goes into effect. Make sure your restart policy is not Never, because that will make the probe useless.

There are two other types of probe:

- `TcpSocket` – Just check that a port is open
- `Exec` – Run a command that returns 0 for success

Using readiness probes to manage dependencies

Readiness probes are used for different purpose. Your container may be up-and-running, but it may depend on other services that are unavailable at the moment. For example, Hue-music may depend on access to a data service that contains your listening history. Without access, it is unable to perform its duties. In this case, other services or external clients should not send requests to the Hue music service, but there is no need to restart it. Readiness probes address this use case. When a readiness probe fails for a container, the container's pod will be removed from any service endpoint it is registered with. This ensures that requests don't flood services that can't process them. Note that you can also use readiness probes to temporarily remove pods that are overbooked until they drain some internal queue.

Here is a sample readiness probe. I use the exec probe here to execute a custom command. If the command exits a non-zero exit code, the container will be torn down:

```
readinessProbe:
  exec:
    command:
        - /usr/local/bin/checker
        - --full-check
        - --data-service=hue-multimedia-service
  initialDelaySeconds: 60
  timeoutSeconds: 5
```

It is fine to have both a readiness probe and a liveness probe on the same container as they serve different purposes.

Employing init containers for orderly pod bring-up

Liveness and readiness probes are great. They recognize that, at startup, there may be a period where the container is not ready yet, but shouldn't be considered failed. To accommodate that there is the `initialDelayInSeconds` setting where containers will not be considered failed. But, what if this initial delay is potentially very long? Maybe, in most cases, a container is ready after a couple of seconds and ready to process requests, but because the initial delay is set to five minutes just in case, we waste a lot of time where the container is idle. If the container is part of a high-traffic service, then many instances can all sit idle for five minutes after each upgrade and pretty much make the service unavailable.

Init containers address this problem. A pod may have a set of init containers that run to completion before other containers are started. An init container can take care of all the non-deterministic initialization and let application containers with their readiness probe have minimal delay.

Init containers are in Beta right now, so you specify them in an annotation. Once the feature moves out of Beta they will be properly added to the pod spec:

```
apiVersion: v1
kind: Pod
metadata:
  name: hue-fitness
  annotations:
    pod.beta.kubernetes.io/init-containers: '[
        {
            "name": "install",
            "image": "busybox",
            "command": ["/support/safe_init"],
            "volumeMounts": [
                {
                    "name": "workdir",
                    "mountPath": "/work-dir"
                }
            ]
        }
    ]'
spec:
  ...
```

Sharing with DaemonSet pods

eg one nginx instance per worker

DaemonSet pods are pods that are deployed automatically, one per node (or a designated subset of the nodes). They are typically used for keeping an eye on nodes and ensuring they are operational. This is a very important function, which we covered in *Chapter 3*, *Monitoring, Logging, and Troubleshooting*, when we discussed the node problem detector. But they can be used for much more. The nature of the default Kubernetes scheduler is that it schedules pods based on resource availability and requests. If you have lots of pods that don't require a lot of resources, similarly many pods will be scheduled on the same node. Let's consider a pod that performs a small task and then, every second, sends a summary of all its activities to a remote service. Now, imagine that, on average, 50 of these pods are scheduled on the same node. This means that, every second, 50 pods make 50 network requests with very little data. How about we cut it down by 50× to just a single network request? With a DaemonSet pod, all the other 50 pods can communicate with it instead of talking directly to the remote service. The DaemonSet pod will collect all the data from the 50 pods and, once a second, will report it in aggregate to the remote service. Of course, that requires the remote service API to support aggregate reporting. The nice thing is that the pods themselves don't have to be modified; they will just be configured to talk to the DaemonSet pod on localhost instead of the remote service. The DaemonSet pod serves as an aggregating proxy.

The interesting part about this configuration file is that the `hostNetwork`, `hostPID`, and `hostIPC` options are set to `true`. This enables the pods to communicate efficiently with the proxy, utilizing the fact they are running on the same physical host:

```
apiVersion: extensions/v1beta1
kind: DaemonSet
metadata:
  name: hue-collect-proxy
  labels:
    tier: stats
    app: hue-collect-proxy
spec:
  template:
    metadata:
      labels:
        hue-collect-proxy
    spec:
      hostPID: true
      hostIPC: true
```

```
hostNetwork: true
containers:
    image: the_g1g1/hue-collect-proxy
    name: hue-collect-proxy
```

Evolving the Hue platform with Kubernetes

In this section, we'll discuss other ways to extend the Hue platform and service additional markets and communities. The question is always, what Kubernetes features and capabilities can we use to address new challenges or requirements?

Utilizing Hue in the enterprise

The enterprise often can't run in the Cloud, either due to security and compliance reasons, or for performance reasons because the system has work with data and legacy systems that are not cost-effective to move to the Cloud. Either way, Hue for enterprise must support on-premise clusters and/or bare-metal clusters.

While Kubernetes is most often deployed on the Cloud, and even has a special Cloud-provider interface, it doesn't depend on the Cloud and can be deployed anywhere. It does require more expertise, but enterprise organizations that already run systems on their own datacenters have that expertise.

 CoreOS provides a lot of material regarding deploying Kubernetes clusters on bare-metal lusters.

Advancing science with Hue

Hue is so great at integrating information from multiple sources that it would be a boon for the scientific community. Consider how Hue can help multi-disciplinary collaborations between scientists from different areas.

A network of scientific communities might require deployment across multiple geographically distributed clusters. Enter cluster federation. Kubernetes has this use use case in mind and evolves its support. We will discuss it at length in a later chapter.

Educating the kids of the future with hue

Hue can be utilized for education and provide many services to online education systems. But, privacy concerns may prevent deploying Hue for kids as a single, centralized system. One possibility is to have a single cluster, with namespaces for different schools. Another deployment option is that each school or county has its own Hue Kubernetes cluster. In the second case, Hue for education must be extremely easy to operate to cater for schools without a lot of technical expertise. Kubernetes can help a lot by providing self-healing and auto-scaling features and capabilities for Hue, to be as close to zero-administration as possible.

Summary

In this chapter, we designed and planned the development, deployment, and management of the Hue platform – an imaginary omniscient and omnipotent service – built on microservices architecture. We used Kubernetes as the underlying orchestration platform, of course, and delved into many of its concepts and resources. In particular, we focused on deploying pods for long-running services as opposed to jobs for launching short-term or cron jobs, explored internal services versus external services, and also used namespaces to segment a Kubernetes cluster. Then we looked at the management of a large system such as Hue with liveness and readiness probes, init containers, and DaemonSets.

You should now feel comfortable architecting web-scale systems composed of microservices and understand how to deploy and manage them in a Kubernetes cluster.

In *Chapter 7, Handling Kubernetes Storage*, we will look into the super-important area of storage. Data is king, but often the least flexible element of the system. Kubernetes provides a storage model, and many options for storing and accessing data.

Handling Kubernetes Storage

In this chapter, we'll look at how Kubernetes manages storage. Storage is very different from compute, but at a high level they are both resources. Kubernetes as a generic platform takes the approach of abstracting storage behind a programming model and a set of plugins for storage providers. First, we'll go in to detail about the storage conceptual model and how storage is made available to containers in the cluster. Then, we'll cover the common case cloud platform storage providers, such as AWS, GCE, and Azure. Then we'll look at a prominent open source storage provider (GlusterFS from Red Hat), which provides a distributed filesystem. We'll also look into an alternative solution – Flocker – that manages your data in containers as part of the Kubernetes cluster. Finally, we'll see how Kubernetes supports integration of existing enterprise storage solutions.

At the end of this chapter, you'll have a solid understanding of how storage is represented in Kubernetes, the various storage options in each deployment environment (local testing, public cloud, enterprise), and how to choose the best option for your use case.

Persistent volumes walkthrough

In this section, we will understand the Kubernetes storage conceptual model and see how to map persistent storage into containers so they can read and write. Let's start by understanding the problem of storage. Containers and pods are ephemeral. Anything a container writes to its own filesystem gets wiped out when the container dies. Containers can also mount directories from their host node and read or write. That will survive container restarts, but the nodes themselves are not immortal.

There are other problems, such as ownership for mounted hosted directories when the container dies. Just imagine a bunch of containers writing important data to various data directories on their host and then go away leaving all that data all over the nodes with no direct way to tell what container wrote what data. You can try to record this information, but where would you record it? It's pretty clear that for a large-scale system, you need persistent storage accessible from any node to reliably manage the data.

Volumes

The basic Kubernetes storage abstraction is the volume. Containers mount volumes that bind to their pod and they access the storage wherever it may be as if it's in their local filesystem. This is nothing new, and it is great because, as a developer who writes applications that need access to data, you don't have to worry about where and how the data is stored.

Using emptyDir for intra-pod communication

It is very simple to share data between containers in the same pod using a shared volume. Container 1 and container 2 simply mount the same volume and can communicate by reading and writing to this shared space. The most basic volume is the `emptyDir`. An `emptyDir` volume is an `empty` directory on the host. Note that it is not persistent because when the pod is removed from the node, the contents are erased. If a container just crashes, the pod will stick around and you can access it later. Another very interesting option is to use a RAM disk, by specifying the medium as `Memory`. Now, your containers communicate through shared memory, which is much faster but more volatile of course. If the node is restarted, the `emptyDir`'s volume contents are lost.

Here is a `pod` configuration file that has two containers that mount the same volume called `shared-volume`. The containers mount it in different paths, but when the hue-global-listener container is writing a file to `/notifications`, the `hue-job-scheduler` will see that file under `/incoming`:

```
apiVersion: v1
kind: Pod
metadata:
  name: hue-scheduler
spec:
  containers:
  - image: the_g1g1/hue-global-listener
    name: hue-global-listener
```

```
    volumeMounts:
    - mountPath: /notifications
      name: shared-volume
  - image: the_g1g1/hue-job-scheduler
    name: hue-job-scheduler
    volumeMounts:
    - mountPath: /incoming
      name: shared-volume
volumes:
- name: shared-volume
  emptyDir: {}
```

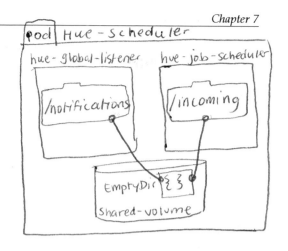

To use the shared memory option, we just need to add `medium: Memory` to the `emptyDir` section:

```
volumes:
- name: shared-volume
  emptyDir:
    medium: Memory
```

Using HostPath for intra-node communication

Sometimes you want your pods to get access to some host information (for example, the Docker Daemon) or you want pods on the same node to communicate with each other. This is useful if the pods know they are on the same host. Since Kubernetes schedules pods based on available resources, pods usually don't know what other pods they share the node with. There are two cases where a pod can rely on other pods being scheduled with it on the same node:

- In a single-node cluster all pods obviously share the same node
- DaemonSet pods always share a node with any other pod that matches their selector

For example, in *Chapter 6, Using Critical Kubernetes Resources*, we discussed a DeamonSet pod that serves as an aggregating proxy to other pods. Another way to implement this behavior is for the pods to simply write their data to a mounted volume that is bound to a `host` directory and the DaemonSet pod can directly read it and act on it.

Before you decide to use HostPath volume, make sure you understand
the limitations:

- The behavior of pods with the same configuration might be different if they
  are data-driven and the files on their host are different.

- It can violate resource-based scheduling (coming soon to Kubernetes)
  because Kubernetes can't monitor HostPath resources.

- The containers that access host directories must have a security context
  with `privileged` set to `true` or, on the host side, you need to change the
  permissions to allow writing.

Here is a configuration file that mounts the `/coupons` directory into the `hue-coupon-hunter` container, which is mapped to the host's `/etc/hue/data/coupons` directory:

```
apiVersion: v1
kind: Pod
metadata:
  name: hue-coupon-hunter
spec:
  containers:
  - image: the_g1g1/hue-coupon-hunter
    name: hue-coupon-hunter
    volumeMounts:
    - mountPath: /coupons
      name: coupons-volume
  volumes:
  - name: coupons-volume
    host-path:
        path: /etc/hue/data/coupons
```

Since the pod doesn't have a `privileged` security context, it will not be able to
write to the `host` directory. Let's change the container spec to enable it by adding
a security context:

```
  - image: the_g1g1/hue-coupon-hunter
    name: hue-coupon-hunter
    volumeMounts:
    - mountPath: /coupons
      name: coupons-volume
    securityContext:
        privileged: true
```

In the following diagram, you can see that each container has its own local storage area inaccessible to other containers or pods and the host's /data directory is mounted as a volume into both container 1 and container 2:

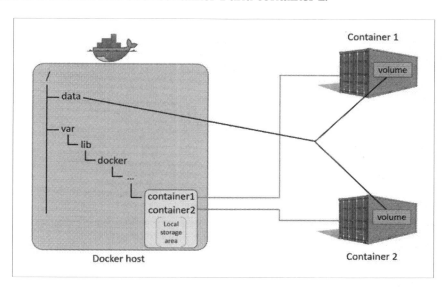

Provisioning persistent volumes

While emptyDir volumes can be mounted and used by containers, they are not persistent and don't require any special provisioning because they use existing storage on the node. HostPath volumes persist on the original node, but if a pod is restarted on a different node, it can't access the HostPath volume from its previous node. Real persistent volumes use storage provisioned ahead of time by administrators. In cloud environments, the provisioning may be very streamlined but it is still required, and as a Kubernetes cluster administrator you have to at least make sure your storage quota is adequate and monitor usage versus quota diligently.

Remember that persistent volumes are resources that the Kubernetes cluster is using similar to nodes. As such they are not managed by the Kubernetes API server.

You can provision resources statically or dynamically.

Provisioning persistent volumes statically

Static provisioning is straightforward. The cluster administrator creates persistent volumes backed up by some storage media ahead of time, and these persistent volumes can be claimed by containers.

Provisioning persistent volumes dynamically

Dynamic provisioning may happen when a persistent volume claim doesn't match any of the statically provisioned persistent volumes. If the claim specified a storage class and the administrator configured that class for dynamic provisioning, then a persistent volume may be provisioned on the fly. We will see examples later when we discuss persistent volume claims and storage classes.

Creating persistent volumes

Here is the configuration file for an NFS persistent volume:

```
apiVersion: v1
kind: PersistentVolume
metadata:
  name: pv-1
  annotations:
    volume.beta.kubernetes.io/storage-class: "normal"
  labels:
     release: stable
     capacity: 100Gi
spec:
  capacity:
    storage: 100Gi
  accessModes:
    - ReadWriteOnce
   - ReadOnlyMany
  persistentVolumeReclaimPolicy: Recycle
  nfs:
    path: /tmp
    server: 172.17.0.8
```

A persistent volume has a spec and metadata that includes the name and possibly an annotation of a storage class. The storage class annotation will become an attribute when storage classes get out of beta. Note that persistent volumes are at v1, but storage classes are still in beta. More on storage classes later. Let's focus on the spec here. There are four sections: capacity, access mode, reclaim policy, and the volume type (nfs in the example).

Capacity

Each volume has a designated amount of storage. Storage claims may be satisfied by persistent volumes that have at least that amount of storage. In the example, the persistent volume has a capacity of 100 Gibibytes (2^{30} bytes). It is important when allocating static persistent volumes to understand the storage request patterns. For example, if you provision 20 persistent volumes with 100 GiB capacity and a container claims a persistent volume with 150 GiB, then this claim will not be satisfied even though there is enough capacity overall:

```
capacity:
    storage: 100Gi
```

Access modes

There are three access modes:

- `ReadOnlyMany`: Can be mounted read-only by many nodes
- `ReadWriteOnce`: Can be mounted as read-write by a single node
- `ReadWriteMany`: Can be mounted as read-write by many nodes

The storage is mounted to nodes, so even with `ReadWriteOnce` multiple containers on the same node can mount the volume and write to it. If that causes a problem, you need to handle it though some other mechanism (for example, claim the volume only in DaemonSet pods that you know will have just one per node).

Different storage providers support some subset of these modes. When you provision a persistent volume, you can specify which modes it will support. For example, NFS supports all modes, but in the example, only these modes were enabled:

```
accessModes:
    - ReadWriteMany
    - ReadOnlyMany
```

Reclaim policy

The reclaim policy determines what happens when a persistent volume claim is deleted. There are three different policies:

- **Retain** – the volume will need to be reclaimed manually
- **Delete** – the associated storage asset such as AWS EBS, GCE PD, Azure disk, or OpenStack Cinder volume is deleted
- **Recycle** – delete content only (`rm -rf /volume/*`)

The `Retain` and `Delete` policies mean the persistent volume is not available anymore for future claims. The `recycle` policy allows the volume to be claimed again.

Currently, only NFS and HostPath support recycling. AWS EBS, GCE PD, Azure disk, and Cinder volumes support deletion. Dynamically provisioned volumes are always deleted.

Volume type

The volume type is specified by name in the spec. There is no `volumeType` section. In the preceding example, `nfs` is the volume type:

```
nfs:
    path: /tmp
    server: 172.17.0.8
```

Each volume type may have its own set of parameters. In this case, it's a `path` and `server`.

We will go over various volume types later.

Making persistent volume claims

When containers want access to some persistent storage they make a claim (or rather, the developer and cluster administrator coordinate on necessary storage resources to claim). Here is a sample claim that matches the persistent volume from the previous section:

```
kind: PersistentVolumeClaim
apiVersion: v1
metadata:
  name: storage-claim
  annotations:
    volume.beta.kubernetes.io/storage-class: "normal"
spec:
  accessModes:
    - ReadWriteOnce
  resources:
    requests:
      storage: 80Gi
  selector:
```

```
matchLabels:
  release: "stable"
matchExpressions:
  - {key: capacity, operator: In, values: [80Gi, 100Gi]}
```

In the metadata, you can see the storage class annotation. The name `storage-claim` will be important later when mounting the claim into a container.

The access mode in the spec is `ReadWriteOnce`, which means if the claim is satisfied no other claim with the `ReadWriteOnce` access mode can be satisfied, but claims for `ReadOnlyMany` can still be satisfied.

The resources section requests 80 GiB. This can be satisfied by our persistent volume, which has a capacity of 100 Gi. But, this is a little bit of a waste because 20 Gi will not be used by definition.

The selector section allows you to filter available volumes further. For example, here the volume must match the label `release: stable` and also have a label with either `capacity: 80 Gi` or `capacity: 100 Gi`. Imagine that we have several other volumes provisioned with capacities of 200 Gi and 500 Gi. We don't want to claim a 500 Gi volume when we only need 80 Gi.

Kubernetes always tries to match the smallest volume that can satisfy a claim, but if there are no 80 Gi or 100 Gi volumes then the labels will prevent assigning a 200 Gi or 500 Gi volume and use dynamic provisioning instead.

It's important to realize that claims don't mention volumes by name. The matching is done by Kubernetes based on storage class, capacity, and labels.

Finally, persistent volume claims belong to a namespace. Binding a persistent volume to a claim is exclusive. That means that a persistent volume will be bound to a namespace. Even if the access mode is `ReadOnlyMany` or `ReadWriteMany`, all the pods that mount the persistent volume claim must be from that claim's namespace.

Mounting claims as volumes

OK. We have provisioned a volume and claimed it. It's time to use the claimed storage in a container. This turns out to be pretty simple. First, the persistent volume claim must be used as a volume in the pod and then the containers in the pod can mount it, just like any other volume. Here is a `pod` configuration file that specifies the persistent volume claim we created earlier (bound to the NFS persistent volume we provisioned):

```
kind: Pod
apiVersion: v1
metadata:
```

```
  name: the-pod
spec:
  containers:
    - name: the-container
      image: some-image
      volumeMounts:
      - mountPath: "/mnt/data"
        name: persistent-volume
  volumes:
    - name: persistent-volume
      persistentVolumeClaim:
        claimName: storage-claim
```

The key is in the `persistentVolumeClaim` section under `volumes`. The claim name (`storage-claim` here) uniquely identifies within the current namespace the specific claim and makes it available as a volume named `persistent-volume` here. Then, the container can refer to it by its name and mount it to `/mnt/data`.

Storage classes

Storage classes let an administrator configure your cluster with custom persistent storage (as long as there is a proper plugin to support it). A storage class has a name in the metadata (it must be specified in the annotation to claim), a provisioner, and parameters.

The storage class is still `in beta` as of Kubernetes 1.5. Here is a sample storage class:

```
kind: StorageClass
apiVersion: storage.k8s.io/v1beta1
metadata:
  name: standard
provisioner: kubernetes.io/aws-ebs
parameters:
  type: gp2
```

You may create multiple storage classes for the same provisioner with different parameters. Each provisioner has its own parameters.

The currently supported volume types are as follows:

- `emptyDir`
- `hostPath`
- `gcePersistentDisk`
- `awsElasticBlockStore`
- `nfs`
- `iscsi`
- `flocker`
- `glusterfs`
- `rbd`
- `cephfs`
- `gitRepo`
- `secret`
- `persistentVolumeClaim`
- `downwardAPI`
- `azureFileVolume`
- `azureDisk`
- `vsphereVolume`
- `Quobyte`

This list contains both persistent volumes and other volume types, such as `gitRepo` or `secret`, that are not backed by your typical network storage. This area of Kubernetes is still in flux and, in the future, it will be decoupled further and the design will be cleaner, where the plugins are not part of Kubernetes itself. Utilizing volume types intelligently is a major part of architecting and managing your cluster.

Default storage class

The cluster administrator can also assign a default storage class. When a default storage class is assigned and the `DefaultStorageClass` admission plugin is turned on, then claims with no storage class will be dynamically provisioned using the default storage class. If the default storage class is not defined or the admission plugin is not turned on, then claims with no storage class can only match volumes with no storage class.

Demonstrating persistent volume storage end to end

To illustrate all the concepts, let's do a mini demonstration where we create a HostPath volume, claim it, mount it, and have containers write to it.

Let's start by creating a `hostPath` volume. Save the following in `persistent-volume.yaml`:

```
kind: PersistentVolume
apiVersion: v1
metadata:
  name: persistent-volume-1
spec:
  capacity:
    storage: 1Gi
  accessModes:
    - ReadWriteMany
  hostPath:
    path: "/tmp/data"
```

```
> kubectl create -f persistent-volume.yaml
persistentvolume "persistent-volume-1" created
```

To check out the available volumes, you can use the resource type `persistentvolumes` or `pv` for short:

```
> kubectl get pv
NAME                    CAPACITY   ACCESSMODES   RECLAIMPOLICY   STATUS
CLAIM        REASON     AGE
persistent-volume-1     1Gi        RWX           Retain          Available
6m
```

The capacity is 1 GiB as requested. The reclaim policy is `Retain` because host path volumes are retained. The status is `Available` because the volume has not been claimed yet. The access mode is specified a `RWX`, which means `ReadWriteMany`. All access modes have a shorthand version:

- **RWO** – `ReadWriteOnce`
- **ROX** – `ReadOnlyMany`
- **RWX** – `ReadWriteMany`

We have a persistent volume. Let's create a claim. Save the following to `persistent-volume-claim.yaml`:

```
kind: PersistentVolumeClaim
apiVersion: v1
metadata:
  name: persistent-volume-claim
spec:
  accessModes:
    - ReadWriteOnce
  resources:
    requests:
      storage: 1Gi
```

Then, run the following command:

```
> kubectl create -f  .\persistent-volume-claim.yaml
persistentvolumeclaim "persistent-volume-claim" created
```

Let's check the `claim` and the `volume`:

```
k get pvc
NAME                      STATUS    VOLUME                CAPACITY
ACCESSMODES    AGE
persistent-volume-claim   Bound     persistent-volume-1   1Gi        RWX
27s
```

```
> k get pv
NAME                  CAPACITY   ACCESSMODES   RECLAIMPOLICY   STATUS
CLAIM                              REASON    AGE
persistent-volume-1   1Gi        RWX                           Retain          Bound
default/persistent-volume-claim              40m
```

As you can see, the `claim` and the volume are bound to each other. The final step is to create a `pod` and assign the `claim` as a `volume`. Save the following to `shell-pod.yaml`:

```
kind: Pod
apiVersion: v1
metadata:
  name: just-a-shell
  labels:
```

```
      name: just-a-shell
spec:
  containers:
    - name: a-shell
      image: ubuntu
      command: ["/bin/bash", "-c", "while true ; do sleep 10 ; done"]
      volumeMounts:
      - mountPath: "/data"
        name: pv
    - name: another-shell
      image: ubuntu
      command: ["/bin/bash", "-c", "while true ; do sleep 10 ; done"]
      volumeMounts:
      - mountPath: "/data"
        name: pv
  volumes:
    - name: pv
      persistentVolumeClaim:
        claimName: persistent-volume-claim
```

This pod has two containers that use the Ubuntu image and both run a shell command that just sleeps in an infinite loop. The idea is that the container will keep running, so we can connect to it later and check its filesystem. The pod mounts our persistent volume claim with a volume name of pv. Both containers mount it into their /data directory.

Let's create the pod and verify that both containers are running:

```
> kubectl create -f shell-pod.yaml
pod "just-a-shell" created


> kubectl get pods
NAME            READY     STATUS     RESTARTS     AGE
just-a-shell    2/2       Running    0            1h
```

Then, `ssh` to the node. This is the host whose `/tmp/data` is the pod's volume that mounted as `/data` into each of the running containers:

```
> minikube ssh
```

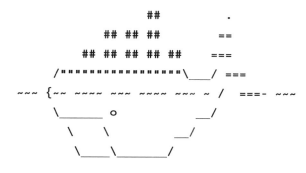

```
Boot2Docker version 1.11.1, build master : 901340f - Fri Jul  1 22:52:19
UTC 2016
Docker version 1.11.1, build 5604cbe
docker@minikube:~$
```

Inside the node, we can communicate with the containers using Docker commands. Let's look at the last two running containers:

```
docker@minikube:~$ docker ps -n=2
CONTAINER ID        IMAGE               COMMAND                 CREATED
STATUS              PORTS               NAMES
3c91a46b834a        ubuntu              "/bin/bash -c 'while "  About
an hour ago    Up About an hour                   k8s_another-
shell.b64b3aab_just-a-shell_default_ebf12a22-cee9-11e6-a2ae-
4ae3ce72fe94_8c7a8408
f1f9de10fdfd        ubuntu              "/bin/bash -c 'while "  About an
hour ago    Up About an hour                   k8s_a-shell.1a38381b_
just-a-shell_default_ebf12a22-cee9-11e6-a2ae-4ae3ce72fe94_451fa9ec
```

Then, let's create a file in the `/tmp/data` directory on the host. It should be visible by both containers via the mounted volume:

```
docker@minikube:~$ sudo touch /tmp/data/1.txt
```

Let's execute a `shell` on one of the containers, verify that the file `1.txt` is indeed visible, and create another file, `2.txt`:

```
docker@minikube:~$ docker exec -it 3c91a46b834a /bin/bash

root@just-a-shell:/# ls /data

1.txt

root@just-a-shell:/# touch /data/2.txt

root@just-a-shell:/# exit

Finally, we can run a shell on the other container and verify that both
1.txt and 2.txt are visible:

docker@minikube:~$ docker exec -it f1f9de10fdfd /bin/bash

root@just-a-shell:/# ls /data

1.txt   2.txt
```

Public storage volume types - GCE, AWS, and Azure

In this section, we'll look at some of the common volume types available in the leading public cloud platforms. Managing storage at scale is a difficult task that eventually involves physical resources, similar to nodes. If you choose to run your Kubernetes cluster on a public cloud platform, you can let your cloud provider deal with all these challenges and focus on your system. But it's important to understand the various options, constraints, and limitations of each volume type.

AWS Elastic Block Store (EBS)

AWS provides the elastic block store as persistent storage for EC2 instances. An AWS Kubernetes cluster can use AWS EBS as persistent storage with the following limitations:

- The pods must run on AWS EC2 instances as nodes
- Pods can only access EBS volumes provisioned in their availability zone
- An EBS volume can be mounted on a single EC2 instance.

Those are severe limitations. The restriction for a single availability zone, while great for performance, eliminates the ability to share storage at scale or across a geographically distributed system without custom replication and synchronization. The limit of a single EBS volume to a single EC2 instance means even within the same availability zone pods can't share storage (even for reading) unless you make sure they run on the same node.

With all the disclaimers out of the way, let's see how to mount an EBS volume:

```
apiVersion: v1
kind: Pod
metadata:
  name: some-pod
spec:
  containers:
  - image: some-container
    name: some-container
    volumeMounts:
    - mountPath: /ebs
      name: some-volume
  volumes:
  - name: some-volume
    awsElasticBlockStore:
      volumeID: <volume-id>
      fsType: ext4
```

You must create the EBS volume in AWS and then you just mount it into the pod. There is no need for a claim or storage class because you mount the volume directly by ID. The `awsElasticBlockStore` volume type is known to Kubernetes.

AWS Elastic File System (EFS)

AWS recently released a new service called the Elastic File System. This is really a managed NFS service. It's using NFS 4.1 protocol and it has many benefits over EBS:

- Multiple EC2 instances can access the same files across multiple availability zones (but within the same region)
- Capacity is automatically scaled up and down based on actual usage
- You pay only for what you use
- You can connect on-premise servers to EFS over VPN
- EFS runs off SSD drives that are automatically replicated across availability zones

That said, EFS is more expansive than EBS even when you consider the automatic replication to multiple AZs (assuming you fully utilize your EBS volumes). From a Kubernetes point of view, AWS EFS is just an NFS volume. You provision it as such:

```
apiVersion: v1
kind: PersistentVolume
metadata:
  name: efs-share
spec:
  capacity:
    storage: 200Gi
  accessModes:
    - ReadWriteMany
  nfs:
    server: eu-west-1b.fs-64HJku4i.efs.eu-west-1.amazonaws.com
    path: "/"
```

Once the persist volume exists, you can create a claim for it, attach the claim as a volume to multiple pods (`ReadWriteMany` access mode), and mount it into containers.

GCE persistent disk

The `gcePersistentDisk` volume type is very similar to `awsElasticBlockStore`. You must provision the disk ahead of time. It can only be used by GCE instances in the same project and zone. But the same volume can be used as read-only on multiple instances. This means it supports `ReadWriteOnce` and `ReadOnlyMany`. You can use a GCE persistent disk to share data as read-only between multiple pods in the same zone.

The pod that's using a persistent disk in `ReadWriteOnce` mode must be controlled by a replication controller, a replica set, or a deployment with a replica count of `0` or `1`. Trying to scale beyond `1` will fail for obvious reasons:

```
apiVersion: v1
kind: Pod
metadata:
  name: some-pod
spec:
  containers:
  - image: some-container
```

```
  name: some-container
  volumeMounts:
  - mountPath: /pd
    name: some-volume
volumes:
- name: some-volume
  gcePersistentDisk:
    pdName: <persistent disk name>
    fsType: ext4
```

Azure data disk

The Azure data disk is a virtual hard disk stored in Azure storage. It's similar in capabilities to AWS EBS. Here is a sample pod configuration file:

```
apiVersion: v1
kind: Pod
metadata:
 name: some-pod
spec:
 containers:
   - image: some-container
     name: some-container
     volumeMounts:
       - name: some-volume
         mountPath: /azure
 volumes:
       - name: some-volume
         azureDisk:
           diskName: test.vhd
           diskURI: https://someaccount.blob.microsoft.net/vhds/test.vhd
```

In addition to the mandatory diskName and diskURI parameters, it also has a few optional parameters:

- cachingMode: The disk caching mode. This must be one of None, ReadOnly, or ReadWrite. The default is None.
- fsType: The filesystem type set to mount. The default is ext4.
- readOnly: Whether the filesystem is used as readOnly. The default is false.

Azure data disks are limited to 1,023 GB. Each Azure VM can have up to 16 data disks. You can attach an Azure data disk to a single Azure VM.

Azure file storage

In addition to the data disk, Azure has also a shared filesystem similar to AWS EFS. However, Azure file storage uses the SMB/CIFS protocol (it supports SMB 2.1 and SMB 3.0). It is based on the Azure storage platform and has the same availability, durability, scalability, and geo-redundancy capabilities as Azure Blob, Table, or Queue.

In order to use Azure file storage, you need to install on each client VM the `cifs-utils` package. You also need to create a `secret`, which is a required parameter:

```
apiVersion: v1
kind: Secret
metadata:
  name: azure-file-secret
type: Opaque
data:
  azurestorageaccountname: <base64 encoded account name>
  azurestorageaccountkey: <base64 encoded account key>
```

Here is a configuration file for Azure file storage:

```
apiVersion: v1
kind: Pod
metadata:
 name: some-pod
spec:
 containers:
  - image: some-container
    name: some-container
    volumeMounts:
      - name: some-volume
        mountPath: /azure
 volumes:
      - name: some-volume
        azureFile:
```

```
    secretName: azure-file-secret
  shareName: azure-share
    readOnly: false
```

Azure file storage supports sharing within the same region as well as connecting on-premise clients. Here is a diagram that illustrates the workflow:

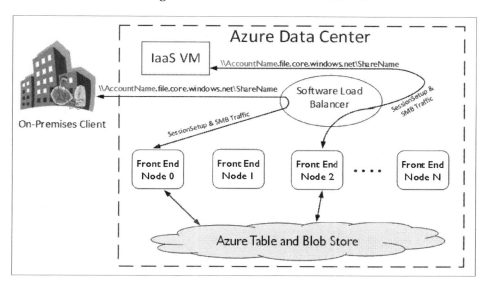

GlusterFS and Ceph volumes in Kubernetes

GlusterFS and Ceph are two distributed persistent storage systems. GlusterFS is at its core a network filesystem. Ceph is at the core an object store. Both expose block, object, and filesystem interfaces. Both use the xfs filesystem under the covers to store the data and metadata as xattr attributes. There are several reasons why you may want to use GlusterFs or Ceph as persistent volumes in your Kubernetes cluster:

- You may have a lot of data and applications that access the data in GlusterFS or Ceph
- You have administrative and operational expertise managing GlusterFS or Ceph
- You run in the cloud, but the limitations of the cloud platform persistent storage are a non-starter

Using GlusterFS

GlusterFS is intentionally simple, exposing the underlying directories as they are and leaving it to clients (or middleware) to handle high availability, replication, and distribution. Gluster organizes the data into logical volumes, which encompass multiple nodes (machines) that contain bricks, which store files. Files are allocated to bricks according to DHT (distributed hash table). If files are renamed or the GlusterFS cluster is expanded or rebalanced, files may be moved between bricks. The following diagram shows the GlusterFS building blocks:

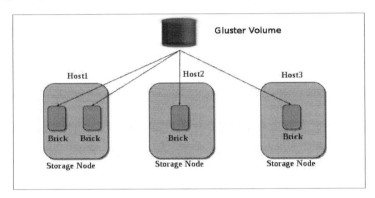

To use a GlusterFS cluster as persistent storage for Kubernetes (assuming you have an up and running GlusterFS cluster), you need to follow several steps. In particular, the GlusterFS nodes are managed by the plugin as a Kubernetes service (although as an application developer it doesn't concern you).

Creating endpoints

Here is an example of an endpoints resource that you can create as a normal Kubernetes resource using `kubectl create`:

```
{
  "kind": "Endpoints",
  "apiVersion": "v1",
  "metadata": {
    "name": "glusterfs-cluster"
  },
  "subsets": [
    {
      "addresses": [
        {
          "ip": "10.240.106.152"
```

```
            }
        ],
        "ports": [
            {
                "port": 1
            }
        ]
    },
    {
        "addresses": [
            {
                "ip": "10.240.79.157"
            }
        ],
        "ports": [
            {
                "port": 1
            }
        ]
    }
    ]
}
```

Adding a GlusterFS Kubernetes service

To make the endpoints persistent, you use a Kubernetes service with no selector to indicate the endpoints are managed manually:

```
{
    "kind": "Service",
    "apiVersion": "v1",
    "metadata": {
        "name": "glusterfs-cluster"
    },
    "spec": {
        "ports": [
            {"port": 1}
        ]
    }
}
```

Creating pods

Finally, in the pod spec's `volumes` section, provide the following information:

```
"volumes": [
        {
            "name": "glusterfsvol",
            "glusterfs": {
                "endpoints": "glusterfs-cluster",
                "path": "kube_vol",
                "readOnly": true
            }
        }
    ]
```

The containers can then mount `glusterfsvol` by name.

The `endpoints` tell the GlusterFS volume plugin how to find the storage nodes of the GlusterFS cluster.

Using Ceph

Ceph's object store can be accessed using multiple interfaces. Kubernetes supports the **RBD** (block) and **CEPHFS** (filesystem) interfaces. The following diagram shows how RADOS – the underlying object store – can be accessed in multiple days. Unlike GlusterFS, Ceph does a lot of work automatically. It does distribution, replication, and self-healing all on its own:

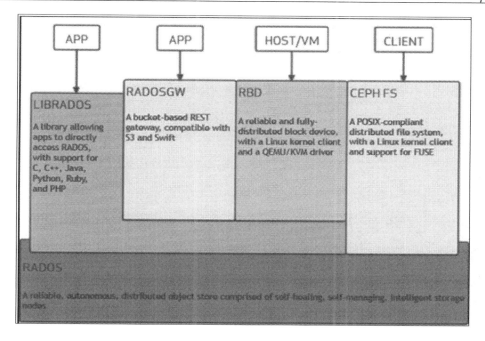

Connecting to Ceph using RBD

Kubernetes supports Ceph via the **Rados Block Device (RBD)** interface. You must install ceph-common on each node in the Kubernetes cluster. Once you have your Ceph cluster up and running, you need to provide some information required by the Ceph RBD volume plugin in the pod configuration file:

- monitors: Ceph monitors.
- pool: The name of the RADOS pool. If not provided, the default RBD pool is used.
- image: The image name that RBD has created.
- user: The RADOS user name. If not provided, the default admin is used.
- keyring: The path to the keyring file. If not provided, the default /etc/ceph/keyring is used.
- secretName: The name of the authentication secrets. If provided, secretName overrides keyring. Note, see the following paragraph about how to create a secret.
- fsType: The filesystem type (ext4, xfs, and so on) that is formatted on the device.
- readOnly: Whether the filesystem is used as readOnly.

If the Ceph authentication `secret` is used, you need to create a `secret` object:

```
apiVersion: v1
kind: Secret
metadata:
  name: ceph-secret
type: "kubernetes.io/rbd"
data:
  key: QVFCMTZWMVZvRjVtRXhBQTVrQ1FzN2JCCajhWVUxSdzI2Qzg0SEE9PQ==
```

> The secret type is kubernetes.io/rbd.

The pod spec's volumes section looks same as this:

```
"volumes": [
    {
        "name": "rbdpd",
        "rbd": {
            "monitors": [
          "10.16.154.78:6789",
    "10.16.154.82:6789",
          "10.16.154.83:6789"
      ],
            "pool": "kube",
            "image": "foo",
            "user": "admin",
            "secretRef": {
        "name": "ceph-secret"
      },
            "fsType": "ext4",
            "readOnly": true
        }
    }
]
```

Ceph RBD supports `ReadWriteOnce` and `ReadOnlyMany` access modes.

Connecting to Ceph using CephFS

If your Ceph cluster is already configured with CephFS, then you can assign it very easily to pods. Also CephFS supports `ReadWriteMany` access modes.

The configuration is similar to Ceph RBD, except you don't have a pool, image, or filesystem type. The secret can be a reference to a Kubernetes `secret` object (preferred) or a `secret` file:

```
apiVersion: v1
kind: Pod
metadata:
  name: cephfs
spec:
  containers:
  - name: cephfs-rw
    image: kubernetes/pause
    volumeMounts:
    - mountPath: "/mnt/cephfs"
      name: cephfs
  volumes:
  - name: cephfs
    cephfs:
      monitors:
      - 10.16.154.78:6789
      - 10.16.154.82:6789
      - 10.16.154.83:6789
      user: admin
      secretFile: "/etc/ceph/admin.secret"
      readOnly: true
```

You can also provide a path as a parameter in the `cephfs` system. The default is `/`.

Flocker as a clustered container data volume manager

So far, we have discussed storage solutions that stored the data outside the Kubernetes cluster (except for `emptyDir` and HostPath, which are not persistent). Flocker is a little different. It is Docker-aware. It was designed to let Docker data volumes transfer with their container when the container is moved between nodes. You may want to use the Flocker volume plugin if you're migrating a Docker-based system that use a different orchestration platform, such as Docker compose or Mesos, to Kubernetes and you use Flocker for orchestrating storage. Personally, I feel that there is a lot of duplication between what Flocker does and what Kubernetes does to abstract storage.

Flocker has a control service and agents on each node. Its architecture is very similar to Kubernetes with its API server and the Kubelet running on each node. The Flocker control service exposes a REST API and manages the configuration of the state across the cluster. The agents are responsible for ensuring that the state of their node matches the current configuration. For example, if a dataset needs to be on node X, then the Flocker agent on node X will create it.

The following diagram showcases the Flocker architecture:

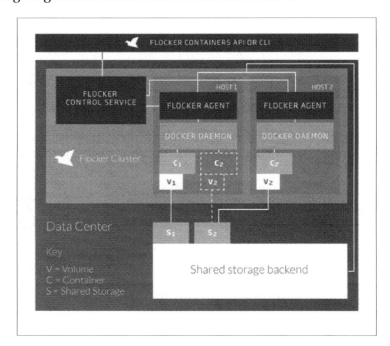

In order to use Flocker as persistent volumes in Kubernetes, you first must have a properly configured Flocker cluster. Flocker can work with many backing stores (again, very similar to Kubernetes persistent volumes).

Then you need to create Flocker datasets and at that point you're ready to hook it up as a persistent volume. After all your hard work, this part is easy and you just need to specify the Flocker dataset name:

```
apiVersion: v1
kind: Pod
metadata:
  name: some-pod
spec:
  containers:
    - name: some-container
      image: kubernetes/pause
      volumeMounts:
          # name must match the volume name below
          - name: flocker-volume
            mountPath: "/flocker"
  volumes:
    - name: flocker-volume
      flocker:
        datasetName: some-flocker-dataset
```

Integrating enterprise storage into Kubernetes

If you have an existing **Storage Area Network (SAN)** exposed over the iSCSI interface, Kubernetes has a volume plugin for you. It follows the same model as other shared persistent storage plugins we've seen earlier. You must configure the iSCSI initiator, but you don't have to provide any initiator information. All you need to provide is the following:

- IP address of the iSCSI target and port (if not the default 3260)
- Target's iqn (iSCSI qualified name) – typically reversed domain name
- **LUN** – logical unit number
- Filesystem type
- Readonly Boolean flag

The `iSCSI` plugin supports `ReadWriteOnce` and `ReadonlyMany`. Note that you can't partition your device at this time. Here is the volume spec:

```
volumes:
  - name: iscsi-volume
    iscsi:
      targetPortal: 10.0.2.34:3260
      iqn: iqn.2001-04.com.example:storage.kube.sys1.xyz
      lun: 0
      fsType: ext4
      readOnly: true
```

Torus – the new kid on the block

CoreOS recently released Torus – a new network storage system designed for Kubernetes. It takes advantage of the Kubernetes networking model and utilizes ATA over Ethernet. It is optimized for distributing storage across a large number of commodity hardware compared to the traditional approach of a relatively small number of specialized hardware. Torus uses `etcd` to store the storage state and can be connected to Kubernetes via the Flex volume plugin. It's still early days but Torus can become the right storage solution for fresh Kubernetes deployments. It will be very interesting to follow its progress.

Here is a diagram that shows how Torus is organized and deployed:

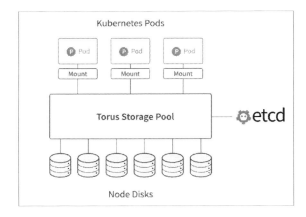

Summary

In this chapter, we took a deep look into storage in Kubernetes. We've looked at the generic conceptual model based on volumes, claims, and storage classes, as well as the implementation as volume plugins. Kubernetes eventually maps all storage systems into mounted filesystems in containers. This straightforward model allows administrators to configure and hook up any storage system from local host directories through cloud-based shared storage all the way to enterprise storage systems. You should now have a clear understanding of how storage is modeled and implemented in Kubernetes and be able to make intelligent choices of how to implement storage in your Kubernetes cluster.

In the *Chapter 8, Running Stateful Application with Kubernetes*, we'll see how Kubernetes can raise the level of abstraction and on top of storage help in developing, deploying, and operating stateful applications using concepts such as stateful sets.

8

Running Stateful Applications with Kubernetes

In this chapter, we will look into what it takes to run stateful applications on Kubernetes. Kubernetes is taking a lot of work off our hands by automatically starting and restarting pods across the cluster nodes as needed, based on complex requirements and configurations such as namespaces, limits, and quotas. But, when pods run storage-aware software, such as databases and queues, relocating a pod can cause the system to break. First, we'll understand the essence of stateful pods and why they are much more complicated to manage in Kubernetes. We will look at a few ways to manage the complexity such as shared environment variables and DNS records. In some situations, a redundant in-memory state, a DaemonSet, or persistent storage claims can do the trick. The main solution that Kubernetes promotes for state-aware pods is the **StatefulSet** (previously called **PetSet**) resource that allows managing an indexed collection of pods with stable properties. Finally, we will dive deep into a full-fledged example of running a Cassandra cluster on top of Kubernetes.

Stateful versus stateless applications in Kubernetes

A stateless Kubernetes application is an application that doesn't manage its state in the Kubernetes cluster. All of the state is stored outside the cluster and the cluster containers access it in some manner. In this section, we'll understand why state management is critical to the design of a distributed system and the benefits of managing states within the Kubernetes cluster.

Understanding the nature of distributed data-intensive apps

Let's start from the basics here. Distributed applications are a collection of processes that run on multiple machines, process inputs, manipulate data, expose APIs, and possibly have other side effects. Each process is a combination of its program, its runtime environment, and its inputs and outputs. The programs you write at school get their input as command line arguments, maybe read a file or access a database, and then write their results to the screen or a file or a database. Some programs keep states in memory and can serve requests over the network. Simple programs run on a single machine, can hold all their states in memory or read from a file. Their runtime environment is their operating system. If they crash, the user has to restart them manually. They are tied to their machine. A distributed application is a different animal. A single machine is not enough to process all the data or serve all the requests fast enough. A single machine can't hold all the data. The data that needs to be processed is so large that it can't be downloaded cost-effectively into each processing machine. Machines can fail and need to be replaced. Upgrades need to be performed over all the processing machines. Users may be distributed across the globe.

Taking all these issues into account, it becomes clear that the traditional approach doesn't work. The limiting factor becomes the data. Users/client must receive only summary or processed data. All massive data processing must be done close to the data itself because transferring data is prohibitively slow and expensive. Instead, the bulk of processing code must run in the same data center and network environment of the data.

Why manage states in Kubernetes?

The main reason to manage states in Kubernetes itself as opposed to a separate cluster is that a lot of the infrastructure needed to monitor, scale, allocate, secure and operate a storage cluster is already provided by Kubernetes. Running a parallel storage cluster will lead to a lot of duplicated effort.

Why manage states outside of Kubernetes?

Let's not rule out the other option. It may be better in some situations to manage states in a separate non-Kubernetes cluster, as long as it shares the same internal network (data proximity trumps everything).

Some valid reasons are:

- You already have a separate storage cluster and you don't want to rock the boat
- Your storage cluster is used by other non-Kubernetes applications
- Kubernetes support for your storage cluster is not stable or mature enough

You may want to approach stateful apps in Kubernetes incrementally, starting with a separate storage cluster and integrating more tightly with Kubernetes later.

Shared environment variables versus DNS records for discovery

Kubernetes provides several mechanisms for global discovery across the cluster. If your storage cluster is not managed by Kubernetes, you still need to tell Kubernetes pods how to find it and access it. There are two main methods:

- DNS
- Environment variables

In some cases, you may want to use both where environment variables can override DNS.

Accessing external data stores via DNS

The DNS approach is simple and straightforward. Assuming your external storage cluster is load balanced and can provide a stable endpoint, then pods can just hit directly that endpoint and connect to the external cluster.

Accessing external data stores via environment variables

Another simple approach is to use environment variables to pass connection information to an external storage cluster. Kubernetes offers the ConfigMap resource as a way to keep configuration separate from the container image. The configuration is a set of key-value pairs. The configuration information can be exposed as an environment variable inside the container as well as volumes. You may prefer to use secrets for sensitive connection information.

Creating a ConfigMap

The following configuration file will create a configuration file that keeps a list of addresses:

```
apiVersion: v1
kind: ConfigMap
metadata:
  name: db-config
  namespace: default
data:
  db-ip-addresses: 1.2.3.4,5.6.7.8
```

```
> kubectl create -f .\configmap.yaml
configmap "db-config" created
```

The `data` section contains all the key value pairs. In this case, just a single pair with a key name of `db-ip-addresses`. It will be important later when consuming the `configmap` in a pod. You can check out the content to make sure it's OK:

```
> kubectl get configmap db-config -o yaml
apiVersion: v1
data:
  db-ip-addresses: 1.2.3.4,5.6.7.8
kind: ConfigMap
metadata:
  creationTimestamp: 2017-01-09T03:14:07Z
  name: db-config
  namespace: default
  resourceVersion: "551258"
  selfLink: /api/v1/namespaces/default/configmaps/db-config
  uid: aebcc007-d619-11e6-91f1-3a7ae2a25c7d
```

There are other ways to create `ConfigMap`. You can directly create them using the `--from-value` or `--from-file` command line arguments.

Consuming a ConfigMap as an environment variable

When you are creating a pod, you can specify a ConfigMap and consume its values in several ways. Here is how to consume our configuration map as an environment variable:

```
apiVersion: v1
kind: Pod
metadata:
  name: some-pod
spec:
  containers:
    - name: some-container
      image: busybox
      command: [ "/bin/sh", "-c", "env" ]
      env:
        - name: DB_IP_ADDRESSES
          valueFrom:
            configMapKeyRef:
              name: db-config
              key: db-ip-addresses
  restartPolicy: Never
```

This pod runs the busybox minimal container and executes an env bash command and immediately exists. The db-ip-addresses key from the db-config map is mapped to the environment variable, DB_IP_ADDRESSES, and is reflected in the output:

```
> kubectl logs some-pod
HUE_REMINDERS_SERVICE_PORT=80
HUE_REMINDERS_PORT=tcp://10.0.0.238:80
KUBERNETES_PORT=tcp://10.0.0.1:443
KUBERNETES_SERVICE_PORT=443
HOSTNAME=some-pod
SHLVL=1
HOME=/root
HUE_REMINDERS_PORT_80_TCP_ADDR=10.0.0.238
HUE_REMINDERS_PORT_80_TCP_PORT=80
HUE_REMINDERS_PORT_80_TCP_PROTO=tcp
DB_IP_ADDRESSES=1.2.3.4,5.6.7.8
```

```
HUE_REMINDERS_PORT_80_TCP=tcp://10.0.0.238:80
KUBERNETES_PORT_443_TCP_ADDR=10.0.0.1
PATH=/usr/local/sbin:/usr/local/bin:/usr/sbin:/usr/bin:/sbin:/bin
KUBERNETES_PORT_443_TCP_PORT=443
KUBERNETES_PORT_443_TCP_PROTO=tcp
KUBERNETES_SERVICE_PORT_HTTPS=443
KUBERNETES_PORT_443_TCP=tcp://10.0.0.1:443
HUE_REMINDERS_SERVICE_HOST=10.0.0.238
PWD=/
KUBERNETES_SERVICE_HOST=10.0.0.1
```

Using a redundant in-memory state

In some cases, you may want to keep a transient state in memory. Distributed caching is a common case. Time-sensitive information is another one. For these use cases, there is no need for persistent storage and multiple pods accessed through a service may be just the right solution. We can use standard Kubernetes techniques such as labeling to identify pods that belong to the store redundant copies of the same state and expose it through a service. If a pod dies, Kubernetes will create a new one and until it catches up the other pods will serve the state. We can even use the pod anti-affinity Alpha feature to ensure that pods who maintain redundant copies of the same state are not scheduled to the same node.

Using DaemonSet for redundant persistent storage

Some stateful applications such as distributed databases or queues manage their state redundantly and sync their nodes automatically (we'll take a very deep look into Cassandra later). In these cases, it is important that pods are scheduled to separate nodes. It is also important that pods are scheduled to nodes with particular hardware configuration or are even dedicated for the stateful application. The DaemonSet feature is perfect for this use case. We can label a set of nodes and make sure that the stateful pods are scheduled on a one-by-one basis to the selected group of nodes.

Applying persistent volume claims

If the stateful application can use effectively shared persistent storage, then using a persistent volume claim in each pod is the way to go, as we demonstrated in *Chapter 7, Handling Kubernetes Storage*. The stateful application will be presented with a mounted volume that looks just like a local filesystem.

Utilizing StatefulSet

The StatefulSet controller is a relatively new addition to Kubernetes (introduced as StatefulSet in Kubernetes 1.3 and renamed to StatefulSet in Kubernetes 1.5). It is especially designed to support distributed stateful applications where the identities of the members is important and if a pod is restarted it must retain its identity in the set. It provides ordered deployment and scaling. Unlike regular pods, the pods of a stateful set are associated with persistent storage.

When to use StatefulSet

StatefulSet is great for applications that require one or more of the following:

- Stable, unique network identifiers
- Stable, persistent storage
- Ordered, graceful deployment, and scaling
- Ordered, graceful deletion, and termination

The components of StatefulSet

There are several pieces that need to be configured correctly in order to have a working StatefulSet:

- A headless service responsible for managing the network identity of the StatefulSet pods
- The StatefulSet itself with a number of replicas
- Persistent storage provision dynamically or by an administrator

Here is an example of a service called `nginx` that will be used for a StatefulSet:

```
apiVersion: v1
kind: Service
metadata:
  name: nginx
  labels:
    app: nginx
spec:
  ports:
  - port: 80
    name: web
```

```
  clusterIP: None
  selector:
    app: nginx
```

Now, the `StatefulSet` configuration file will reference the service:

```
apiVersion: apps/v1beta1
kind: StatefulSet
metadata:
  name: web
spec:
  serviceName: "nginx"
  replicas: 3
  template:
    metadata:
      labels:
        app: nginx
```

The next part is the pod template that includes a mounted volume named www:

```
  spec:
    terminationGracePeriodSeconds: 10
    containers:
    - name: nginx
      image: gcr.io/google_containers/nginx-slim:0.8
      ports:
      - containerPort: 80
        name: web
      volumeMounts:
      - name: www
        mountPath: /usr/share/nginx/html
```

Last but not least, the `volumeClaimTemplates` use a claim named www matching the mounted volume. The claim requests `1Gib` of `storage` with `ReadWriteOnce` access:

```
  volumeClaimTemplates:
  - metadata:
      name: www
    spec:
```

```
accessModes: [ "ReadWriteOnce" ]
resources:
  requests:
    storage: 1Gib
```

Running a Cassandra cluster in Kubernetes

In this section, we will explore in detail a very large example of configuring a Cassandra cluster to run on a Kubernetes cluster. The full example can be accessed here:

```
https://github.com/kubernetes/kubernetes/tree/master/examples/
storage/cassandra.
```

First, we'll learn a little bit about Cassandra itself and its idiosyncrasies and then follow a step-by-step procedure to get it running using several of the techniques and strategies we've covered in the previous section.

Quick introduction to Cassandra

Cassandra is a distributed columnar data store. It was designed from the get go for big data. Cassandra is fast, robust (no single point of failure), highly-available, and linearly scalable. It also has multi-data center support. It achieves all this by having a laser focus and carefully crafting the features it supports—and just as importantly— the features it doesn't support. In a previous company, I ran a Kubernetes cluster that used Cassandra as the main data store for a sensors data (about 100 TB). Cassandra allocates the data to a set of nodes (node ring) based on a DHT algorithm. The cluster nodes talk to each other via a gossip protocol and learn quickly about the overall state of the cluster (what nodes joined and what nodes left or are unavailable). Cassandra constantly compacts the data and balances the cluster. The data is typically replicated multiple times for redundancy, robustness, and high-availability. From a developer's point of view, Cassandra is very good for time-series data and provides a flexible model where you can specify the consistency level in each query. It is also idempotent (a very important feature for a distributed database), which means repeated inserts or updates are allowed.

Here is a diagram that shows how a Cassandra cluster is organized and how a client can access any node and the request will be forwarded automatically to the nodes that have the requested data:

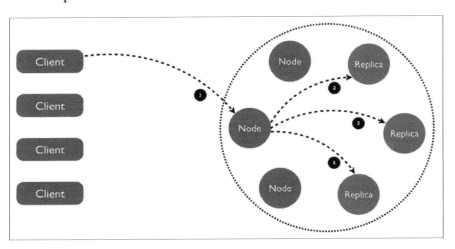

The Cassandra Docker image

Deploying Cassandra on Kubernetes as opposed to a standalone Cassandra cluster deployment requires a special Docker image. This is an important step because it means we can use Kubernetes to keep track of our Cassandra pods. The image is available here:

```
https://github.com/kubernetes/kubernetes/tree/master/examples/
storage/cassandra/image.
```

Here are the essential parts of the Docker file.

The image is based on Debian Jessie:

```
FROM google/debian:jessie
```

Add and copy the necessary files (Cassandra.jar, various configuration files, run script, and read-probe script), create a data directory for Cassandra to store its SSTables, and mount it:

```
ADD files /
RUN mv /java.list /etc/apt/sources.list.d/java.list \
  && mv /cassandra.list /etc/apt/sources.list.d/cassandra.list \
  && chmod a+rx /run.sh /sbin/dumb-init /ready-probe.sh \
```

```
&& mkdir -p /cassandra_data/data \
&& mv /logback.xml /cassandra.yaml /jvm.options /etc/cassandra/
```

```
VOLUME ["/cassandra_data"]
```

Expose important ports for accessing Cassandra and to let Cassandra nodes gossip with each other:

```
# 7000: intra-node communication
# 7001: TLS intra-node communication
# 7199: JMX
# 9042: CQL
EXPOSE 7000 7001 7199 9042
```

Finally, the command, which uses dumb-init, a simple container init system from yelp, eventually runs the run.sh script:

```
CMD ["/sbin/dumb-init", "/bin/bash", "/run.sh"]
```

Exploring the run.sh script

The run.sh script requires some shell skills but it's worth the effort. Since Docker allows running only one command, it is very common with non-trivial applications to have a launcher script that sets up the environment and prepares for the actual application. In this case, the image supports several deployment options (stateful set, replication controller, DaemonSet) that we'll cover later and the run script accommodates all by being very configurable via environment variables.

First, some local variables are set for the Cassandra configuration file at /etc/cassandra/cassandra.yaml. The CASSANDRA_CFG variable will be used in the rest of the script:

```
set -e
CASSANDRA_CONF_DIR=/etc/cassandra
CASSANDRA_CFG=$CASSANDRA_CONF_DIR/cassandra.yaml
```

If no CASSANDRA_SEEDS were specified, then set the HOSTNAME, which is used in the stateful set solution:

```
# we are doing StatefulSet or just setting our seeds
if [ -z "$CASSANDRA_SEEDS" ]; then
  HOSTNAME=$(hostname -f)
Fi
```

Then comes a long list of environment variables with defaults. The syntax, ${VAR_ NAME:-<default>}, uses the environment variable, VAR_NAME, if it's defined, or the default value.

A similar syntax: ${VAR_NAME:=<default>}, does the same thing, but also assigns the default value to the environment variable if not defined.

Both variations are used here:

```
CASSANDRA_RPC_ADDRESS="${CASSANDRA_RPC_ADDRESS:-0.0.0.0}"
CASSANDRA_NUM_TOKENS="${CASSANDRA_NUM_TOKENS:-32}"
CASSANDRA_CLUSTER_NAME="${CASSANDRA_CLUSTER_NAME:='Test Cluster'}"
CASSANDRA_LISTEN_ADDRESS=${POD_IP:-$HOSTNAME}
CASSANDRA_BROADCAST_ADDRESS=${POD_IP:-$HOSTNAME}
CASSANDRA_BROADCAST_RPC_ADDRESS=${POD_IP:-$HOSTNAME}
CASSANDRA_DISK_OPTIMIZATION_STRATEGY="${CASSANDRA_DISK_OPTIMIZATION_
STRATEGY:-ssd}"
CASSANDRA_MIGRATION_WAIT="${CASSANDRA_MIGRATION_WAIT:-1}"
CASSANDRA_ENDPOINT_SNITCH="${CASSANDRA_ENDPOINT_SNITCH:-SimpleSnitch}"
CASSANDRA_DC="${CASSANDRA_DC}"
CASSANDRA_RACK="${CASSANDRA_RACK}"
CASSANDRA_RING_DELAY="${CASSANDRA_RING_DELAY:-30000}"
CASSANDRA_AUTO_BOOTSTRAP="${CASSANDRA_AUTO_BOOTSTRAP:-true}"
CASSANDRA_SEEDS="${CASSANDRA_SEEDS:false}"
CASSANDRA_SEED_PROVIDER="${CASSANDRA_SEED_PROVIDER:-org.apache.cassandra.
locator.SimpleSeedProvider}"
CASSANDRA_AUTO_BOOTSTRAP="${CASSANDRA_AUTO_BOOTSTRAP:false}"


# Turn off JMX auth
CASSANDRA_OPEN_JMX="${CASSANDRA_OPEN_JMX:-false}"
# send GC to STDOUT
CASSANDRA_GC_STDOUT="${CASSANDRA_GC_STDOUT:-false}"
```

Then comes a section where all the variables are printed to the screen. Let's skip most of it:

```
echo Starting Cassandra on ${CASSANDRA_LISTEN_ADDRESS}
echo CASSANDRA_CONF_DIR ${CASSANDRA_CONF_DIR}

...
```

The next section is very important. By default, Cassandra uses a simple snitch, which is unaware of racks and data centers. This is not optimal when the cluster spans multiple data centers and racks. Cassandra is rack and data center aware and can optimize both for redundancy and high-availability while limiting communication across data centers appropriately:

```
# if DC and RACK are set, use GossipingPropertyFileSnitch
if [[ $CASSANDRA_DC && $CASSANDRA_RACK ]]; then
   echo "dc=$CASSANDRA_DC" > $CASSANDRA_CONF_DIR/cassandra-rackdc.
properties
   echo "rack=$CASSANDRA_RACK" >> $CASSANDRA_CONF_DIR/cassandra-rackdc.
properties
   CASSANDRA_ENDPOINT_SNITCH="GossipingPropertyFileSnitch"
fi
```

Memory management is important and you can control the maximum heap size to ensure Cassandra doesn't start thrashing and swapping to disk:

```
if [ -n "$CASSANDRA_MAX_HEAP" ]; then
   sed -ri "s/^(#)?-Xmx[0-9]+.*/-Xmx$CASSANDRA_MAX_HEAP/" "$CASSANDRA_
CONF_DIR/jvm.options"
   sed -ri "s/^(#)?-Xms[0-9]+.*/-Xms$CASSANDRA_MAX_HEAP/" "$CASSANDRA_
CONF_DIR/jvm.options"
fi
```

```
if [ -n "$CASSANDRA_REPLACE_NODE" ]; then
   echo "-Dcassandra.replace_address=$CASSANDRA_REPLACE_NODE/" >>
"$CASSANDRA_CONF_DIR/jvm.options"
fi
```

The rack and data center information is stored in a simple Java `properties` file:

```
for rackdc in dc rack; do
  var="CASSANDRA_${rackdc^^}"
  val="${!var}"
  if [ "$val" ]; then
  sed -ri 's/^('"$rackdc"'=).*/\1 '"$val"'/' "$CASSANDRA_CONF_DIR/
cassandra-rackdc.properties"
  fi
done
```

The next section loops over all the variables defined earlier, finds the corresponding key in the Cassandra.yaml configuration files, and overwrites them. That ensures that each configuration file is customized on the fly just before it launches Cassandra itself:

```
for yaml in \
  broadcast_address \
  broadcast_rpc_address \
  cluster_name \
  disk_optimization_strategy \
  endpoint_snitch \
  listen_address \
  num_tokens \
  rpc_address \
  start_rpc \
  key_cache_size_in_mb \
  concurrent_reads \
  concurrent_writes \
  memtable_cleanup_threshold \
  memtable_allocation_type \
  memtable_flush_writers \
  concurrent_compactors \
  compaction_throughput_mb_per_sec \
  counter_cache_size_in_mb \
  internode_compression \
  endpoint_snitch \
  gc_warn_threshold_in_ms \
  listen_interface \
  rpc_interface \
  ; do
  var="CASSANDRA_${yaml^^}"
  val="${!var}"
  if [ "$val" ]; then
    sed -ri 's/^(# )?('"$yaml"':).*/\2 '"$val"'/' "$CASSANDRA_CFG"
  fi
done


echo "auto_bootstrap: ${CASSANDRA_AUTO_BOOTSTRAP}" >> $CASSANDRA_CFG
```

The next section is all about setting the seeds or seed provider depending on the deployment solution (stateful set or not). There is a little trick for the first pod to bootstrap as its own seed:

```
# set the seed to itself.  This is only for the first pod, otherwise
# it will be able to get seeds from the seed provider
if [[ $CASSANDRA_SEEDS == 'false' ]]; then
  sed -ri 's/- seeds:.*/- seeds: "'"$POD_IP"'"/' $CASSANDRA_CFG
else # if we have seeds set them.  Probably StatefulSet
  sed -ri 's/- seeds:.*/- seeds: "'"$CASSANDRA_SEEDS"'"/' $CASSANDRA_CFG
fi


sed -ri 's/- class_name: SEED_PROVIDER/- class_name: '"$CASSANDRA_SEED_
PROVIDER"'/' $CASSANDRA_CFG
```

The following section sets up various options for remote management and JMX monitoring. It's critical in complicated distributed systems to have proper administration tools. Cassandra has deep support for the ubiquitous **Java Management Extensions (JMX)** standard:

```
# send gc to stdout
if [[ $CASSANDRA_GC_STDOUT == 'true' ]]; then
  sed -ri 's/ -Xloggc:\/var\/log\/cassandra\/gc\.log//' $CASSANDRA_CONF_
DIR/cassandra-env.sh
fi


# enable RMI and JMX to work on one port
echo "JVM_OPTS=\"\$JVM_OPTS -Djava.rmi.server.hostname=$POD_IP\"" >>
$CASSANDRA_CONF_DIR/cassandra-env.sh


# getting WARNING messages with Migration Service
echo "-Dcassandra.migration_task_wait_in_seconds=${CASSANDRA_MIGRATION_
WAIT}" >> $CASSANDRA_CONF_DIR/jvm.options

echo "-Dcassandra.ring_delay_ms=${CASSANDRA_RING_DELAY}" >> $CASSANDRA_
CONF_DIR/jvm.options


if [[ $CASSANDRA_OPEN_JMX == 'true' ]]; then
  export LOCAL_JMX=no

  sed -ri 's/ -Dcom\.sun\.management\.jmxremote\.authenticate=true/
-Dcom\.sun\.management\.jmxremote\.authenticate=false/' $CASSANDRA_CONF_
DIR/cassandra-env.sh
```

```
sed -ri 's/ -Dcom\.sun\.management\.jmxremote\.password\.file=\/etc\/
cassandra\/jmxremote\.password//' $CASSANDRA_CONF_DIR/cassandra-env.sh
fi
```

Finally, the `class` path is set to the Cassandra JAR file and it launches Cassandra itself in the foreground (not Daemonized):

```
export CLASSPATH=/kubernetes-cassandra.jar

cassandra -R -f
```

Hooking up Kubernetes and Cassandra

Connecting Kubernetes and Cassandra takes some work because Cassandra was designed to be very self-sufficient, but we want to let it hook Kubernetes at the right time to provide capabilities such as automatically restarting failed nodes, monitoring, allocating Cassandra pods, and providing a unified view of the Cassandra pods side by side of other pods. Cassandra is a complicated beast and has many knobs to control it. It comes with a `Cassandra.yaml` configuration file and you can override all the options with environment variables.

Digging into the Cassandra configuration

There are two settings that are particularly relevant: the seed provider and the snitch. The seed provider is responsible for publishing a list of IP addresses (seeds) of nodes in the cluster. Every node that starts running connects to the seeds (there are usually at least three) and if it successfully reaches one of them they immediately exchange information about all the nodes in the cluster. This information is updated constantly for each node as the nodes gossip with each other.

The default seed provider configured in `Cassandra.yaml` is just a static list of IP addresses, in this case just the loopback interface:

```
seed_provider:
    - class_name: SEED_PROVIDER
      parameters:
          # seeds is actually a comma-delimited list of addresses.
          # Ex: "<ip1>,<ip2>,<ip3>"
          - seeds: "127.0.0.1"
```

The other important setting is the snitch. It has two roles:

- It teaches Cassandra enough about your network topology to route requests efficiently.

- It allows Cassandra to spread replicas around your cluster to avoid correlated failures. It does this by grouping machines into data centers and racks. Cassandra will do its best not to have more than one replica on the same rack (which may not actually be a physical location).

Cassandra comes pre-loaded with several snitch classes, but none of them are Kubernetes aware. The default is SimpleSnitch, but can be overridden:

```
# You can use a custom Snitch by setting this to the full class
# name of the snitch, which will be assumed to be on your # classpath.
endpoint_snitch: SimpleSnitch
```

The custom seed provider

When running Cassandra nodes as pods in Kubernetes, Kubernetes may move pods around including seeds. To accommodate that, a Cassandra seed provider needs to interact with the Kubernetes API server.

Here is a short snippet from the custom KubernetesSeedPRovider Java class that implements the Cassandra SeedProvider API:

```
public class KubernetesSeedProvider implements SeedProvider {
    ...
    /**
     * Call kubernetes API to collect a list of seed providers
     * @return list of seed providers
     */
    public List<InetAddress> getSeeds() {
        String host = getEnvOrDefault("KUBERNETES_PORT_443_TCP_ADDR",
"kubernetes.default.svc.cluster.local");
        String port = getEnvOrDefault("KUBERNETES_PORT_443_TCP_PORT",
"443");
        String serviceName = getEnvOrDefault("CASSANDRA_SERVICE",
"cassandra");
        String podNamespace = getEnvOrDefault("POD_NAMESPACE",
"default");
        String path = String.format("/api/v1/namespaces/%s/endpoints/",
podNamespace);
```

```
        String seedSizeVar = getEnvOrDefault("CASSANDRA_SERVICE_NUM_
SEEDS", "8");

        Integer seedSize = Integer.valueOf(seedSizeVar);

        String accountToken = getEnvOrDefault("K8S_ACCOUNT_TOKEN", "/var/
run/secrets/kubernetes.io/serviceaccount/token");


        List<InetAddress> seeds = new ArrayList<InetAddress>();
        try {
            String token = getServiceAccountToken(accountToken);


            SSLContext ctx = SSLContext.getInstance("SSL");
            ctx.init(null, trustAll, new SecureRandom());


            String PROTO = "https://";
            URL url = new URL(PROTO + host + ":" + port + path +
serviceName);
            logger.info("Getting endpoints from " + url);
            HttpsURLConnection conn = (HttpsURLConnection)url.
openConnection();


            conn.setSSLSocketFactory(ctx.getSocketFactory());
            conn.addRequestProperty("Authorization", "Bearer " + token);
            ObjectMapper mapper = new ObjectMapper();
            Endpoints endpoints = mapper.readValue(conn.getInputStream(),
Endpoints.class);        }
            ...
        }
        ...


    return Collections.unmodifiableList(seeds);
}
```

Creating a Cassandra headless service

The role of the headless service is to allow clients in the Kubernetes cluster to connect to the Cassandra cluster through a standard Kubernetes service instead of keeping track of the network identities of the nodes or putting a dedicated load balancer in front of all the nodes. Kubernetes provides all that out of the box through its services.

Here is the configuration file:

```
apiVersion: v1
kind: Service
metadata:
  labels:
    app: cassandra
  name: cassandra
spec:
  clusterIP: None
  ports:
    - port: 9042
  selector:
    app: Cassandra
```

The `app: Cassandra` label will group all the pods to participate in the service. Kubernetes will create endpoint records and the DNS will return a record for discovery. The `clusterIP` is `None`, which means the service is headless and Kubernetes will not do any load balancing or proxying. This is important because Cassandra nodes do their own communication directly.

The `9042` port is used by Cassandra to serve CQL requests. Those can be queries, inserts/updates (it's always an upsert with Cassandra), or deletes.

Using statefulSet to create the Cassandra cluster

Declaring a stateful set is not trivial. It is arguably the most complex Kubernetes resource. It has a lot of moving parts: standard metadata, the stateful set spec, the pod template (which is often pretty complex itself), and volume claim templates.

Dissecting the stateful set configuration file

Let's go methodically over this example stateful set configuration file that declares a three-node Cassandra cluster.

Here is the basic metadata. Note the `apiVersion` string starting with `apps/`:

```
apiVersion: "apps/v1beta1"
kind: StatefulSet
metadata:
  name: cassandra
```

The stateful set `spec` defines the headless service name, how many pods there are in the stateful set, and the pod template (explained later). The `replicas` field specifies how many pods are in the stateful set:

```
spec:
  serviceName: cassandra
  replicas: 3
  template: …
```

The term `replicas` for the pods is an unfortunate choice because the pods are NOT replicas of each other. They share the same pod template, but they have a unique identity and they are responsible for different subsets of the state in general. This is even more confusing in the case of Cassandra, which uses the same term `replicas` to refer to groups of nodes that redundantly duplicate some subset of the state (but are not identical, because each can manage additional states too). I opened a GitHub issue with the Kubernetes project to change the term from `replicas` to `members`:

`https://github.com/kubernetes/kubernetes.github.io/issues/2103`.

The pod template contains a single container based on the custom Cassandra image. Here is the pod template, with the `app: cassandra` label:

```
template:
  metadata:
    labels:
      app: cassandra
  spec:
    containers: …
```

The container spec has multiple important parts. It starts with a `name` and the `image` we looked at earlier:

```
containers:
  - name: cassandra
    image: gcr.io/google-samples/cassandra:v11
    imagePullPolicy: Always
```

Then it defines multiple container ports needed for external and internal communication by Cassandra nodes:

```
ports:
  - containerPort: 7000
    name: intra-node
  - containerPort: 7001
```

```
    name: tls-intra-node
  - containerPort: 7199
    name: jmx
  - containerPort: 9042
    name: cql
```

The resources section specifies the CPU and memory needed by the container. This is critical because the storage management layer should never be a performance bottleneck due to cpu or memory.

```
resources:
  limits:
    cpu: "500m"
    memory: 1Gi
  requests:
    cpu: "500m"
    memory: 1Gi
```

Cassandra needs access to IPC, which the container requests through the security content's capabilities:

```
securityContext:
capabilities:
  add:
        - IPC_LOCK
```

The *env* section specifies environment variables that will be available inside the container. The following is a partial list of the necessary variables. The CASSANDRA_SEEDS variable is set to the headless service, so a Cassandra node can talk to seeds on startup and discover the whole cluster. Note that in this configuration, we don't use the special Kubernetes seed provider. The POD_IP is interesting because it utilizes the Downward API to populate its value via the field reference to status.podIP:

```
env:
  - name: MAX_HEAP_SIZE
    value: 512M
  - name: CASSANDRA_SEEDS
    value: "cassandra-0.cassandra.default.svc.cluster.local"
  - name: POD_IP
    valueFrom:
      fieldRef:
        fieldPath: status.podIP
```

The container has a readiness probe too to ensure the Cassandra node doesn't receive requests before it's fully online:

```
readinessProbe:
  exec:
    command:
    - /bin/bash
    - -c
    - /ready-probe.sh
  initialDelaySeconds: 15
  timeoutSeconds: 5
```

Cassandra needs to read and write the data of course. The `cassandra-data` volume mount is where it's at:

```
volumeMounts:
- name: cassandra-data
  mountPath: /cassandra_data
```

That's it for the container spec. The last part is the volume claim template. In this case, dynamic provisioning is used. It's highly recommended to use SSD drives for Cassandra storage and especially its journal. The requested storage in this example is 1 Gi. I discovered through experimentation that 1-2 TB is ideal for a single Cassandra node. The reason is that Cassandra does a lot of data shuffling under the covers, compacting and rebalancing the data. If a node leaves the cluster or a new one joins the cluster, you have to wait until the data is properly rebalanced before the data from the node that left is properly re-distributed or a new node is populated. Note that Cassandra needs a lot of disk space to do all this shuffling. It is recommended to have 50% free disk space. When you consider that you also need replication (typically 3X) then the required storage space can be 6X your data size. You can get by with 30% free space if you're adventurous and maybe use just 2X replication depending on your use case. But, don't get below 10% free disk space even on a single node. I learned the hard way that Cassandra will be simply stuck and unable to compact and rebalance such nodes without extreme measures.

The access mode is of course `ReadWriteOnce`:

```
volumeClaimTemplates:
- metadata:
    name: cassandra-data
    annotations:
      volume.alpha.kubernetes.io/storage-class: anything
```

```
spec:
  accessModes: [ "ReadWriteOnce" ]
  resources:
    requests:
      storage: 1Gi
```

When deploying a stateful set, Kubernetes creates the pod in order per its index number. When scaling up or down, it also does it in order. For Cassandra, this is not important because it can handle nodes joining or leaving the cluster in any order. When a Cassandra pod is destroyed, the persistent volume remains. If a pod with the same index is created later, the original persistent volume will be mounted into it. This stable connection between a particular pod and its storage enables Cassandra to manage the state properly.

Using a replication controller to distribute Cassandra

A stateful set is great, but as mentioned earlier, Cassandra is already a sophisticated distributed database. It has a lot of mechanisms for automatically distributing and balancing and replicating the data around the cluster. These mechanisms are not optimized for working with network persistent storage. Cassandra was designed to work with the data stored directly on the nodes. When a node dies, Cassandra can recover having redundant data stored on other nodes. Let's look at a different way to deploy Cassandra on a Kubernetes cluster, which is more aligned with Cassandra's semantics. Another benefit of this approach is that if you have an existing Kubernetes cluster; you don't have to upgrade it to the latest and greatest just to use a stateful set.

We will still use the headless service, but instead of a stateful set we'll use a regular replication controller. There are some important differences:

- Replication controller instead of a stateful set
- Storage on the node the pod is scheduled to
- The custom Kubernetes seed provider class is used

Dissecting the replication controller configuration file

The metadata is pretty minimal, with just a name (labels are not required):

```
apiVersion: v1
kind: ReplicationController
```

```
metadata:
  name: cassandra
  # The labels will be applied automatically
  # from the labels in the pod template, if not set
  # labels:
    # app: Cassandra
```

The `spec` specifies the number of `replicas`:

```
spec:
  replicas: 3
  # The selector will be applied automatically
  # from the labels in the pod template, if not set.
  # selector:
    # app: Cassandra
```

The pod template's metadata is where the `app: Cassandra` label is specified. The replication controller will keep track and make sure that there are exactly three pods with that label:

```
template:
  metadata:
    labels:
      app: Cassandra
```

The pod template's `spec` describes the list of containers. In this case, there is just one container. It uses the same Cassandra Docker image named `cassandra` and runs the `run.sh` script:

```
spec:
  containers:

    - command:
        - /run.sh
      image: gcr.io/google-samples/cassandra:v11
      name: cassandra
```

The resources section just requires `0.5` units of CPU in this example:

```
resources:
        limits:
            cpu: 0.5
```

The environment section is a little different. The CASSANDRA_SEED_PROVDIER specifies the custom Kubernetes seed provider class we examined earlier. Another new addition here is POD_NAMESPACE, which uses the Downward API again to fetch the value from the metadata:

```
env:
    - name: MAX_HEAP_SIZE
      value: 512M
    - name: HEAP_NEWSIZE
      value: 100M
    - name: CASSANDRA_SEED_PROVIDER
      value: "io.k8s.cassandra.KubernetesSeedProvider"
    - name: POD_NAMESPACE
      valueFrom:
        fieldRef:
          fieldPath: metadata.namespace
    - name: POD_IP
      valueFrom:
        fieldRef:
          fieldPath: status.podIP
```

The `ports` section is identical, exposing the intra-node communication ports: 7000 and 7001, the 7199 JMX port used by external tools such as Cassandra OpsCenter to communicate with the Cassandra cluster, and of course the 9042 CQL port through which clients communicate with the cluster:

```
ports:
    - containerPort: 7000
      name: intra-node
    - containerPort: 7001
      name: tls-intra-node
    - containerPort: 7199
      name: jmx
    - containerPort: 9042
      name: cql
```

Once again, the volume is mounted into `/cassandra_data`. This is important because the same Cassandra image configured properly just expects its `data` directory to be at a certain path. Cassandra doesn't care about the backing storage (although you should care as the cluster administrator). Cassandra will just read and write using filesystem calls:

```
volumeMounts:
  - mountPath: /cassandra_data
    name: data
```

The `volumes` section is the biggest difference from the stateful set solution. A stateful set uses persistent storage claims to connect a particular pod with stable identity to a particular persistent volume. The replication controller solution just uses an `emptyDir` on the hosting node:

```
volumes:
  - name: data
    emptyDir: {}
```

This has many ramifications. You have to provision enough storage on each node. If a Cassandra pod dies, its storage goes away. Even if the pod is restarted on the same physical (or virtual) machine the data on disk will be lost because `emptyDir` is deleted once its pod is removed. Note that container restarts are OK, because `emptyDir` survives container crashes. So, what happens when the pod dies? The replication controller will start a new pod with empty data. Cassandra will detect that a new node was added to the cluster, assign it some portion of the data, and start rebalancing automatically by moving data from other nodes. This is where Cassandra shines. It constantly compacts, rebalances, and distributes the data evenly across the cluster. It will just figure out what to do on your behalf.

Assigning pods to nodes

The main problem with the replication controller approach is that multiple pods can get scheduled on the same Kubernetes node. What if you have a replication factor of three and all three pods that are responsible for some range of the keyspace are all scheduled to the same Kubernetes node? First, all requests for read or writes of that range of keys will go to the same node, creating more pressure. But, even worse, we just lost our redundancy. We have a **single point of failure (SPOF)**. If that node dies, the replication controller will happily start three new pods on some other Kubernetes node, but all of them will have no data and no other Cassandra node in the cluster (the other pods) will have the data to copy from.

This can be solved using a Kubernetes 1.4 Alpha concept called anti-affinity. When assigning pods to nodes, a pod can be annotated such that the scheduler will not schedule it to a node that already had a pod with a particular set of labels. Here is how to ensure that at most a single Cassandra pod will be assigned to a node:

```
annotations:
    scheduler.alpha.kubernetes.io/affinity: >
      {
        "nodeAffinity": {
          "requiredDuringSchedulingIgnoredDuringExecution": {
            "nodeSelectorTerms": [
              {
                "matchExpressions": [
                  {
                    "key": "app",
                    "operator": "NotIn",
                    "values": ["cassandra"]
                  }
                ]
              }
            ]
          }
        }
      }
```

Using DaemonSet to distribute Cassandra

A better solution to the problem of assigning Cassandra pods to different nodes is to use a DaemonSet. A DaemonSet has a pod template like a replication controller. But, a DaemonSet has a node selector that determines on which nodes to schedule its pods. It doesn't have a certain number of replicas, it just schedules a pod on each node that matches its selector. The simplest case is to schedule a pod on each node in the Kubernetes cluster. But, the node selector can also use match expressions against labels to deploy to a particular subset of nodes. Let's create a DaemonSet for deploying our Cassandra cluster onto the Kubernetes cluster:

```
DaemonSet is still a beta resource:
apiVersion: extensions/v1beta1
kind: DaemonSet
metadata:
  name: cassandra-daemonset
```

The `spec` of the DaemonSet contains a regular pod template. The `nodeSelector` section is where the magic happens and ensures that one and exactly one pod will always be scheduled to each node with a label of `app: Cassandra`:

```
spec:
  template:
    metadata:
      labels:
        app: cassandra
    spec:
      # Filter only nodes with the label "app: cassandra":
      nodeSelector:
        app: cassandra
      containers:
```

The rest is identical to the replication controller. Note that `nodeSelector` is expected to be deprecated in favor of affinity. When that happens, it's not clear.

Summary

In this chapter, we covered the topic of stateful applications and how to integrate them with Kubernetes. We discovered that stateful applications are complicated and considered several mechanisms for discovery such as DNS and environment variables. We also discussed several state management solutions such as in-memory redundant storage and persistent storage. The bulk of the chapter revolved around deploying a Cassandra cluster inside a Kubernetes cluster using several options such as a stateful set, a replication controller, and a DaemonSet. Each approach has its own pros and cons. At this point, you should have a thorough understanding of stateful applications and how to apply them in your Kubernetes-based system. You are armed with multiple methods for various use cases and maybe you've even learned a little bit about Cassandra.

In *Chapter 9, Rolling Updates, Scalability, and Quotas*, we will continue our journey and explore the important topic of scalability and in particularly auto-scalability and how to deploy and do live upgrades and updates as the cluster dynamically grows. These issues are very intricate, especially when the cluster has stateful apps running on it.

Rolling Updates, Scalability, and Quotas

In this chapter, we will explore the automated pod scalability that Kubernetes provides, how it affects rolling updates, and how it interacts with quotas. We will touch on the important topic of provisioning and how to choose and manage the size of the cluster. Finally, we will go over how the Kubernetes team tests the limits of Kubernetes with a 2,000 node cluster. Here are the main points we will cover:

- Horizontal pod autoscaling
- Performing rolling updates with autoscaling
- Handling scarce resources with quotas and limits
- Pushing the envelope with Kubernetes performance

At the end of this chapter, you will have the ability to plan a large-scale cluster, provision it economically, and make informed decisions about the various trade-offs between performance, cost, and availability. You will also understand how to set up horizontal pod auto-scaling and use resource quotas intelligently to let Kubernetes automatically handle intermittent fluctuations in volume.

Horizontal pod autoscaling

Kubernetes can watch over your pods and scale them when the CPU utilization or some other metric crosses a threshold. The autoscaling resource specifies the details (percentage of CPU, how often to check) and the corresponding autoscale controller adjusts the number of replicas, if needed.

The following diagram illustrates the different players and their relationships:

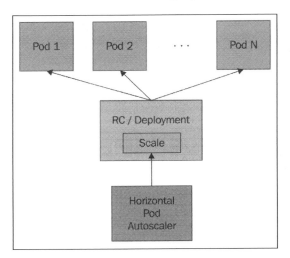

As you can see, the horizontal pod autoscaler doesn't create or destroy pods directly. It relies instead on the replication controller or deployment resources. This is very smart because you don't need to deal with situations where autoscaling conflicts with the replication controller or deployments trying to scale the number of pods, unaware of the autoscaler efforts.

The autoscaler automatically does what we had to do ourselves before. Without the autoscaler, if we had a replication controller with replicas set to 3, but we determined that based on average CPU utilization we actually needed 4, then we would update the replication controller from 3 to 4 and keep monitoring the CPU utilization manually in all pods. The autoscaler will do it for us.

Declaring horizontal pod autoscaler

To declare a horizontal pod autoscaler, we need a replication controller, or a deployment, and an autoscaling resource. Here is a simple replication controller configured to maintain 3 nginx pods:

```
apiVersion: v1
 kind: ReplicationController
 metadata:
   name: nginx
 spec:
   replicas: 3
```

```
template:
  metadata:
    labels:
      run: nginx
  spec:
    containers:
    - name: nginx
      image: nginx
      ports:
      - containerPort: 80
```

The `autoscaling` resource references the Nginx replication controller in `scaleTargetRef`:

```
apiVersion: autoscaling/v1
kind: HorizontalPodAutoscaler
metadata:
  name: nginx
  namespace: default
spec:
  maxReplicas: 4
  minReplicas: 2
  targetCPUUtilizationPercentage: 90
  scaleTargetRef:
    apiVersion: v1
    kind: ReplicationController
    name: nginx
```

The `minReplicas` and `maxReplicas` specify the range of scaling. This is needed to avoid runaway situations that could occur because of some problem. Imagine that, due to some bug, every pod immediately uses 100% CPU regardless of the actual load. Without the `maxReplicas` limit, Kubernetes will keep creating more and more pods until all cluster resources are exhausted. If we are running in a cloud environment with autoscaling of VMs then we will incur a significant cost. The other side of this problem is that, if there is no `minReplicas` and there is a lull in activity, then all pods could be terminated, and when new requests come in all the pods will have to be created and scheduled again. If there are patterns of on and off activity, then this cycle can repeat multiple times. Keeping the minimum of replicas running can smooth this phenomenon. In the preceding example, `minReplicas` is set to 2 and `maxReplicas` is set to 4. Kubernetes will ensure that there are always between 2 to 4 Nginx instances running.

The target CPU utilization percentage is a mouthful. Let's abbreviate it to TCUP. You specify a single number, but Kubernetes doesn't start scaling up and down immediately when the threshold is crossed. This could lead to constant thrashing if the average load hovers around the TCUP. Instead, Kubernetes has a tolerance, which is currently (Kubernetes 1.5) hardcoded to 0.1. That means that, if TCUP is 90%, then scaling up will occur only when average CPU utilization goes above *99% (90 + 0.1 * 90)* and scaling down will occur only if average CPU utilization goes below 81%.

Custom metrics

CPU utilization is an important metric to gauge if pods that are bombarded with too many requests should be scaled up, or if they are mostly idle and can be scaled down. But CPU is not the only and sometimes not even the best metric to keep track of. Memory may be the limiting factor, or even more specialized metrics, such as the depth of a pod's internal on-disk queue, the average latency on a request, or the average number of service timeouts.

The horizontal pod custom metrics are an alpha extension added in version 1.2. The ENABLE_CUSTOM_METRICS environment variable must be set to true when the cluster is started to enable custom metrics. Since it's an alpha feature, it is specified as annotations in the autoscaler spec.

Kubernetes requires that the custom metrics have a cAdvisor endpoint configured. This is a standard interface that Kubernetes understands. When you're exposing your application metrics as a cAdvisor metrics endpoint, Kubernetes can work with your metrics just like it works with its own built-in metrics. The mechanism to configure the custom metrics endpoint is to create a ConfigMap with a definition.json file that will be consumed as a volume mounted at /etc/custom-metrics.

Here is a sample ConfigMap:

```
apiVersion: v1
kind: ConfigMap
metadata:
  name: cm-config
data:
  definition.json: "{\"endpoint\" : \"http://localhost:8080/metrics\"}"
```

Since cAdvisor operates at the node level, the localhost endpoint is a node endpoint that requires the containers inside the pod to request both a host port and a container port:

```
ports:
- hostPort: 8080
  containerPort: 8080
```

The custom metrics are specified as annotations due to the beta status of the feature. When custom metrics reach v1 status they will be added as regular fields.

The value in the annotation is interpreted as a target metric value averaged over all running pods. For example, a **queries per second (qps)** custom metric can be added as follows:

```
annotations:

    alpha/target.custom-metrics.podautoscaler.kubernetes.io:
'{"items":[{"name":"qps", "value": "10"}]}'
```

At this point, the custom metrics can be handled just like the built-in CPU utilization percentage. If the average value across all pods exceeds the target value, then more pods will be added up to the max limit. If the average value drops below the target value, then pods will be destroyed up to the minimum.

When multiple metrics are present, the horizontal pod autoscaler will scale up to satisfy the most demanding one. For example, if metric A can be satisfied by three pods and metric B can be satisfied by four pods, then the pods will be scaled up to four replicas.

By default, the target CPU percentage is 80. Sometimes, CPU can be all over the place, and you may want to scale your pods based on some other metric. To make the CPU irrelevant for autoscaling decisions, you can set it to a ludicrous value that will never be reached, such as 999,999. Now, the autoscaler will only consider the other metrics because CPU utilization will always be below the target CPU utilization.

Autoscaling with Kubectl

Kubectl can create an autoscale resource using the standard `create` command accepting a configuration file. But Kubectl also has a special command, `autoscale`, that lets you easily set an autoscaler in one command without a special configuration file.

1. First, let's start a replication controller that makes sure there are three replicas of a simple pod that just runs an infinite `bash` loop:

```
apiVersion: v1

kind: ReplicationController

metadata:

    name: bash-loop-rc

spec:

    replicas: 3
```

```
        template:
          metadata:
            labels:
              name: bash-loop-rc
          spec:
            containers:
              - name: bash-loop
                image: ubuntu
                command: ["/bin/bash", "-c", "while true; do sleep 10;
                      done"]
```

2. Let's create a replication controller:

```
> kubectl create -f bash-loop-rc.yaml
replicationcontroller "bash-loop-rc" created
```

3. Here is the resulting replication controller:

```
> kubectl get rc
```

NAME	DESIRED	CURRENT	READY	AGE
bash-loop-rc	3	3	3	1m

4. You can see that the desired and current count are both three, meaning three pods are running. Let's make sure:

```
> kubectl get pods
```

NAME	READY	STATUS	RESTARTS	AGE
bash-loop-rc-61k87	1/1	Running	0	50s
bash-loop-rc-7bdtz	1/1	Running	0	50s
bash-loop-rc-smfrt	1/1	Running	0	50s

5. Now, let's create an autoscaler. To make it interesting, we'll set the minimum number of replicas to 4 and the maximum number to 6:

```
> kubectl  autoscale rc bash-loop-rc --min=4 --max=6 --cpu-
percent=50
replicationcontroller "bash-loop-rc" autoscaled
```

6. Here is the resulting horizontal pod autoscaler (you can use hpa). It shows the referenced replication controller, the target and current CPU percentage, and the min/max pods. The name matches the referenced replication controller:

```
> kubectl get hpa
```

NAME	REFERENCE	TARGET	CURRENT	MINPODS	MAXPODS	AGE
bash-loop-rc	bash-loop-rc	50%	0%	4	6	7s

7. Originally, the replication controller was set to have three replicas, but the autoscaler has a minimum of four pods. What's the effect on the replication controller? That's right. Now the desired number of replicas is four. If the average CPU utilization goes above 50%, then it may climb to five or even six:

```
> kubectl get rc

NAME          DESIRED   CURRENT   READY   AGE
bash-loop-rc  4         4         4       7m
```

8. Just to make sure everything works, here is another look at the pods. Note the new pod (58 seconds old) that was created because of the autoscaling:

```
> kubectl get pods

NAME                   READY   STATUS    RESTARTS   AGE
bash-loop-rc-61k87     1/1     Running   0          8m
bash-loop-rc-7bdtz     1/1     Running   0          8m
bash-loop-rc-smfrt     1/1     Running   0          8m
bash-loop-rc-z0xrl     1/1     Running   0          58s
```

9. When we delete the horizontal pod autoscaler, the replication controller retains the last desired number of replicas (four in this case). Nobody remembers that the replication controller was created with three replicas:

```
> kubectl  delete hpa bash-loop-rc

horizontalpodautoscaler "bash-loop-rc" deleted
```

10. As you can see, the replication controller wasn't reset and still maintains four pods even when the autoscaler is gone:

```
> kubectl get rc

NAME          DESIRED   CURRENT   READY   AGE
bash-loop-rc  4         4         4       9m
```

Let's try something else. What happens if we create a new horizontal pod autoscaler with a range of 2 to 6 and the same CPU target of 50%?

```
> kubectl autoscale rc bash-loop-rc --min=2 --max=6 --cpu-percent=50
replicationcontroller "bash-loop-rc" autoscaled
```

Well, the replication controller still maintains its four replicas, which is within the range:

```
> kubectl get rc
NAME          DESIRED   CURRENT   READY   AGE
bash-loop-rc  4         4         4       9m
```

However, the actual CPU utilization is zero, or close to zero. The replica count should have been scaled down to two replicas. Let's check out the horizontal pod autoscaler itself:

```
> kubectl get hpa
NAME             REFERENCE        TARGET   CURRENT     MINPODS MAXPODS   AGE
bash-loop-rc     bash-loop-rc 50%          <waiting> 2         6         1m
```

The secret is in the current CPU metric, which is <waiting>. That means that the autoscaler hasn't received up-to-date information from Heapster yet, so it has no reason to scale the number of replicas in the replication controller.

Performing rolling updates with autoscaling

Rolling updates are the cornerstone of managing large clusters. Kubernetes support rolling updates at the replication controller level and by using deployments. Rolling updates using replication controllers are incompatible with the horizontal pod autoscaler. The reason is that, during the rolling deployment, a new replication controller is created and the horizontal pod autoscaler remains bound to the old replication controller. Unfortunately, the intuitive Kubectl rolling-update command triggers a replication controller rolling update.

Since rolling updates are such an important capability, I recommend that you always bind horizontal pod autoscalers to a deployment object instead of a replication controller or a replica set. When the horizontal pod autoscaler is bound to a deployment, it can set the replicas in the deployment spec and let the deployment take care of the necessary underlying rolling update and replication.

Here is a deployment configuration file we've used for deploying the hue-reminders service:

```
apiVersion: extensions/v1beta1
kind: Deployment
metadata:
  name: hue-reminders
spec:
  replicas: 2
  template:
    metadata:
      name: hue-reminders
```

```
    labels:
      app: hue-reminders
  spec:
    containers:
    - name: hue-reminders
      image: g1g1/hue-reminders:v2.2
      ports:
      - containerPort: 80
```

To support it with autoscaling and ensure we always have between 10 to 15 instances running, we can create an autoscaler configuration file:

```
apiVersion: autoscaling/v1
 kind: HorizontalPodAutoscaler
 metadata:
   name: hue-reminders
   namespace: default
 spec:
   maxReplicas: 15
   minReplicas: 10
   targetCPUUtilizationPercentage: 90
   scaleTargetRef:
     apiVersion: v1
     kind: Deployment
     name: hue-reminders
```

The kind of the scaleTargetRef field is now Deployment instead of ReplicationController. This is important because we may have a replication controller with the same name. To disambiguate and ensure that the horizontal pod autoscaler is bound to the correct object, the kind and the name must match.

Alternatively, we can use the kubectl autoscale command:

```
> kubectl autoscale deployment hue-reminders --min=10--max=15
  --cpu-percent=90
```

Handling scarce resources with limits and quotas

With the horizontal pod autoscaler creating pods on the fly, we need to think about managing our resources. Scheduling can easily get out of control, and inefficient use of resources is a real concern. There are several factors that can interact with each other in subtle ways:

- Overall cluster capacity
- Resource granularity per node
- Division of workloads per namespace
- Daemon sets
- Stateful sets

First, let's understand the core issue. The Kubernetes scheduler has to take into account all these factors when it schedules pods. If there are conflicts or a lot of overlapping requirements, then Kubernetes may have a problem finding room to schedule new pods. For example, a very extreme yet simple scenario is that a DaemonSet runs on every node a pod that requires 50% of the available memory. Now, Kubernetes can't schedule any pod that needs more than 50% memory because the DaemonSet pod gets priority. Even if you provision new nodes, the DaemonSet will immediately commandeer half of the memory.

Stateful sets are similar to DaemonSets in that they require new nodes to expand. The trigger to adding new members to the stateful set is growth in data, but the impact is taking resources from the pool available for Kubernetes to schedule other members. In a multi-tenant situation, the noisy neighbor problem can raise its head in a provisioning or resource allocation context. You may plan exact rations meticulously in your namespace between different pods and their resource requirements, but you share the actual nodes with your neighbors from other namespaces that you may not even have visibility into.

Most of these problems can be mitigated by judiciously using namespace resource quotas and careful management of the cluster capacity across multiple resource types such as CPU, memory, and storage.

Enabling resource quotas

Most Kubernetes distributions support Resource Quota out of the box. The API servers' `--admission-control` flag must have `ResourceQuota` as one of its arguments. You will also have to create a `ResourceQuota` object to enforce it. Note that there may be at most one `ResourceQuota` object per namespace to prevent potential conflicts. This is enforced by Kubernetes.

Resource quota types

There are different types of quota we can manage and control. The categories are compute, storage, and objects.

Compute resource quota

Compute resources are CPU and memory. For each one, you can specify a limit or request a certain amount. Here is the list of compute related fields. Note that `requests.cpu` can be specified as just `cpu`, and `requests.memory` can be specified as just `memory`:

- `limits.cpu`: Across all pods in a non-terminal state, the sum of CPU limits cannot exceed this value

- `limits.memory`: Across all pods in a non-terminal state, the sum of memory limits cannot exceed this value

- `requests.cpu`: Across all pods in a non-terminal state, the sum of CPU requests cannot exceed this value

- `requests.memory`: Across all pods in a non-terminal state, the sum of memory requests cannot exceed this value

Storage resource quota

The storage resource quota type is a little more complicated. There are two entities you can restrict per namespace: the amount of storage and the number of persistent volume claims. However, in addition to just globally setting the quota on total storage or total number of persistent volume claims, you can also do that per `storage` class. The notation for `storage` class resource quota is a little verbose, but it gets the job done:

- `requests.storage`: Across all persistent volume claims, the sum of storage requests cannot exceed this value

- `persistentvolumeclaims`: The total number of persistent volume claims that can exist in the namespace

- `<storage-class>.storageclass.storage.k8s.io/requests.storage`: Across all persistent volume claims associated with the storage-class-name, the sum of storage requests cannot exceed this value

- `<storage-class >.storageclass.storage.k8s.io/persistentvolumeclaims`: Across all persistent volume claims associated with the storage-class-name, this is the total number of persistent volume claims that can exist in the namespace

Object count quota

Kubernetes has another category of resource quotas, which is API objects. My guess is that the goal is to protect the Kubernetes API server from having to manage too many objects. Remember that Kubernetes does a lot of work under the hood. It often has to query multiple objects to authenticate, authorize, and ensure that an operation doesn't violate any of the many policies that may be in place. A simple example is pod scheduling based on replication controllers. Imagine that you have 1,000,000,000 replication controller objects. Maybe you just have three pods and most of the replication controllers have zero replicas. Still, Kubernetes will spend all its time just verifying that indeed all those billion replication controllers have no replicas of their pod template and that they don't need to kill any pods. This is an extreme example, but the concept applies. Too many API objects means a lot of work for Kubernetes.

The overage of objects that can be restricted is a little spotty. For example, you can limit the number of replication controller, but not replica sets, which are almost an improved version of replication controller, but can do exactly the same damage if too many of them are around.

The most glaring omission is namespaces. There is no limit to the number of namespaces. Since all limits are per namespace, you can easily overwhelm Kubernetes by creating too many namespaces, where each namespace has only a small number of API objects.

Here are all the supported objects:

- `ConfigMaps`: The total number of config maps that can exist in the namespace
- `PersistentVolumeClaims`: The total number of persistent volume claims that can exist in the namespace
- `Pods`: The total number of pods in a non-terminal state that can exist in the namespace. A pod is in a terminal state if `status.phase` in (`Failed`, `Succeeded`) is `true`
- `ReplicationControllers`: The total number of replication controllers that can exist in the namespace

[handwritten margin notes: What is the max # of pods per ns? How were we able to spin up ~1500 for ingress testing?]

- `ResourceQuotas`: The total number of resource quotas that can exist in the namespace
- `Services`: The total number of services that can exist in the namespace
- `Services.LoadBalancers`: The total number of load balancer services that can exist in the namespace
- `Services.NodePorts`: The total number of node port services that can exist in the namespace
- `Secrets`: The total number of secrets that can exist in the namespace

Quota scopes

Some resources, such as pods, may be in different states, and it is useful to have different quotas for these different states. For example, if there are many pods that are terminating (this happens a lot during rolling updates) then it is OK to create more pods even if the total number exceeds the quota. This can be achieved by only applying a pod object `count` `quota` to `non-terminating` pods. Here are the existing scopes:

- `Terminating`: Match pods where `spec.activeDeadlineSeconds >= 0`
- `NotTerminating`: Match pods where `spec.activeDeadlineSeconds` is nil
- `BestEffort`: Match pods that have best effort quality of service
- `NotBestEffort`: Match pods that do not have best effort quality of service

While the `BestEffort` scope applies only to pods, the `Terminating`, `NotTerminating`, and `NotBestEffort` scopes apply to CPU and memory too. This is interesting because a resource quota limit can prevent a pod from terminating. Here are the supported objects:

- `cpu`
- `limits.cpu`
- `limits.memory`
- `memory`
- `pods`
- `requests.cpu`
- `requests.memory`

Requests and limits

The meaning of requests and limits in the context of resource quotas is that it requires the containers to make it explicitly specify the target attribute. This way, Kubernetes can manage the total quota because it knows exactly what range of resources is allocated to each container.

Working with quotas

Let's create a namespace first:

```
> kubectl create namespace ns

namespace "ns" created
```

Using namespace-specific context

When working with namespaces other than default, I prefer to use a context, so I don't have to keep typing --namespace=ns for every command:

```
> kubctl config set-context ns –cluster=minikube –user=minikube –
namespace=ns

Context "ns" set.

> kubectl config use-context ns

Switched to context "ns".
```

Creating quotas

1. Then create a compute quota object:

   ```
   apiVersion: v1
   kind: ResourceQuota
   metadata:
     name: compute-quote
   spec:
     hard:
       pods: "2"
       requests.cpu: "1"
       requests.memory: 20Mi
       limits.cpu: "2"
       limits.memory: 2Gi


   > kubectl create -f compute-quota.
   resourcequota "compute-quota" created
   ```

2. Next, let's add count quota object:

```
apiVersion: v1
kind: ResourceQuota
metadata:
  name: object-counts-quota
spec:
  hard:
    configmaps: "10"
    persistentvolumeclaims: "4"
    replicationcontrollers: "20"
    secrets: "10"
    services: "10"
    services.loadbalancers: "2"


> kubectl create -f .\object-count-quota.yaml
resourcequota "object-counts" created
```

3. We can observe all the quotas:

```
> kubectl get quota
NAME                 AGE
compute-resources    16m
object-counts        3m
```

4. And we can even get all the information using describe:

```
kubectl describe quota compute-resources
Name:             compute-resources
Namespace:        ns
Resource          Used     Hard
--------          ----     ----
limits.cpu        0        2
limits.memory     0        2Gi
pods              0        2
requests.cpu      0        1
requests.memory   0        20Mi
```

```
> kubectl describe quota object-counts
Name:                          object-counts
Namespace:                     ns
Resource                       Used   Hard
--------                       ----   ----
configmaps                     0      10
persistentvolumeclaims         0      4
replicationcontrollers         0      20
secrets                        1      10
services                       0      10
services.loadbalancers         0      2
```

This view gives us an instant understanding of global resource usage of important resources across the cluster without diving into too many separate objects.

1. Let's add an Nginx server to our namespace:

```
> kubectl run nginx --image=nginx --replicas=1
deployment "nginx" created
> kubectl get pods
No resources found.
```

2. Uh-oh. No resources found. But, there was no error when the deployment was created. Let's check out the deployment then:

```
> kubectl describe deployment nginx
Name:                   nginx
Namespace:              ns
CreationTimestamp:      Wed, 25 Jan 2017 20:34:25 +0800
Labels:                 run=nginx
Selector:               run=nginx
Replicas:               0 updated | 1 total | 0 available | 1
unavailable
StrategyType:           RollingUpdate
MinReadySeconds:        0
RollingUpdateStrategy:  1 max unavailable, 1 max surge
Conditions:
```

```
      Type                      Status   Reason
      ----                      ------   ------
      Available                 True     MinimumReplicasAvailable
      ReplicaFailure            True     FailedCreate
  OldReplicaSets:               <none>
  NewReplicaSet:                nginx-1790024440 (0/1 replicas created)
```

There it is, all highlighted. The `ReplicationFailure` status is `True` and the reason is `FailedCreate`. You can see that the deployment created a new replica set called `nginx-1790024440`, but it couldn't create the pod it was supposed to create. We still don't know why. Let's check out the replica set:

```
> kubectl describe replicaset nginx-1790024440
Name:         nginx-1790024440
Namespace:    ns
Image(s):     nginx
Selector:     pod-template-hash=1790024440,run=nginx
Labels:       pod-template-hash=1790024440
              run=nginx
Replicas:     0 current / 1 desired
Pods Status:  0 Running / 0 Waiting / 0 Succeeded / 0 Failed
No volumes.
Events:
```

FirstSeen SubObjectPath	LastSeen Type	Count Reason	From Message
--------- -------------	------- -------	----- ------	---- -------
3m }	1m Warning	16 FailedCreate	{replicaset-controller Error creating:

```
pods "nginx-1790024440-" is forbidden: failed quota: compute-quote: must
specify limits.cpu,limits.memory,requests.cpu,requests.memory
```

The output is very wide, so it overlaps several lines, but the message is crystal clear. Since there is a compute quota in the namespace, every container must specify its CPU, memory requests, and limit. The quota controller must account for every container compute resources usage to ensure the total namespace quota is respected.

OK. We understand the problem, but how to resolve it? One way is to create a dedicated `deployment` object for each pod type we want to use and carefully set the CPU and memory requests and limit. But what if we're not sure? What if there are many pod types and we don't want to manage a bunch of `deployment` configuration files?

Another solution is to specify the limit on the command line when we run the `deployment`:

```
kubectl run nginx \
  --image=nginx \
  --replicas=1 \
  --requests=cpu=100m,memory=4Mi \
  --limits=cpu=200m,memory=8Mi \
  --namespace=ns
```

That works, but creating deployments on the fly with lots of arguments is a very fragile way to manage your cluster:

```
> kubectl get pods
NAME                      READY   STATUS    RESTARTS   AGE
nginx-2199160687-zkc2h    1/1     Running   0          2m
```

Using limit ranges for default compute quotas

1. A better way is to specify default compute limits. Enter limit ranges. Here is a configuration file that sets some defaults for containers:

    ```
    apiVersion: v1
    kind: LimitRange
    metadata:
      name: limits
    spec:
      limits:
      - default:
          cpu: 200m
          memory: 6Mi
        defaultRequest:
          cpu: 100m
    ```

```
        memory: 5Mi
    type: Container


> kubectl create -f limits.yaml
limitrange "limits" created
```

2. Here are the current default `limits`:

```
kubectl describe limits limits
Name:           limits
Namespace:      quota-example
Type        Resource   Min  Max  Default Request   Default Limit
Max Limit/Request Ratio
----        --------   ---  ---  ---------------   -------------
----------------------
Container memory     -    -    5Mi               6Mi             -
Container cpu        -    -    100m              200m
```

3. Now, let's run Nginx again without specifying any CPU or memory requests and limits. But first, let's delete the current Nginx deployment:

```
> kubectl delete deployment nginx
deployment "nginx" deleted
> kubectl run nginx --image=nginx --replicas=1
deployment "nginx" created
```

Let's see if the pod was created. Yes it was!

```
> kubectl get pods
NAME                   READY   STATUS    RESTARTS   AGE
nginx-701339712-41856  1/1     Running   0          1m
```

Choosing and managing the cluster capacity

With Kubernetes' horizontal pod autoscaling, DaemonSets, stateful sets, and quotas, we can scale and control our pods, storage, and other objects. However, in the end, we're limited by the physical (virtual) resources available to our Kubernetes cluster. If all your nodes are running at 100% capacity, you need to add more nodes to your cluster. There is no way around it. Kubernetes will just fail to scale. On the other hand, if you have very dynamic workloads then Kubernetes can scale down your pods, but if you don't scale down your nodes correspondingly you will still pay for the excess capacity. In the cloud you can stop and start instances.

Choosing your node types

The simplest solution is to choose a single node type with a known quantity of CPU, memory, and local storage. But that is typically not the most efficient and cost-effective solution. It makes capacity planning simple because the only question is how many nodes are needed. Whenever you add a node, you add a known quantity of CPU and memory to your cluster, but most Kubernetes clusters and components within the cluster handle different workloads. We may have a stream processing pipeline where many pods receive some data and process it in one place. This workload is CPU-heavy and may or may not need a lot of memory. Other components, such as a distributed memory cache, need a lot of memory, but very little CPU. Other components, such as a Cassandra cluster, need multiple SSD disks attached to each node.

For each type of node you should consider proper labeling and making sure that Kubernetes schedules the pods that are designed to run on that node type.

Choosing your storage solutions

Storage is a huge factor in scaling a cluster. There are three categories of scalable storage solution:

- Roll your own
- Use your cloud platform storage solution
- Use an out-of-cluster solution

When you use roll your own, you install some type of storage solution in your Kubernetes cluster. The benefits are flexibility and full control, but you have to manage and scale it yourself.

When you use your cloud platform storage solution, you get a lot out of the box, but you lose control, you typically pay more, and depending on the service you may be locked in to that provider.

When you use an out-of-cluster solution, the performance and cost of data transfer may be much greater. You typically use this option if you need to integrate with an existing system.

Of course, large clusters may have multiple data stores from all categories. This is one of the most critical decisions you have to make, and your storage needs may change and evolve over time.

Trading off cost and response time

If money is not an issue you can just over-provision your cluster. Every node will have the best hardware configuration available, you'll have way more nodes than are needed to process your workloads, and you'll have copious amounts of available storage. Guess what? Money is always an issue!

You may get by with over-provisioning when you're just starting and your cluster doesn't handle a lot of traffic. You may just run five nodes, even if two nodes are enough most of the time. Multiply everything by 1,000 and someone will come asking questions if you have thousands of idle machines and petabytes of empty storage.

OK. So, you measure and optimize carefully and you get 99.99999% utilization of every resource. Congratulations, you just created a system that can't handle an iota of extra load or the failure of a single node without dropping requests on the floor or delaying responses.

You need to find the middle ground. Understand the typical fluctuations of your workloads and consider the cost/benefit ratio of having excess capacity versus having reduced response time or processing ability.

Sometimes, if you have strict availability and reliability requirements, you can build redundancy into the system and then you over-provision by design. For example, you want to be able to hot swap a failed component with no downtime and no noticeable effects. Maybe you can't lose even a single transaction. In this case, you'll have a live backup for all critical components, and that extra capacity can be used to mitigate temporary fluctuations without any special actions.

Using effectively multiple node configurations

Effective capacity planning requires you to understand the usage patterns of your system and the load each component can handle. That may include a lot of data streams generated inside the system. When you have a solid understanding of the typical workloads, you can look at workflows and which components handle which parts of the load. Then you can compute the number of pods and their resource requirements. In my experience, there are some relatively fixed workloads, some workloads that vary predictively (such as office hours versus non-office hours), and then you have your completely crazy workloads that behave erratically. You have to plan according for each workload, and you can design several families of node configurations that can be used to schedule pods that match a particular workload.

Benefiting from elastic cloud resources

Most cloud providers let you scale instances automatically, which is a perfect complement to Kubernetes' horizontal pod autoscaling. If you use cloud storage, it also grows magically without you having to do anything. However, there are some gotchas that you need to be aware of.

Autoscaling instances

All the big cloud providers have instance autoscaling in place. There are some differences, but scaling up and down based on CPU utilization is always available, and sometimes custom metrics are available too. Sometimes, load balancing is offered as well. As you can see, there is some overlap with Kubernetes here. If your cloud provider doesn't have adequate autoscaling with proper control, it is relatively easy to roll your own, where you monitor your cluster resource usage and invoke cloud APIs to add or remove instances. You can extract the metrics from Kubernetes.

Here is a diagram that shows how two new instances are added based on a CPU load monitor:

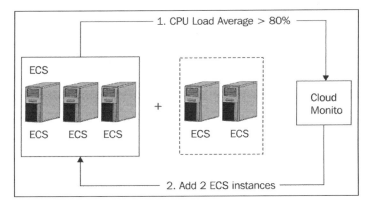

Mind your cloud quotas

When working with cloud providers, some of the most annoying things are quotas. I've worked with four different cloud providers (AWS, GCP, Azure, and Alibaba cloud) and I was always bitten by quotas at some point. The quotas exist to let the cloud providers do their own capacity planning, but from your point of view it is yet one more thing that can trip you up. Imagine that you set up a beautiful autoscaling system that works like magic, and suddenly the system doesn't scale when you hit 100 nodes. You quickly discover that you are limited to 100 nodes and you open a quota to increase support. However, a human must approve quota requests, and that can take a day or two. In the meantime, your system is unable to handle the load.

Manage regions carefully

Cloud platforms are organized in regions and availability zones. Some services and machine configurations are available only in some regions. Cloud quotas are also managed at the regional level. Performance and cost of data transfers within regions is much lower (often free) than across regions. When planning your cluster, you should consider carefully your geo-distribution strategy. If you need to run your cluster across multiple regions, you may have some tough decisions to make regarding redundancy, availability, performance, and cost.

Considering Hyper.sh

Hyper.sh is a container-aware hosting service. You just start containers. The service takes care of allocating the hardware. Containers start within seconds. You never need to wait minutes for a new VM. Hypernetes is Kubernetes on Hyper.sh, and it completely eliminates the need to scale the nodes because there are no nodes as far as you're concerned. There are only containers (or pods).

In the following diagram, you can see on the right how **Hyper Containers** run directly on a multi-tenant bare-metal container cloud:

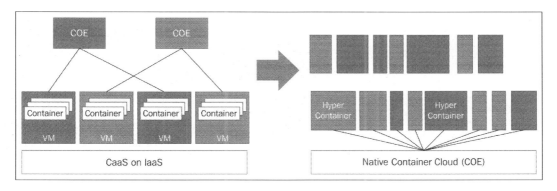

Pushing the envelope with Kubernetes

In this section, we will see how the Kubernetes team pushes Kubernetes to its limit. The numbers are quite telling, but some of the tools and techniques, such as Kubemark, are ingenious, and you may even use them to test your clusters. In the wild, there are some Kubernetes clusters with 3,000 nodes. Recently, at CERN, the OpenStack team achieved 2 million requests per second:

```
http://superuser.openstack.org/articles/scaling-magnum-and-
kubernetes-2-million-requests-per-second/.
```

Mirantis conducted a performance and scaling test in their scaling lab where they deployed 5,000 Kubernetes nodes (in VMs) on 500 physical servers. More details here: http://bit.ly/2oijqQY.

At the end of this section you'll appreciate the effort and creativeness that goes into improving Kubernetes on a large scale, you will know how far you can push a single Kubernetes cluster and what performance to expect, and you'll get an inside look at some tools and techniques that can help you evaluate the performance of your own Kubernetes clusters.

Improving the performance and scalability of Kubernetes

The Kubernetes team focused heavily on performance in a large-scale of the API server and its scalability during their work on Kubernetes 1.2 and 1.3. When Kubernetes 1.2 was released, it supported clusters of up to 1,000 nodes within the Kubernetes service level objectives. Kubernetes 1.3 doubled the number to 2,000 nodes. We will get into the numbers later, but first let's look under the hood and see how Kubernetes achieved these impressive improvements.

Caching reads in the API server

Kubernetes keeps the state of the system in etcd, which is very reliable, though not superfast. The various Kubernetes components operate on snapshots of that state and don't rely on real-time updates. That fact allows the trading of some latency for throughput. All the snapshots used to be updated by etcd watches. Now, the API server has an in-memory read cache that is used for updating state snapshots. The in-memory read cache is updated by etcd watches. These schemes significantly reduces the load on etcd and increase the overall throughput of the API server.

The pod lifecycle event generator

Increasing the number of nodes in a cluster is key for horizontal scalability, but pod density is crucial too. Pod density is the number of pods that the Kubelet can manage efficiently on one node. If pod density is low, then you can't run too many pods on one node. That means that you might not benefit from more powerful nodes (more CPU and memory per node) because the Kubelet will not be able to manage more pods. The other alternative is to force the developers to compromise their design and create coarse-grained pods that do more work per pod. Ideally, Kubernetes should not force your hand when it comes to pod granularity. The Kubernetes team understands this very well and invested a lot of work in improving pod density.

In Kubernetes 1.1, the official (tested and advertised) number was 30 pods per node. I actually ran 40 pods per node on Kubernetes 1.1, but I paid for it in excessive Kubelet overhead that stole CPU from the worker pods. In Kubernetes 1.2, the number jumped to 100 pods per node.

The Kubelet used to poll the container runtime constantly for each pod in its own goroutine. That put a lot of pressure on the container runtime that during peaks to performance has reliability issues, in particular CPU utilization. The solution was the **Pod Lifecycle Event Generator (PLEG)**. The way the PLEG works is that it lists the state of all the pods and containers and compares it to the previous state. This is done once for all the pods and containers. Then, by comparing the state to the previous state, the PLEG knows which pods need to sync again and invokes only those pods. That change resulted in a significant four times lower CPU usage by the Kubelet and the container runtime. It also reduced the polling period, which improves responsiveness.

The following diagram shows the **CPU utilization for 120 pods** on Kubernetes 1.1 versus Kubernetes 1.2. You can see the 4X factor very clearly:

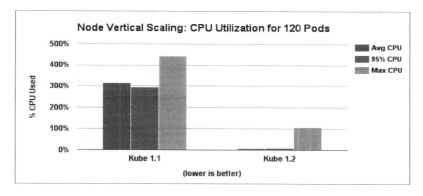

Serializing API objects with protocol buffers

The API server has a REST API. REST APIs typically use JSON as their serialization format, and the Kubernetes API server was no different. However, JSON serialization implies marshaling and unmarshaling JSON to native data structures. This is an expensive operation. In a large-scale Kubernetes cluster, a lot of components need to query or update the API server frequently. The cost of all that JSON parsing and composition adds up quickly. In Kubernetes 1.3, the Kubernetes team added an efficient protocol buffers serialization format. The JSON format is still there, but all internal communication between Kubernetes components uses the protocol buffers serialization format. There are plans to migrate to etcd v3, which has several Kubernetes-motivated changes (such as using gRPC instead of HTTP+JSON for etcd API). This change may provide an additional 30% improvement.

Measuring the performance and scalability of Kubernetes

In order to improve performance and scalability, you need a sound idea of what you want to improve and how you're going to measure the improvements. You must also make sure that you don't violate basic properties and guarantees in the quest for improved performance and scalability. What I love about performance improvements is that they often buy you scalability improvements for free. For example, if a pod needs 50% of the CPU of a node to do its job and you improve performance so that the pod can do the same work using 33% CPU, then you can suddenly run three pods instead of two on that node, and you've improved the scalability of your cluster by 50% overall (or reduced your cost by 33%).

The Kubernetes SLOs

Kubernetes has **Service Level Objectives (SLOs)**. Those guarantees must be respected when trying to improve performance and scalability. Kubernetes has a one-second response time for API calls. That's 1,000 milliseconds. It actually achieves an order of magnitude faster response times most of the time.

Measuring API responsiveness

The API has many different endpoints. There is no simple API responsiveness number. Each call has to be measured separately. In addition, due to the complexity and the distributed nature of the system, not to mention networking issues, there can be a lot of volatility to the results. A solid methodology is to break the API measurements into separate endpoints and then run a lot of tests over time and look at percentiles (which is standard practice).

It's also important to use enough hardware to manage a large number of objects. The Kubernetes team used a 32-core VM with 120 GB for the master in this test.

The following diagram describes the 50th, 90th, and 99th percentile of various important API call latencies. You can see that the 90th percentile is very low, below 20 milliseconds. Even the 99th percentile is less than 125 milliseconds for the **DELETE** pods operation, and less than 100 milliseconds for all other operations:

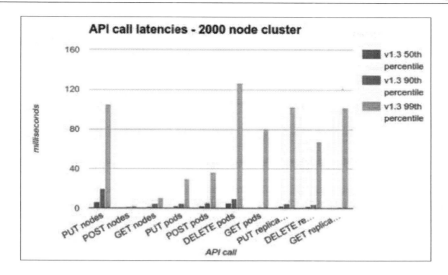

Another category of API calls is LIST operations. Those calls are more expansive because they need to collect a lot of information in a large cluster, compose the response, and send a potential large response. This is where performance improvements such as the in-memory read-cache and the protocol buffers serialization really shine. The response time is understandably greater than the single API calls, but it is still way below the SLO of one second (1,000 milliseconds):

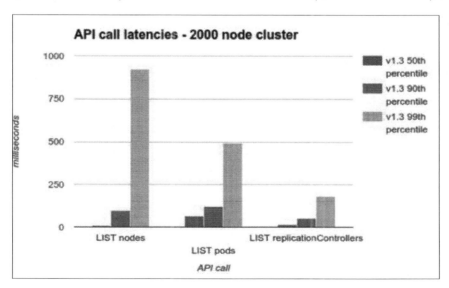

Measuring end to end pod startup time

One of the most important performance characteristics of a large dynamic cluster is end-to-end pod startup time. Kubernetes creates, destroys, and shuffles pods around all the time. You could say that the primary function of Kubernetes is to schedule pods.

In the following diagram, you can see that pod startup time is less volatile than API calls. This makes sense since there is a lot of work that needs to be done, such as launching a new instance of a runtime, that doesn't depend on cluster size. With Kubernetes 1.2 on a 1,000-node cluster, the **99th percentile** end-to-end time to launch a pod was less than 3 seconds. With Kubernetes 1.3, the **99th percentile** end-to-end time to launch a pod was a little over 2.5 seconds. It's remarkable that the time is very close, but a little better with Kubernetes 1.3 on a 2,000-node cluster versus a 1,000-node cluster:

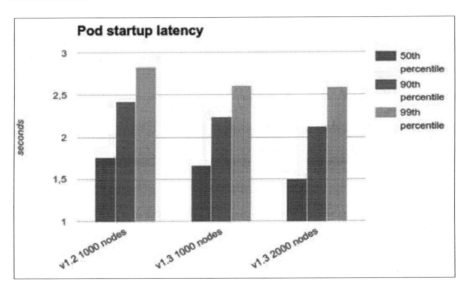

Testing Kubernetes at scale

Clusters with thousands of nodes are expensive. Even a project such as Kubernetes that enjoys the support of Google and other industry giants still needs to come up with reasonable ways to test without breaking the bank.

The Kubernetes team runs a full-fledged test on a real cluster at least once per release to collect real-world performance and scalability data. However, there is also a need for a lightweight and cheaper way to experiment with potential improvements and to detect regressions. Enter the Kubemark.

Introducing the Kubemark tool

The Kubemark is a Kubernetes cluster that runs mock nodes called hollow nodes used for running lightweight benchmarks against large-scale (hollow) clusters. Some of the Kubernetes components that are available on a real node such as the Kubelet are replaced with a hollow Kubelet. The hollow Kubelet fakes a lot of the functionality of a real Kubelet. A hollow Kubelet doesn't actually start any containers, and it doesn't mount any volumes. But from the Kubernetes cluster point of view - the state stored in etcd - all those objects exist and you can query the API server. The hollow Kubelet is actually the real Kubelet with an injected mock Docker client that doesn't do anything.

Another important hollow component is the hollow-proxy, which mocks the Kubeproxy component. It again uses the real Kubeproxy code with a mock proxier interface that does nothing and avoids touching iptables.

Setting up a Kubemark cluster

A Kubemark cluster uses the power of Kubernetes. To set up a Kubemark cluster, perform the following steps:

1. Create a regular Kubernetes cluster where we can run N hollow-nodes.
2. Create a dedicated VM to start all master components for the Kubemark cluster.
3. Schedule N hollow-node pods on the base Kubernetes cluster. Those hollow-nodes are configured to talk to the Kubemark API server running on the dedicated VM.
4. Create add-on pods by scheduling them on the base cluster and configuring them to talk to the Kubemark API server.

A full-fledged guide on GCP is available at `http://bit.ly/2nPMkwc`.

Comparing a Kubemark cluster to a real-world cluster

The performance of Kubemark clusters is mostly similar to the performance of real clusters. For the pod startup end-to-end latency, the difference is negligible. For the API-responsiveness, the differences are higher, though generally less than a factor of two. However, trends are exactly the same: an improvement/regression in a real cluster is visible as a similar percentage drop/increase in metrics in Kubemark.

Summary

In this chapter, we've covered many topics relating to scaling Kubernetes clusters. We discussed how the horizontal pod autoscaler can automatically manage the number of running pods based CPU utilization or other metrics, how to perform rolling updates correctly and safely in the context of auto-scaling, and how to handle scarce resources via resource quotas. Then we moved on to overall capacity planning and management of the cluster's physical or virtual resources. Finally, we delved into a real-world example of scaling a single Kubernetes cluster to handle 2,000 nodes.

At this point, you have a good understanding of all the factors that come into play when a Kubernetes cluster is facing dynamic and growing workloads. You have multiple tools to choose from for planning and designing your own scaling strategy.

In *Chapter 10, Advanced Kubernetes Networking*, we will dive into advanced Kubernetes networking. Kubernetes has a networking model based on the **Common Networking Interface (CNI)** and supports multiple providers.

10
Advanced Kubernetes Networking

In this chapter, we will examine the important topic of networking. Kubernetes as an orchestration platform manages containers/pods running on different machines (physical or virtual) and requires an explicit networking model. We will look at the following topics:

- Kubernetes networking model
- Standard interfaces that Kubernetes supports, such as EXEC, Kubenet, and in particular, CNI
- Various networking solutions that satisfy the requirements of Kubernetes networking
- Network policies and load balancing options
- Writing a custom CNI plugin

At the end of this chapter, you will understand the Kubernetes approach to networking and be familiar with the solution space for aspects such as standard interfaces, networking implementations, and load balancing. You will even be able to write your very own CNI plugin if you wish.

Understanding the Kubernetes networking model

The Kubernetes networking model is based on a flat address space. All pods in a cluster can directly see each other. Each pod has its own IP address. There is no need to configure any NAT. In addition, containers in the same pod share their pod's IP address and can communicate with each other through localhost. This model is pretty opinionated, but once set up, it simplifies life considerably both for developers and administrators. It makes it particularly easy to migrate traditional network applications to Kubernetes. A pod represents a traditional node and each container represents a traditional process.

Intra-pod communication (container to container)

A running pod is always scheduled on one (physical or virtual) node. That means that all the containers run on the same node and can talk to each other in various ways, such as the local filesystem, any IPC mechanism, or using localhost and well-known ports. There is no danger of port collision between different pods because each pod has its own IP address and when a container in the pod uses localhost, it applies to the pod's IP address only. So if container 1 in pod 1 connects to port 1234 that container 2 listens to on pod 1, it will not conflict with another container in pod 2 running on the same node that also listens on port 1234. The only caveat is that if you're exposing ports to the host then you should be careful about pod to node affinity. This can be handled using several mechanisms, such as DaemonSet and pod anti-affinity.

Inter-pod communication (pod to pod)

Pods in Kubernetes are allocated a network-visible IP address (not private to the node). Pods can communicate directly without the aid of network address translation, tunnels, proxies, or any other obfuscating layer. Well-known port numbers can be used for a configuration-free communication scheme. The pod's internal IP address is the same as its external IP address that other pods see (within the cluster network; not exposed to the outside world). That means that standard naming and discovery mechanisms such as DNS work out of the box.

Pod to service communication

Pods can talk to each other directly using their IP addresses and well-known ports, but that requires the pods to know each other's IP addresses. In a Kubernetes cluster, pods can be destroyed and created constantly. The service provides a layer of indirection that is very useful because the service is stable even if the set of actual pods that respond to requests is ever-changing. In addition, you get automatic, highly available load balancing because the Kube-proxy on each node takes care of redirecting traffic to the correct pod:

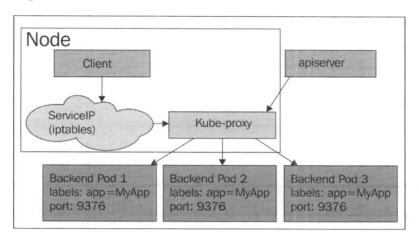

External access

Eventually, some containers need be accessible from the outside world. The pod IP addresses are not visible externally. The service is the right vehicle, but external access typically requires two redirects. For example, cloud provider load balancers are Kubernetes aware, so they can't direct traffic to a particular service directly to a node that runs a pod that can process the request. Instead, the public load balancer just directs traffic to any node in the cluster and the Kube-proxy on that node will redirect again to an appropriate pod if the current node doesn't run the necessary pod.

The following diagram shows how all that the external load balancer on the right side does is send traffic to all nodes that reach the proxy, which takes care of further routing if needed:

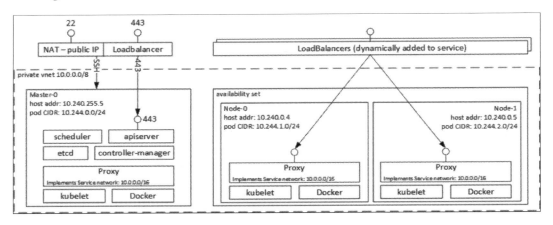

Kubernetes networking versus Docker networking

Docker networking follows a different model, although over time, it starts to gravitate towards the Kubernetes model. In Docker networking, each container has its own private IP address from the 172.xxx.xxx.xxx address space confined to its own node. It can talk to other containers on the same node via their own 172.xxx.xxx.xxx different IP addresses. This makes sense for Docker because it doesn't have the notion of a pod with multiple interacting containers, so it models every container as lightweight VMs that have their own network identity. Note that with Kubernetes, containers from different pods that run on the same node can't connect over localhost (unless exposing host ports, which is discouraged). The whole idea is that, in general, Kubernetes can kill and create pods anywhere, so different pods shouldn't rely, in general, on other pods available on the node. DaemonSets are a notable exception, but the Kubernetes networking model is designed to work for all use cases and doesn't add special cases for direct communication between different pods on the same node.

How do Docker containers communicate across nodes? The container must publish ports to the host. This obviously requires port coordination because if two containers try to publish the same host port, they'll conflict with each other. Then containers (or other processes) connect to the host's port that get channeled into the container. A big downside is that containers can't self-register with external services because they don't know what's their host's IP address. You could work around it by passing the host's IP address as an environment variable when you run the container, but that requires external coordination and complicates the process.

The following diagram shows the networking setup with Docker. Each container has its own IP address; Docker creates the docker0 bridge on every node:

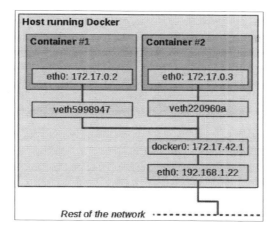

Lookup and discovery

In order for pods and containers to communicate with each other, they need to find each other. There are several ways for containers to locate other containers or announce themselves. There are also some architectural patterns that allow containers to interact indirectly. Each approach has its own pros and cons.

Self-registration

We've mentioned self-registration several times. Let's understand what it means exactly. When a container runs, it knows its pod's IP address. Each container that wants to be accessible to other containers in the cluster can connect to some registration service and register its IP address and port. Other containers can query the registration service for the IP addresses and port of all registered containers and connect to them. When a container is destroyed (gracefully), it will unregister itself. If a container dies ungracefully then some mechanism need to be established to detect that. For example, the registration service can periodically ping all registered containers, or the containers are required periodically to send a keepalive message to the registration service.

The benefit of self-registration is that once the generic registration service is in place (no need to customize it for different purposes), there is no need to worry about keeping track of containers. Another huge benefit is that containers can employ sophisticated policies and decide to unregister temporarily if they are unavailable based on local conditions; for example, if a container is busy and doesn't want to receive any more requests at the moment. This sort of smart and decentralized dynamic load balancing can be very difficult to achieve globally. The downside is that the registration service is yet another non-standard component that containers need to know about in order to locate other containers.

Services and endpoints

Kubernetes services can be considered as a registration service. Pods that belong to a service are registered automatically based on their labels. Other pods can look up the endpoints to find all the service pods or take advantage of the service itself and directly send a message to the service that will get routed to one of the backend pods.

Loosely coupled connectivity with queues

What if containers can talk to each other without knowing their IP addresses and ports? What if most of the communication can be asynchronous and decoupled? In many cases, systems can be composed of loosely coupled components that are not only unaware of the identities of other components, but they are unaware that other components even exist. Queues facilitate such loosely coupled systems. Components (containers) listen to messages from the queue, respond to messages, perform their jobs, and post messages to the queue, on progress, completion status, and error. Queues have many benefits:

- Easy to add processing capacity without coordination, just add more containers that listen to the queue
- Easy to keep track of overall load by queue depth
- Easy to have multiple versions of components running side by side by versioning messages and/or topics
- Easy to implement load balancing as well as redundancy by having multiple consumers process requests in different modes

The downsides of queues are the following:

- Need to make sure that the queue provides appropriate durability and high-availability so it doesn't become a critical SPOF

- Containers need to work with the async queue API (could be abstracted away)
- Implementing request-response requires a somewhat cumbersome listening on response queues

Overall, queues are an excellent mechanism for large-scale systems and they can be utilized in large Kubernetes clusters to ease coordination.

Loosely coupled connectivity with data stores

Another loosely coupled method is to use a data store (for example, Redis) to store messages and then other containers can read them. While possible, this is not the design objective of data stores and the result is often cumbersome, fragile, and doesn't have the best performance. Data stores are optimized for data storage and not for communication. That being said, data stores can be used in conjunction with queues, where a component stores some data in a data store and then sends a message to the queue that data is ready for processing. Multiple components listen to the message and all start processing the data in parallel.

Kubernetes ingress

Kubernetes offers an ingress resource and controller that is designed to expose Kubernetes services to the outside world. You can do it yourself, of course, but many tasks involved in defining ingress are common across most applications for a particular type of ingress such as a web application, CDN, or DDoS protector. You can also write your own ingress objects.

The `ingress` object is often used for smart load balancing and TLS termination. Instead of configuring and deploying your own Nginx server, you can benefit from the built-in ingress. If you need a refresher, hop on to *Chapter 6, Using Critical Kubernetes Resources*, where we discussed the ingress resource with examples.

Kubernetes network plugins

Kubernetes has a network plugin system since networking is so diverse and different people would like to implement it in different ways. Kubernetes is flexible enough to support any scenario. The primary network plugin is CNI, which we will discuss in depth. But Kubernetes also comes with a simpler network plugin called Kubenet. Before we go over the details, let's get on the same page with the basics of Linux networking (just the tip of the iceberg).

Basic Linux networking

Linux, by default, has a single shared network space. The physical network interfaces are all accessible in this namespace. But the physical namespace can be divided into multiple logical namespaces, which is very relevant to container networking.

IP addresses and ports

Network entities are identified by their IP address. Servers can listen to incoming connections on multiple ports. Clients can connect (TCP) or send data (UDP) to servers within their network.

Network namespaces

Namespaces group a bunch of network devices such that they can reach other servers in the same namespace, but not other servers even if they are physically on the same network. Linking networks or network segments can be done via bridges, switches, gateways, and routing.

Virtual Ethernet devices

Virtual Ethernet (veth) devices represent physical network devices. When you create a veth that's linked to a physical device you can assign that veth (and by extension the physical device) into a namespace where devices from other namespaces can't reach it directly, even if physically they are on the same local network.

Bridges

Bridges connect multiple network segments to an aggregate network, so all the nodes can communicate with each other. Bridging is done at the L1 (physical) and L2 (data link) layers of the OSI network model.

Routing

Routing connects separate networks, typically based on routing tables that instruct network devices how to forward packets to their destination. Routing is done through various network devices, such as routers, bridges, gateways, switches, and firewalls, including regular Linux boxes.

Maximum transmission unit

The **maximum transmission unit** (**MTU**) determines how big packets can be. On Ethernet networks, for example, the MTU is 1,500 bytes. The bigger the MTU, the better the ration between payload and headers, which is a good thing. But the downside is that minimum latency is reduced because you have to wait for the entire packet to arrive and, furthermore, in case of failure, you have to retransmit the entire big packet.

Pod networking

Here is a diagram that describes the relationship between pod, host, and the global Internet at networking level via veth0:

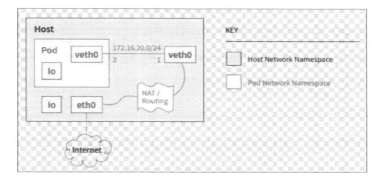

Kubenet

Back to Kubernetes. Kubenet is a network plugin. It's very rudimentary and just creates a Linux bridge called cbr0 and a veth for each pod. Cloud providers typically use it to set up routing rules for communication between nodes, or in single-node environments. The veth pair connects each pod to its host node using an IP address from the host's IP addresses range.

Requirements

The Kubenet plugin has the following requirements:

- The node must be assigned a subnet to allocate IP addresses for its pods
- The standard CNI bridge, lo, and host-local plugins are required at version 0.2.0 or greater
- The Kubelet must be run with the --network-plugin=kubenet argument
- The Kubelet must be run with the --non-masquerade-cidr=<clusterCidr> argument

Setting the MTU

The MTU is critical for network performance. Kubernetes network plugins such as Kubenet make their best efforts to deduce optimal MTU, but sometimes they need help. For example, if an existing network interface (for example, the Docker `docker0` bridge) sets a small MTU then Kubenet will reuse it. Another example is IPSEC, that requires lowering the MTU due to the extra overhead from IPSEC encapsulation overhead, but the Kubenet network plugin doesn't take it into consideration. The solution is to avoid relying on the automatic calculation of the MTU and just tell the Kubelet what MTU should be used for network plugins via the `--network-plugin-mtu` command-line switch that is provided to all network plugins. Although, at the moment, only the Kubenet network plugin accounts for this command-line switch.

Container networking interface

Container Networking Interface (CNI) is a specification as well as a set of libraries for writing network plugins to configure network interfaces in Linux containers (not just Docker). The specification actually evolved from the rkt network proposal. There is a lot of momentum behind CNI and it's on a fast track to become the established industry standard. Some of the organizations that use CNI are:

- Rkt
- Kubernetes
- Kurma
- Cloud foundry
- Mesos

The CNI team maintains some core plugins, but there are a lot of third-party plugins too that contribute to the success of CNI:

- **Project Calico**: A layer 3 virtual network
- **Weave**: A multi-host Docker network
- **Contiv networking**: Policy-based networking
- **Infoblox**: Enterprise IP address management for containers

Container runtime

CNI defines a plugin spec for networking application containers, but the plugin must be plugged into a container runtime that provides some services. In the context of CNI, an application container is a network-addressable entity (has its own IP address). For Docker, each container has its own IP address. For Kubernetes, each pod has its own IP address and the pod is the CNI container and not the containers within the pod.

Likewise, rkt's app containers are similar to Kubernetes pods in that they may contain multiple Linux containers. If in doubt, just remember that a CNI container must have its own IP address. The runtime's job is to configure a network and then execute one or more CNI plugins, passing them the network configuration in JSON format.

The following diagram shows a container runtime using the CNI plugin interface to communicate with multiple CNI plugins:

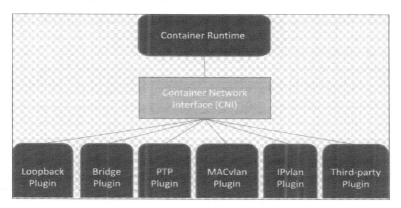

CNI plugin

The CNI plugin's job is to add a network interface into the container network namespace and bridge the container to the host via a veth pair. It should then assign an IP address via an IPAM (IP address management) plugin and setup routes.

The container runtime (rkt or Docker) invokes the CNI plugin as an executable. The plugin needs to support the following operations:

- Add a container to the network
- Remove a container from the network
- Report version

The plugin uses a simple command-line interface, standard input/output, and environment variables. The network configuration in JSON format is passed to the plugin through standard input. The other arguments are defined as environment variables:

- CNI_COMMAND: Indicates the desired operation; ADD, DEL, or VERSION.
- CNI_CONTAINERID: Container ID.
- CNI_NETNS: Path to network namespace file.

- `CNI_IFNAME`: Interface name to set up; plugin must honor this interface name or return an `error`.

- `CNI_ARGS`: Extra arguments passed in by the user at invocation time. Alphanumeric key-value pairs separated by semicolons, for example, `FOO=BAR;ABC=123`.

- `CNI_PATH`: List of paths to search for CNI plugin executables. Paths are separated by an OS-specific list separator, for example `:` on Linux and `;` on Windows.

If the command succeeds, the plugin returns a zero exit code and the generated interfaces (in the case of the ADD command) are streamed to standard output as JSON. This low-tech interface is smart in the sense that it doesn't require any specific programming language or component technology or binary API. CNI plugin writers can use their favorite programming language too.

The result of invoking the CNI plugin with the ADD command looks as follows:

```
{
  "cniVersion": "0.3.0",
  "interfaces": [                    (this key omitted by IPAM plugins)
      {
          "name": "<name>",
          "mac": "<MAC address>", (required if L2 addresses are
meaningful)
          "sandbox": "<netns path or hypervisor identifier>" (required
for container/hypervisor interfaces, empty/omitted for host interfaces)
      }
  ],
  "ip": [
      {
          "version": "<4-or-6>",
          "address": "<ip-and-prefix-in-CIDR>",
          "gateway": "<ip-address-of-the-gateway>",    (optional)
          "interface": <numeric index into 'interfaces' list>
      },
      ...
  ],
  "routes": [                                           (optional)
      {
```

```
            "dst": "<ip-and-prefix-in-cidr>",
            "gw": "<ip-of-next-hop>"                         (optional)
        },
        ...
    ]
    "dns": {
      "nameservers": <list-of-nameservers>                   (optional)
      "domain": <name-of-local-domain>                       (optional)
      "search": <list-of-additional-search-domains>          (optional)
      "options": <list-of-options>                           (optional)
    }
}
```

The input network configuration contains a lot of information: cniVersion, name, type, args (optional), ipMasq (optional), ipam, and dns. The ipam and dns parameters are dictionaries with their own specified keys. Here is an example of a network configuration:

```
{
    "cniVersion": "0.3.0",
    "name": "dbnet",
    "type": "bridge",
    // type (plugin) specific
    "bridge": "cni0",
    "ipam": {
      "type": "host-local",
      // ipam specific
      "subnet": "10.1.0.0/16",
      "gateway": "10.1.0.1"
    },
    "dns": {
      "nameservers": [ "10.1.0.1" ]
    }
}
```

Note that additional plugin-specific elements can be added. In this case, the `bridge:` `cni0` element is a custom one that the specific `bridge` plugin understands.

The `CNI spec` also supports network configuration lists where multiple CNI plugins can be invoked in order.

Later, we will dig into a fully-fledged implementation of a CNI plugin.

Kubernetes networking solutions

Networking is a vast topic. There are many ways to set up networks and connect devices, pods, and containers. Kubernetes can't be opinionated about it. The high-level networking model of a flat address space for Pods is all that Kubernetes prescribes. Within that space, many valid solutions are possible, with various capabilities and policies for different environments. In this section, we'll examine some of the available solutions and understand how they map to the Kubernetes networking model.

Bridging on bare metal clusters

The most basic environment is a raw bare metal cluster with just an L2 physical network. You can connect your containers to the physical network with a Linux bridge device. The procedure is quite involved and requires familiarity with low-level Linux network commands such as `brctl`, `ip addr`, `ip route`, `ip link`, `nsenter`, and so on. If you plan to implement it, this guide can serve as a good start (search for the *With Linux Bridge devices* section): `http://blog.oddbit.com/2014/08/11/four-ways-to-connect-a-docker/`.

Contiv

Contiv is a general-purpose network plugin for container networking and it can be used with Docker directly, Mesos, Docker Swarm, and of course Kubernetes via a CNI plugin. Contiv is focused on network policies that overlap somewhat with Kubernetes' own network policy object. Here are some of the capabilities of the Contiv net plugin:

- Supports both libnetwork's CNM and the CNI specification
- A feature-rich policy model to provide secure, predictable application deployment
- Best-in-class throughput for container workloads
- Multi-tenancy, isolation, and overlapping subnets

- Integrated IPAM and service discovery
- A variety of physical topologies:
  - ° Layer2 (VLAN)
  - ° Layer3 (BGP)
  - ° Overlay (VXLAN)
  - ° Cisco SDN solution (ACI)
- IPv6 support
- Scalable policy and route distribution

Integration with application blueprints, including the following:

- Docker compose
- Kubernetes deployment manager
- Service load balancing is built in east-west microservice load balancing
- Traffic isolation for storage, control (for example, etcd/consul), network, and management traffic

Contiv has many features and capabilities. I'm not sure if it's the best choice for Kubernetes due to its broad surface area.

Open vSwitch

Open vSwitch is a mature software-based virtual switch solution endorsed by many big players. The **Open Virtualization Network (OVN)** solution lets you build various virtual networking topologies. It has a dedicated Kubernetes plugin, but it is not trivial to set up, as demonstrated by this guide: https://github.com/openvswitch/ovn-kubernetes.

Open vSwitch can connect bare metal servers, VMs, and pods/containers using the same logical network. It actually supports both overlay and underlay modes.

Here are some of its key features:

- Standard 802.1Q VLAN model with trunk and access ports
- NIC bonding with or without LACP on upstream switch
- NetFlow, sFlow(R), and mirroring for increased visibility
- QoS (Quality of Service) configuration, plus policing
- Geneve, GRE, VXLAN, STT, and LISP tunneling

- 802.1ag connectivity fault management
- OpenFlow 1.0 plus numerous extensions
- Transactional configuration database with C and Python bindings
- High-performance forwarding using a Linux kernel module

Nuage networks VCS

The **Virtualized Cloud Services (VCS)** product from Nuage networks provides a highly scalable policy-based **Software-Defined Networking (SDN)** platform. It is an enterprise-grade offering that builds on top of the open source open vSwitch for the data plane along with a feature-rich SDN controller built on open standards.

The Nuage platform uses overlays to provide seamless policy-based networking between Kubernetes Pods and non-Kubernetes environments (VMs and bare metal servers). Nuage's policy abstraction model is designed with applications in mind and makes it easy to declare fine-grained policies for applications. The platform's real-time analytics engine enables visibility and security monitoring for Kubernetes applications.

In addition, all of VCS components can be installed in containers. There are no special hardware requirements.

Canal

Canal is a mix of two open source projects: Calico and Flannel. The name **Canal** is a portmanteau of the project names. Flannel by CoreOS is focused on container networking and **Calico** is focused on network policy. Originally, they were developed independently, but users wanted to use them together. The open source Canal project is currently a deployment pattern to install both projects as separate CNI plugins. But a new company called **Tigera** formed by Calico's founders is shepherding both projects now and has plans for tighter integration.

The following diagram demonstrates the present status of Canal and how it relates to container orchestrators such as Kubernetes or Mesos:

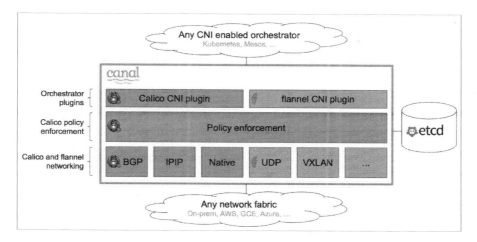

Note that when integrating with Kubernetes, Canal doesn't use **etcd** directly anymore. Instead it relies on the Kubernetes API server.

Flannel

Flannel is a virtual network that gives a subnet to each host for use with container runtimes. It runs a `flaneld` agent on each host that allocates a subnet to the node from a reserved address space stored in **etcd**. Forwarding packets between containers and, ultimately, hosts is done by one of multiple backends. The most common backend uses **UDP** over a TUN device that tunnels through port 8285 by default (make sure it's open in your firewall).

The following diagram describes in detail the various components of Flannel, the virtual network devices it creates, and how they interact with the host and the pod via the `docker0` bridge. It also shows the UDP encapsulation of packets and how they are transmitted between hosts:

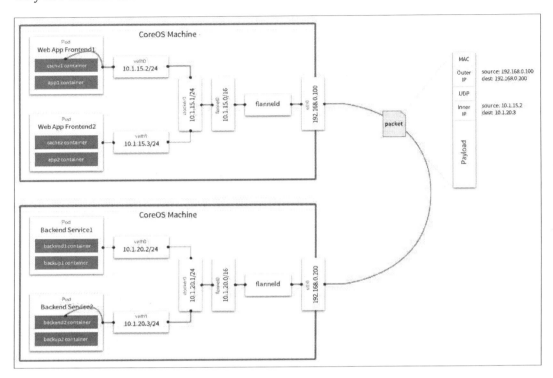

Other backends include the following:

- `vxlan`: Uses in-kernel VXLAN to encapsulate the packets.
- `host-gw`: Creates IP routes to subnets via remote machine IPs. Note that this requires direct layer2 connectivity between hosts running Flannel.
- `aws-vpc`: Creates IP routes in an Amazon VPC route table.
- `gce`: Creates IP routes in a Google compute engine network.
- `alloc`: Only performs subnet allocation (no forwarding of data packets).
- `ali-vpc`: Creates IP routes in an alicloud VPC route table.

Calico project

Calico is a versatile virtual networking and network security solution for containers. Calico can integrate with all the primary container orchestration frameworks and runtimes:

- Kubernetes (CNI plugin)
- Mesos (CNI plugin)
- Docker (libnework plugin)
- OpenStack (Neutron plugin)

Calico can also be deployed on-premises or on public clouds with its full feature set. Calico's network policy enforcement can be specialized for each workload and make sure that traffic is controlled precisely and packets always go from their source to vetted destinations. Calico can map automatically network policy concepts from orchestration platforms to its own network policy. The reference implementation of Kubernetes' network policy is Calico.

Romana

Romana is a modern cloud-native container networking solution. It operates at layer 3, taking advantage of standard IP address management techniques. Whole networks can become the unit of isolation as Romana uses Linux hosts to create gateways and routes to the networks. Operating at layer 3 level means that no encapsulation is needed. Network policy is enforced as a distributed firewall across all endpoints and services. Hybrid deployments across cloud platforms and on-premises deployments are easier as there is no need to configure virtual overlay networks.

Romana claims that their approach brings significant performance improvements. The following diagram shows how Romana eliminates a lot of the overhead associated with VXLAN encapsulation:

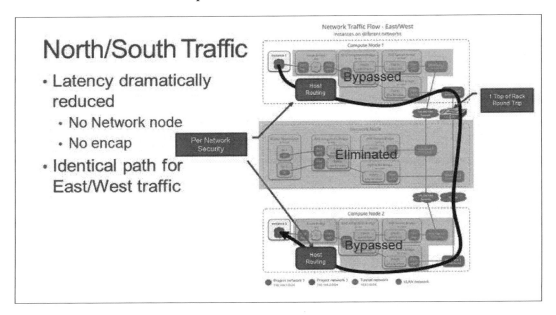

Weave net

Weave net is all about ease of use and zero configuration. It uses VXLAN encapsulation under the covers and micro DNS on each node. As a developer, you operate at a higher abstraction level. You name your containers and Weave net lets you connect to and use standard ports for services. That helps migrating existing applications into containerized applications and microservices. Weave net has a CNI plugin for interfacing with Kubernetes (and Mesos). On Kubernetes 1.4 and higher, you can integrate Weave net with Kubernetes by running a single command that deploys a DaemonSet:

```
kubectl apply -f https://git.io/weave-kube
```

The Weave net pods on every node will take care of attaching any new pod you create to the Weave network. Weave net supports the network policy API as well providing a complete yet easy to set up solution.

Using network policies effectively

The Kubernetes network policy is about managing network traffic to selected pods and namespaces. In a world of hundreds of microservices deployed and orchestrated, as is often the case with Kubernetes, managing networking and connectivity between pods is essential. It's important to understand that it is not primarily a security mechanism. If an attacker can reach the internal network, they will probably be able to create their own pods that comply with the network policy in place and communicate freely with other pods. In the previous section, we looked at different Kubernetes networking solutions and focused on the container networking interface. In this section, the focus is on network policy, although there are strong connections between the networking solution and how network policy is implemented on top.

Understanding the Kubernetes network policy design

A network policy is a specification of how selections of pods can communicate with each other and other network endpoints. NetworkPolicy resources use labels to select pods and define whitelist rules that allow traffic to the selected pods in addition to what is allowed by the isolation policy for a given namespace.

Network policies and CNI plugins

There is an intricate relationship between network policies and CNI plugins. Some CNI plugins implement both network connectivity and network policy, while others implement just one aspect, but they can collaborate with another CNI plugin that implements the other aspect (for example, Calico and Flannel).

Configuring network policies

Network policies are configured via the NetworkPolicy resource. Here is a sample network policy:

```
apiVersion: extensions/v1beta1
kind: NetworkPolicy
metadata:
 name: test-network-policy
 namespace: default
spec:
 podSelector:
```

```
    matchLabels:
      role: db
  ingress:
  - from:
    - namespaceSelector:
        matchLabels:
          project: awesome-project
    - podSelector:
        matchLabels:
          role: frontend
    ports:
    - protocol: tcp
      port: 6379
```

Implementing network policies

While the network policy API itself is generic and is part of the Kubernetes API, the implementation is tightly coupled to the networking solution. That means that on each node, there is a special agent or gatekeeper that does the following:

- Intercepts all traffic coming into the node
- Verifies that it adheres to the network policy
- Forwards or rejects each request

Kubernetes provides the facilities to define and store network policies through the API. Enforcing the network policy is left to the networking solution or a dedicated network policy solution that is tightly integrated with the specific networking solution. Calico and Canal are good examples of this approach. Calico has its own networking solution and a network policy solution that works together. But it can also provide network policy enforcement on top of Flannel as part of Canal. In both cases, there is tight integration between the two pieces. The following diagram shows how the Kubernetes policy controller manages the network policies and how agents on the nodes execute it:

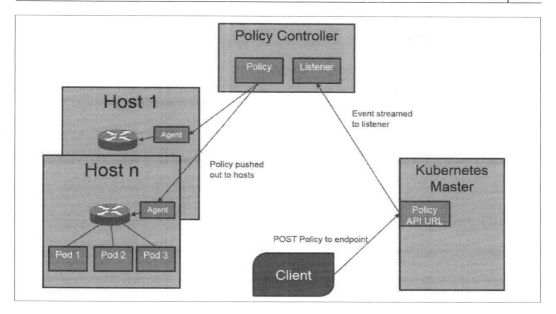

Load balancing options

Load balancing is a critical capability in dynamic systems such as a Kubernetes cluster. Nodes, VMs, and pods come and go, but the clients can't keep track of which individual entities can service their requests. Even if they could, it would require a complicated dance of managing a dynamic map of the cluster, refreshing it frequently, and handling disconnected, unresponsive, or just slow nodes. Load balancing is a battle-tested and well-understood mechanism that adds a layer of indirection that hides the internal turmoil from the clients or consumers outside the cluster. There are options for external as well as internal load balancers. You can also mix and match and use both. The hybrid approach has its own particular pros and cons, such as performance versus flexibility.

External load balancer

An external load balancer is a load balancer that runs outside the Kubernetes cluster, but there must be an external load balancer provider that Kubernetes can interact with to configure the external load balancer with health checks, firewall rules, and to get the external IP address of the load balancer.

The following diagram shows the connection between the load balancer (in the cloud), the Kubernetes API server, and the cluster nodes. The external load balancer has an up-to-date picture of which pods run on which nodes and it can direct external service traffic to the right pods:

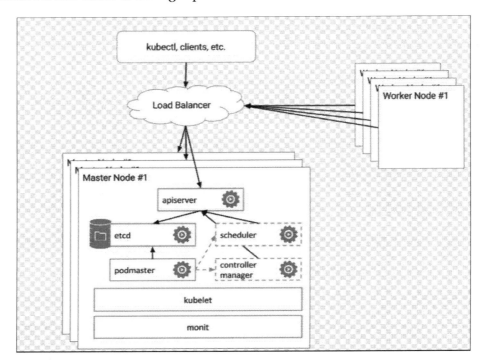

Configuring an external load balancer

The external load balancer is configured via the service configuration file or directly through Kubectl. We use a service type of `LoadBalancer` instead of using a service type of `ClusterIP`, which directly exposes a Kubernetes node as a load balancer. This depends on an external load balancer provider properly installed and configured in the cluster. Google's GKE is the most well-tested provider, but other cloud platforms provide their integrated solution on top of their cloud load balancer.

Via configuration file

Here is an example service configuration file that accomplishes this goal:

```
{
    "kind": "Service",
    "apiVersion": "v1",
```

```
    "metadata": {
       "name": "example-service"
    },
    "spec": {
       "ports": [{
         "port": 8765,
         "targetPort": 9376
       }],
       "selector": {
         "app": "example"
       },
       "type": "LoadBalancer"
    }
}
```

Via Kubectl

You may also accomplish the same result using a direct kubectl command:

```
> kubectl expose rc example --port=8765 --target-port=9376 \
--name=example-service --type=LoadBalancer
```

The decision whether to use a service configuration file or kubectl command is usually determined by the way you set up the rest of your infrastructure and deploy your system. configuration files are more declarative and arguably more appropriate for production usage where you want a versioned, auditable, and repeatable way to manage your infrastructure.

Finding the load balancer IP addresses

The load balancer will have two IP addresses of interest. The internal IP address can be used inside the cluster to access the service. The external IP address is the one clients outside the cluster will use. It's a good practice to create a DNS entry for the external IP address. To get both addresses, use the kubectl describe command. The IP will denote the internal IP address. The LoadBalancer ingress will denote the eternal IP address:

```
> kubectl describe services example-service
    Name:      example-service
    Selector:    app=example
    Type:        LoadBalancer
```

```
IP:       10.67.252.103
LoadBalancer Ingress: 123.45.678.9
Port:       <unnamed> 80/TCP
NodePort:    <unnamed> 32445/TCP
Endpoints:     10.64.0.4:80,10.64.1.5:80,10.64.2.4:80
Session Affinity: None
No events.
```

Identifying client IP addresses

Sometimes, the service may be interested in the source IP address of the clients. Up until Kubernetes 1.5, this information wasn't available. In Kubernetes 1.5, there is a beta feature available only on GKE via an annotation to get the source IP address. In future versions, the capability will be added to other cloud platforms.

Annotating the load balancer for client IP address preservation

Here's how to annotate a service configuration file with the OnlyLocal annotation that triggers the preservation of the client source IP address:

```
{
  "kind": "Service",
  "apiVersion": "v1",
  "metadata": {
    "name": "example-service",
    "annotations": {
        "service.beta.kubernetes.io/external-traffic": "OnlyLocal"
    }
  },
  "spec": {
    "ports": [{
      "port": 8765,
      "targetPort": 9376
    }],
    "selector": {
      "app": "example"
    },
    "type": "LoadBalancer"
  }
}
```

Understanding potential in even external load balancing

External load balancers operate at the node level; while they direct traffic to a particular pod, the load distribution is done at the node level. That means that if your service has four pods, and three of them are on node A and the last one is on node B, then an external load balancer is likely to divide the load evenly between node A and node B. This will have the three pods on node A handle half of the load (1/6 each) and the single pod on node B handle the other half of the load on its own. Weights may be added in the future to address this issue.

Service load balancer

Service load balancing is designed for funneling internal traffic within the Kubernetes cluster and not for external load balancing. This is done by using a service type of clusterIP. It is possible to expose a service load balancer directly via a preallocated port by using service type of NodePort and use it as an external load balancer, but it wasn't designed for that use case. For example, desirable features such as SSL negotiation and HTTP caching will not be readily available.

The following diagram shows how the service load balancer (the yellow clouds) can route traffic to one of the backend pods it manages (via labels of course):

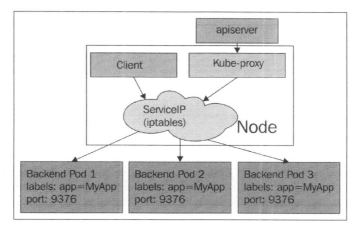

ngress

Ingress in Kubernetes is at its core a set of rules that allow inbound connections to reach cluster services. In addition, some ingress controllers support the following:

- Connection algorithms
- Request limits
- URL rewrites and redirects
- TCP/UDP load balancing
- Access control and authorization

Ingress is specified using an ingress resource and serviced by an ingress controller. It's important to note that ingress is still in beta and it doesn't surface yet all the necessary capabilities. Here is an example of an ingress resource that manages traffic into two services. The rules map the externally visible `http:// foo.bar.com/foo` to the `s1` service and `http://foo.bar.com/bar` to the `s2` service:

```
apiVersion: extensions/v1beta1
kind: Ingress
metadata:
  name: test
spec:
  rules:
  - host: foo.bar.com
    http:
      paths:
      - path: /foo
        backend:
          serviceName: s1
          servicePort: 80
      - path: /bar
        backend:
          serviceName: s2
          servicePort: 80
```

There are two ingress controllers right now. One of them is an L7 ingress controller for GCE only. The other is a more general-purpose Nginx ingress controller that lets you configure Nginx via a ConfigMap. The Nginx ingress controller is very sophisticated and brings to bear a lot of features that are not available yet via the ingress resource directly. It uses the endpoints API to directly forward traffic to pods. For a detailed review, check out `https://github.com/kubernetes/ingress/tree/master/controllers/nginx`.

HAProxy

We discussed using a cloud provider external load balancer using service type `LoadBalancer` and using the internal service load balancer inside the cluster using `ClusterIP`. If we want a custom external load balancer we can create a custom external load balancer provider and use `LoadBalancer` or use the third service type, `NodePort`. **High-Availability (HA)** Proxy is a mature and battle-tested load balancing solution. It is considered the best choice for implementing external load balancing with on-premises clusters. This can be done in several ways:

- Utilize NodePort and carefully manage port allocations
- Implement custom load balancer provider interface
- Run HAProxy inside your cluster as the only target of your frontend servers at the edge of the cluster (load balanced or not)

You can use all approaches with HAProxy. Regardless, it is still recommended to use ingress objects. The `service-loadbalancer` project is a community project that implemented a load balancing solution on top of HAProxy. You can find it here: `https://github.com/kubernetes/contrib/tree/master/service-loadbalancer`.

Utilizing the NodePort

Each service will be allocated a dedicated port from a predefined range. This usually is a high range such as 30,000 and up to avoid clashing with other applications using low known ports. HAProxy will run outside the cluster in this case and it will be configured with the correct port for each service. Then it can just forward any traffic to any nodes and Kubernetes via the internal service, and the load balancer will route it to a proper pod (double load balancing). This is of course sub-optimal because it introduces another hop. The way to circumvent it is to query the Endpoints API and dynamically manage for each service the list of its backend pods and directly forward traffic to the pods.

Custom load balancer provider using HAProxy

This approach is a little more complicated, but the benefit is that it is better integrated with Kubernetes and can make the transition to/from on-premises from/to the cloud easier.

Running HAProxy Inside the Kubernetes cluster

In this approach, we use the internal HAProxy load balancer inside the cluster. There may be multiple nodes running HAProxy and they will share the same configuration to map incoming requests and load balance them across the backend servers (the Apache servers in the following diagram):

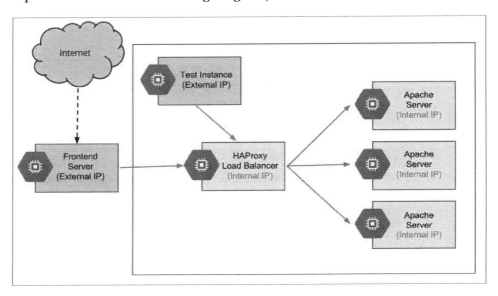

Keepalived VIP

Keepalived `Virtual IP` (`VIP`) is not necessarily a load balancing solution of its own.

It can be a complement to the Nginx ingress controller or the HAProxy-based service `LoadBalancer`. The main motivation is that pods move around in Kubernetes including your load balancer(s). That creates a problem for clients outside the network that require a stable endpoint. DNS is often not good enough due to performance issues. Keepalived provides a high-performance virtual IP address that can serve as the address to the Nginx ingress controller or the HAProxy load balancer. Keepalived utilizes core Linux networking facilities such as IPVS (IP virtual server) and implements high availability via **Virtual Redundancy Router Protocol** (**VRRP**). Everything runs at layer 4 (TCP/UDP). It takes some effort and attention to detail to configure it. Luckily, there is a Kubernetes contrib project that can get you started: `https://github.com/kubernetes/contrib/tree/master/keepalived-vip`.

Writing your own CNI plugin

In this section, we will look at what it takes to actually write your own CNI plugin. First, we will look at the simplest plugin possible – the loopback plugin. Then, we will examine the plugin skeleton that implements most of the boilerplate associated with writing a CNI plugin. Finally, we will review the implementation of the bridge plugin. Before we dive in, here is a quick reminder of what a CNI plugin is:

- A CNI plugin is an executable
- It is responsible for connecting new containers to the network, assigning unique IP addresses to CNI containers, and taking care of routing
- A container is a network namespace (in Kubernetes, a pod is a CNI container)
- Network definitions are managed as JSON files, but stream to the plugin via standard input (no files are being read by the plugin)
- Auxiliary information can be provided via environment variables

First look at the loopback plugin

The loopback plugin simply adds the loopback interface. It is so simple that it doesn't require any network configuration information. Most CNI plugins are implemented in Golang and the loopback CNI plugin is no exception. Let's look at the imports first. There are multiple packages from the container networking project on GitHub that provide many of the building blocks necessary to implement CNI plugins and the `netlink` package for adding and removing interfaces, and setting IP addresses and routes. We will look at the `skel` package soon:

```
package main

import (

    "github.com/containernetworking/cni/pkg/ns"

    "github.com/containernetworking/cni/pkg/skel"

    "github.com/containernetworking/cni/pkg/types/current"

    "github.com/containernetworking/cni/pkg/version"

    "github.com/vishvananda/netlink"

)
```

Then, the plugin implements two commands, cmdAdd and cmdDel, which are called when a container is added to or removed from the network. Here is the add command:

```go
func cmdAdd(args *skel.CmdArgs) error {
  args.IfName = "lo"
  err := ns.WithNetNSPath(args.Netns, func(_ ns.NetNS) error {
    link, err := netlink.LinkByName(args.IfName)
    if err != nil {
      return err // not tested
    }

    err = netlink.LinkSetUp(link)
    if err != nil {
      return err // not tested
    }

    return nil
  })
  if err != nil {
    return err // not tested
  }

  result := current.Result{}
  return result.Print()
}
```

The core of this function is setting the interface name to lo (for loopback) and adding the link to the container's network namespace.

The del command does the opposite:

```go
func cmdDel(args *skel.CmdArgs) error {
  args.IfName = "lo"
  err := ns.WithNetNSPath(args.Netns, func(ns.NetNS) error {
    link, err := netlink.LinkByName(args.IfName)
    if err != nil {
      return err // not tested
    }
```

```
    err = netlink.LinkSetDown(link)
    if err != nil {
      return err // not tested
    }

    return nil
  })
  if err != nil {
    return err // not tested
  }

  return nil
}
```

The main function simply calls the `skel` package, passing the command functions. The `skel` package will take care of running the CNI plugin executable and will invoke the `addCmd` and `delCmd` functions at the right time:

```
func main() {
  skel.PluginMain(cmdAdd, cmdDel, version.All)
}
```

Building on the CNI plugin skeleton

Let's explore the `skel` package and see what it does under the covers. Starting with the `PluginMain()` entry point, it is responsible for invoking `PluginMainWithError()`, catching errors, printing them to standard output, and exiting:

```
func PluginMain(cmdAdd, cmdDel func(_ *CmdArgs) error, versionInfo
version.PluginInfo) {
  if e := PluginMainWithError(cmdAdd, cmdDel, versionInfo); e != nil {
    if err := e.Print(); err != nil {
      log.Print("Error writing error JSON to stdout: ", err)
    }
    os.Exit(1)
  }
}
```

The `PluginErrorWithMain()` instantiates a dispatcher, sets it up with all the I/O streams and the environment, and invokes its `PluginMain()` method:

```go
func PluginMainWithError(cmdAdd, cmdDel func(_ *CmdArgs) error,
versionInfo version.PluginInfo) *types.Error {

  return (&dispatcher{
    Getenv: os.Getenv,
    Stdin:  os.Stdin,
    Stdout: os.Stdout,
    Stderr: os.Stderr,
  }).pluginMain(cmdAdd, cmdDel, versionInfo)
}
```

Here is, finally, the main logic of the skeleton. It gets the `cmd` arguments from the environment (which includes the configuration from standard input), detects which `cmd` is invoked, and calls the appropriate `plugin` function (`cmdAdd` or `cmdDel`). It can also return version information:

```go
func (t *dispatcher) pluginMain(cmdAdd, cmdDel func(_ *CmdArgs) error,
versionInfo version.PluginInfo) *types.Error {
  cmd, cmdArgs, err := t.getCmdArgsFromEnv()
  if err != nil {
    return createTypedError(err.Error())
  }

  switch cmd {
  case "ADD":
    err = t.checkVersionAndCall(cmdArgs, versionInfo, cmdAdd)
  case "DEL":
    err = t.checkVersionAndCall(cmdArgs, versionInfo, cmdDel)
  case "VERSION":
    err = versionInfo.Encode(t.Stdout)
  default:
    return createTypedError("unknown CNI_COMMAND: %v", cmd)
  }

  if err != nil {
    if e, ok := err.(*types.Error); ok {
```

```
        // don't wrap Error in Error
        return e
    }
    return createTypedError(err.Error())
  }
  return nil
}
```

Reviewing the bridge plugin

The bridge plugin is more substantial. Let's look at some of the key parts of its implementation. The full source code is available here: `https://github.com/containernetworking/cni/blob/master/plugins/main/bridge/bridge.go`.

It defines a network configuration `struct` with the following fields:

```
type NetConf struct {
  types.NetConf
  BrName         string  `json:"bridge"`
  IsGW           bool    `json:"isGateway"`
  IsDefaultGW    bool    `json:"isDefaultGateway"`
  ForceAddress   bool    `json:"forceAddress"`
  IPMasq         bool    `json:"ipMasq"`
  MTU            int     `json:"mtu"`
  HairpinMode    bool    `json:"hairpinMode"`
}
```

We will not cover what each parameter does and how it interacts with the other parameters due to space limitations. The goal is to understand the flow and have a starting point if you want to implement your own CNI plugin. The configuration is loaded from JSON via the `loadNetConf()` function. It is called at the beginning of the `cmdAdd()` and `cmdDel()` functions:

```
n, cniVersion, err := loadNetConf(args.StdinData)
```

Here is the core of the `cmdAdd()` that use information from network configuration, sets up a `veth`, interacts with the IPAM plugin to add a proper IP address, and returns the results:

```
hostInterface, containerInterface, err := setupVeth(netns, br, args.
IfName, n.MTU, n.HairpinMode)
  if err != nil {
```

```
    return err
  }


  // run the IPAM plugin and get back the config to apply
  r, err := ipam.ExecAdd(n.IPAM.Type, args.StdinData)
  if err != nil {
    return err
  }


  // Convert the IPAM result was into the current Result type
  result, err := current.NewResultFromResult(r)
  if err != nil {
    return err
  }


  if len(result.IPs) == 0 {
    return errors.New("IPAM returned missing IP config")
  }


  result.Interfaces = []*current.Interface{brInterface, hostInterface,
containerInterface}
```

This is just part of the full implementation. There is also route setting and hardware IP allocation. I encourage you to pursue the full source code, which is quite extensive, to get the full picture.

Summary

In this chapter, we covered a lot of ground. Networking is such a vast topic and there are so many combinations of hardware, software, operating environments, and user skills that coming up with a comprehensive networking solution that is both robust, secure, performs well, and is easy to maintain is a very complicated endeavor. For Kubernetes clusters, the cloud providers mostly solve these issues. But if you run on-premise clusters or need a tailor-made solution, you get a lot of options to choose from. Kubernetes is a very flexible platform, designed for extension. Networking in particular is totally pluggable. The main topics we discussed were the Kubernetes networking model (flat address space where pods can reach other and shared localhost between all containers inside a pod), how lookup and discovery work, the Kubernetes network plugins, various networking solutions at different levels of abstraction (a lot of interesting variations), using network policies effectively to control the traffic inside the cluster, the spectrum of load balancing solutions, and finally we looked at how to write a CNI plugin by dissecting a real-world implementation.

At this point, you are probably overwhelmed, especially if you're not a subject-matter expert. You should have a good grasp of the internals of Kubernetes networking, be aware of all the interlocking pieces required to implement a fully-fledged solution, and can craft your own solution based on trade-offs that make sense for your system.

In *Chapter 11, Running Kubernetes on Multiple Clouds and Cluster Federation*, we will go even bigger and look at running Kubernetes on multiple clusters, cloud providers, and federation. This is an important part of the Kubernetes story for geo-distributed deployments and ultimate scalability. Federated Kubernetes clusters can exceed local limitations, but they bring a whole slew of challenges too.

11
Running Kubernetes on Multiple Clouds and Cluster Federation

In this chapter we'll take it to the next level, with running on multiple clouds and cluster federation. A Kubernetes cluster is a closely-knit unit where all the components run in relative proximity and are connected by a fast network (a physical data center or cloud provider availability zone). This is great for many use cases, but there are several important use cases where systems need to scale beyond a single cluster. Kubernetes federation is a methodical way to combine multiple Kubernetes clusters and interact with them as a single entity. The topics we will cover include the following:

- A deep dive into what cluster federation is all about
- How to prepare, configure, and manage a cluster federation
- How to run a federated workload across multiple clusters

Understanding cluster federation

Cluster federation is conceptually simple. You aggregate multiple Kubernetes clusters and treat them as a single logical cluster. There is a federation control plane that presents to clients a single unified view of the system.

The following diagram demonstrates the big picture of Kubernetes cluster federation:

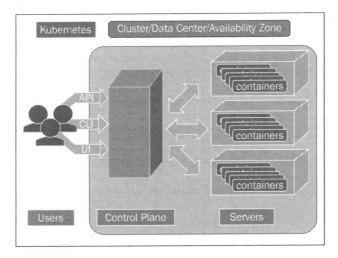

The federation control plane consists of a federation API server and a federation controller manager that collaborate. The federated API server forwards requests to all the clusters in the federation. In addition, the federated controller manager performs the duties of the controller manager across all clusters by routing requests to the individual federation cluster members' changes. In practice, cluster federation is not trivial and can't be totally abstracted away. Cross-pod communication and data transfer may suddenly incur a massive latency and cost overhead. Let's look at the use cases for cluster federation first, understand how the federated components and resources work, and then examine the hard parts: location affinity, cross-cluster scheduling, and federated data access.

Important use cases for cluster federation

There are four categories of use cases that benefit from cluster federation.

Capacity overflow

The public cloud platforms such as AWS, GCE, and Azure are great and provide many benefits, but they are not cheap. Many large organizations have invested a lot in their own data centers. Other organizations work with private service providers such as OVS, Rackspace, or Digital Ocean. If you have the operational capacity to manage and operate infrastructure on your own it makes a lot of economic sense to run your Kubernetes cluster on your infrastructure rather than in the cloud. But what if some of your workloads fluctuate and for a relatively short amount of time require a lot more capacity?

For example, your system maybe hit especially hard on the weekends or maybe during holidays. The traditional approach is to just provision extra capacity. But in many dynamic situations, it is not easy. With capacity overflow, you can run the bulk of your work in a Kubernetes cluster running on an on-premise data center or with a private service provider and have a secondary cloud-based Kubernetes cluster running on one of the big platform providers. Most of the time, the cloud-based cluster will be shut down (stopped instances), but when the need arises you can elastically add capacity to your system by starting some stopped instances. Kubernetes cluster federation can make this configuration relatively straightforward. It eliminates a lot of headaches about capacity planning and paying for hardware that's not used most of the time.

This approach is sometimes called Cloud bursting.

Sensitive workloads

This is almost the opposite of capacity overflow. Maybe you've embraced the cloud native lifestyle and your entire system runs on the cloud, but some data or workloads deal with sensitive information. Regulatory compliance or your organization's security policies may dictate that those data and workloads must run in an environment that's fully controlled by you. Your sensitive data and workloads may be subject to external auditing. It may be critical to ensure no information ever leaks from the private Kubernetes cluster to the cloud-based Kubernetes cluster. But it may be desirable to have visibility into the public cluster and the ability to launch non-sensitive workloads from the private cluster to the cloud-based cluster. If the nature of a workload can change dynamically from non-sensitive to sensitive then it needs to be addressed by coming up with a proper policy and implementation. For example, you may prevent workloads from changing their nature. Alternatively, you may migrate a workload that suddenly became sensitive and ensure that it doesn't run on the cloud-based cluster anymore. Another important instance is national compliance, where certain data is required by law to remain and be accessed only from a designated geographical region (typically a country). In this case, a cluster must be created in that geographical region.

Avoiding vendor lock-in

Large organizations often prefer to have options and not be tied to a single provider. The risk is often too great, because the provider may shut down or be unable to provide the same level of service. Having multiple providers is often good for negotiating prices, too. Kubernetes is designed to be vendor-agnostic. You can run it on different cloud platforms, private service providers, and on-premise data centers.

However, this is not trivial. If you want to be sure that you are able to switch providers quickly or shift some workloads from one provider to the next, you should already be running your system on multiple providers. You can do it yourself or there are some companies that provide the service of running Kubernetes transparently on multiple providers. Since different providers run different data centers, you automatically get some redundancy and protection from vendor-wide outages.

Geo-distributing high availability

High availability means that a service will remain available to users even when some parts of the system fail. In the context of a federated Kubernetes cluster, the scope of failure is an entire cluster, which is typically due to problems with the physical data center hosting the cluster, or perhaps a wider issue with the platform provider. The key to high-availability is redundancy. Geo-distributed redundancy means having multiple clusters running in different locations. It may be different availability zones of the same cloud provider, different regions of the same cloud provider, or even different cloud providers altogether (see the Avowing vendor lock-in section). There are many issues to address when it comes to running a cluster federation with redundancy. We'll discuss some of these issues later. Assuming that the technical and organizational issues have been resolved, high availability will allow the switching of traffic from a failed cluster to another cluster. This should be transparent to the users up to a point (delay during switchover and some in-flight requests or tasks may disappear or fail). The system administrators may need to take extra steps to support the switchover and to deal with the original cluster failure.

The federation control plane

The federation control plane consists of two components that together enable a federation of Kubernetes clusters to appear and function as a single unified Kubernetes cluster.

Federation API server

The federation API server is managing the Kubernetes clusters that together comprise the federation. It manages the federation state (which clusters are part of the federation) in an etcd database the same as a regular Kubernetes cluster, but the state it keeps is just which clusters are members of the federation. The state of each cluster is stored in the etcd database of that cluster. The main purpose of the federation API server job is to interact with the federation controller manager and route requests to the federation member clusters. The federation members don't need to know they are part of a federation: they just work the same.

The following diagram demonstrates the relationships between the federation API server, the federation replication controllers, and the Kubernetes clusters in the federation:

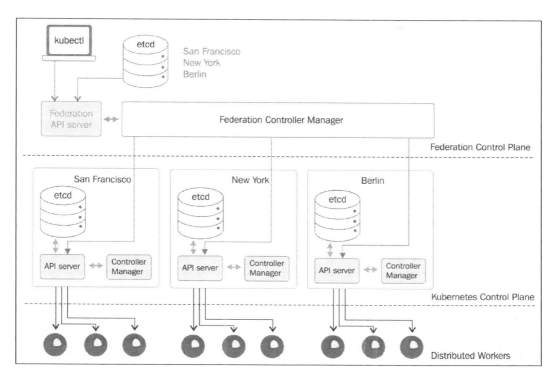

Federation controller manager

The federation controller manager makes sure the federation's desired state matches the actual state. It forwards any necessary changes to the relevant cluster or clusters. The federated controller manager binary contains multiple controllers for all the different federated resources we'll cover later in the chapter. The control logic is similar, though: observes changes and brings cluster state to the desired state when they deviate. This is done for each member in the cluster federation.

The following diagram demonstrates this perpetual control loop:

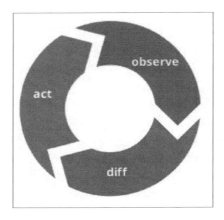

Federated resources

Kubernetes federation is still a work in progress. As of Kubernetes 1.5, only some of the standard resources can be federated. We'll cover them here. To create a federated resource, you use the `--context=federation-cluster` command-line argument to Kubectl. When you use `--context=federation-cluster`, the command goes to the federation API server, which takes care of sending it to all the member clusters.

Federated ConfigMap

Federated ConfigMaps are very useful because they help centralize the configuration of applications that may be spread across multiple clusters.

Creating a federated ConfigMap

Here is an example of creating a federated ConfigMap:

```
> kubectl --context=federation-cluster create -f configmap.yaml
```

As you can see, the only difference from creating a ConfigMap in a single Kubernetes cluster is the context.

When a federated ConfigMap is created, it is stored in the control plane `etcd` database, but a copy is also stored in each member cluster. This way, each cluster can operate independently and doesn't need to access the control plane.

Viewing a federated ConfigMap

You can view ConfigMap by accessing the control plane or by accessing a member cluster. To access a ConfigMap in a member cluster, specify the federation cluster member name in the context:

```
> kubectl --context=cluster-1 get configmap configmap.yaml
```

Updating a federated ConfigMap

It's important to note that, when created through the control plane, the ConfigMap will be identical across all member clusters. However, since it is stored separately in each cluster in addition to the control plane cluster, there is no single source of `true`. It is possible (although not recommended) to later modify the ConfigMap of each member cluster independently. That leads to non-uniform configuration across the federation. There are valid use cases for different configurations for different clusters in the federation, but in those cases I suggest just configuring each cluster directly. When you create a federated ConfigMap you make a statement that means whole clusters should share this configuration. However, you would usually want to update the ConfigMap across all the federation clusters by specifying `--context=federation-cluster`.

Deleting a federated ConfigMap

That's right, you guessed it. You delete as usual, but specify the context:

```
> kubectl --context=federation-cluster delete configmap
```

There is just one little twist. As of Kubernetes 1.5, when you delete a federated ConfigMap, the individual ConfigMaps that were created automatically in each cluster remain. You must delete them separately in each cluster. That is, if you have three clusters in your federation called cluster-1, cluster-2, and cluster-3, you'll have to run these extra three commands to get rid of the ConfigMap across the federation:

```
> kubectl --context=cluster-1 delete configmap
```

```
> kubectl --context=cluster-2 delete configmap
```

```
> kubectl --context=cluster-3 delete configmap
```

This will be rectified in the future.

Federated DaemonSet

A federated DaemonSet is pretty much the same as a regular Kubernetes DaemonSet. You create it and interact with it via the control plane, and the control plane propagates it to all the member clusters. At the end of the day, you can be sure that your Daemons run on every node in every cluster of the federation.

Federated deployment

Federated deployments are a little smarter. When you create a federated deployment with X replicas and you have N clusters, the replicas will be distributed evenly between the clusters by default. If you have three clusters and the federated deployment has 15 pods, then each cluster will run five replicas. As other federated resources, the control plane will store the federated deployment with 15 replicas and then create three deployments (one for each cluster) with five replicas each. You can control the number of replicas per cluster by adding an annotation: `federation.kubernetes.io/deployment-preferences`. Federated deployment is still in alpha as of Kubernetes 1.5. In the future, the annotation will become a proper field in the federated deployment configuration.

Federated events

Federated events are different than the other federated resources. They are only stored in the control plane and are not propagated to the underlying Kubernetes member clusters.

You can query the federation events with `--context=federation-cluster` as usual:

```
> kubectl --context=federation-cluster get events
```

Federated ingress

The federated ingress does more than just create matching ingress objects in each cluster. One of the main features of federated ingress is that if a whole cluster goes down it can direct traffic to other clusters. As of Kubernetes 1.4, federated ingress is supported on Google Cloud Platform, both on GKE and GCE. In the future, hybrid cloud support for federated ingress will be added.

The federated ingress performs the following roles:

- Create Kubernetes ingress objects in each cluster member of the federation
- Provide a one stop logical L7 load balancer with a single IP address for all the cluster ingress objects.
- Monitor the health and capacity of the service backend pods behind the ingress object in each cluster
- Make sure to route client connections to a healthy service endpoint in the face of various failures, such as pod, cluster, availability zone, or a whole region, as long as there is one healthy cluster in the federation

Creating a federated ingress

You create a federated ingress by addressing the federation control plane:

```
> kubectl --context=federation-cluster create -f ingress.yaml
```

The federation control plane will create the corresponding ingress in each cluster. All the clusters will share the same namespace and name for the ingress object:

```
> kubectl --context=cluster-1 get ingress myingress
NAME        HOSTS     ADDRESS          PORTS     AGE
ingress     *         157.231.15.33    80, 443   1m
```

Request routing with a federated ingress

The federated ingress controller will route requests to the closest cluster. Ingress objects expose one or more IP addresses (via the `Status.Loadbalancer.Ingress` field) that remain static for the lifetime of the ingress object. When an internal or external client connects to an IP address of a cluster-specific ingress object, it will be routed to one of the pods in that cluster. However, when a client connects to the IP address of a federated ingress object it will be automatically routed, via the shortest network path, to a healthy pod in the closest cluster to the origin of the request. So, for example, HTTP(S) requests from Internet users in Europe will be routed directly to the closest cluster in Europe that has available capacity. If there are no such clusters in Europe, the request will be routed to the next closest cluster (often in the US).

Handling failures with federated ingress

There are two broad categories of failure:

- Pod failure
- Cluster failure

Pods might fail for many reasons. In a properly configured Kubernetes cluster (a cluster federation member or not), pods will be managed by services and ReplicaSets that can automatically handle pod failures. It shouldn't impact cross-cluster routing and load balancing done by the federated ingress. A whole cluster might fail due to problems with the data center or global connectivity. In this, the federated services and federated ReplicaSets will ensure that the other clusters in the federation run enough pods to handle the workload, and the federated ingress will take care of routing client requests away from the failed cluster. To benefit from this auto-healing capability, clients must always connect to the federation ingress object and not to individual cluster members.

Federated namespace

Kubernetes namespaces are used within a cluster to isolate independent areas and support multi-tenant deployments. Federated namespaces provide the same capabilities across a cluster federation. The API is identical. When a client is accessing the federation control plane, they will only get access to the namespaces they requested and are authorized to access across all the clusters in the federation.

You use the same commands and add `--context=federation-cluster`:

```
> kubectl --context=federation-cluster create -f namespace.yaml
> kubectl --context=cluster-1 get namespaces namespace
> kubectl --context=federation-cluster create -f namespace.yaml
```

Federated ReplicaSet

It is best to use deployments and federated deployments to manage the replicas in your cluster or federation. However, if for some reason you prefer to work directly with ReplicaSets, then Kubernetes supports a federated `ReplicaSet`. There is no federated replication controller because ReplicaSets supersede replication controllers.

When you create a federated ReplicaSets, the job of the control plane is to ensure that the number of replicas across the cluster matches your federated ReplicaSets configuration. The control plane will create a regular ReplicaSet in each federation member. Each cluster will get, by default, an equal (or as close as possible) number of replicas so that the total will add up to the specified number of replicas.

You can control the number of replicas per cluster by specifying using the following annotation: `federation.kubernetes.io/replica-set-preferences`.

The corresponding data structure is as follows:

```
type FederatedReplicaSetPreferences struct {
  Rebalance bool
  Clusters map[string]ClusterReplicaSetPreferences
}
```

If Rebalance is `true`, then running replicas may be moved between clusters as necessary. The clusters map determines the ReplicaSets preferences per cluster. If * is specified as the key, then all unspecified clusters will use that set of preferences. If there is no * entry, then replicas will only run on clusters that show up in the map. Clusters that belong to the federation but don't have an entry will not have pods scheduled (for that pod template).

The individual ReplicaSets preferences per cluster are specified using the following data structure:

```
type ClusterReplicaSetPreferences struct {
  MinReplicas int64
  MaxReplicas *int64
  Weight int64
}
```

MinReplicas is 0 by default. MaxReplicas is unbounded by default. Weight expresses the preference to add an additional replica to this ReplicaSets and defaults to 0.

Federated secrets

Federated secrets are simple. When you create a federated secret as usual through the control plane it gets propagated to the whole cluster. That's it.

The hard parts

So far, federation seems almost straightforward. You group a bunch of clusters together, access them through the control plane, and everything just gets replicated to all the clusters. But there are hard and difficult factors and basic concepts that complicate this simplified view. Much of the power of Kubernetes is derived from its ability to do a lot of work behind the scenes. Within a single cluster deployed fully in a single physical data center or availability zone where all the components are connected with a fast network, Kubernetes is very effective on its own. In a Kubernetes cluster federation, the situation is different. Latency, data transfer costs, and moving pods between clusters all have different trade-offs. Depending on the use case, making federation work may require extra attention, planning, and maintenance on the part of the system designers and operators. In addition, some of the federated resources are not as mature as their local counterparts, and that adds more uncertainty.

Federated unit of work

The unit of work in a Kubernetes cluster is the pod. You can't break a pod in Kubernetes. The entire pod will always be deployed together and be subject to the same lifecycle treatment. Should the pod remain the unit of work for a cluster federation? Maybe it makes more sense to be able to associate a bigger unit, such as a whole ReplicaSet deployment, or service with a specific cluster. If the cluster fails, the entire ReplicaSet deployment, or service is scheduled to a different cluster. How about a collection of tightly coupled ReplicaSets? The answers to these questions are not always easy and may even change dynamically as the system evolves.

Location affinity

Location affinity is a major concern. When can pods be distributed across clusters? What are the relationships between those pods? Are there any requirements for affinity between pods or pods and other resources, such as storage? There are several major categories:

- Strictly-coupled
- Loosely-coupled
- Preferentially-coupled
- Strictly-decoupled
- Uniformly-spread

When designing the system and how to allocate and schedule services and pods across the federation it's important to make sure the location affinity requirements are always respected.

Strictly-coupled

The strictly-coupled requirement applies to applications where the pods must be in the same cluster. If you partition the pods, the application will fail (perhaps due to real-time requirements that can't be met networking across clusters) or the cost may be too high (pods accessing a lot of local data). The only way to move such tightly coupled applications to another cluster is to start a complete copy (including data) on another cluster and then shut down the application on the current cluster. If the data is too large, the application may practically be immovable and sensitive to catastrophic failure. This is the most difficult situation to deal with, and if possible you should architect your system to avoid the strictly-coupled requirement.

Loosely-coupled

Loosely-coupled applications are best when the workload is embarrassingly parallel and each pod doesn't need to know about the other pods or access a lot of data. In these situations, pods can be scheduled to clusters just based on capacity and resource utilization across the federation. If necessary, pods can be moved from one cluster to another without problems. For example, a stateless validation service that performs some calculation and gets all its input in the request itself and doesn't query or write any federation-wide data. It just validates its input and returns a valid/invalid verdict to the caller.

Preferentially-coupled

Preferentially-coupled applications perform better when all the pods are in the same cluster or the pods and the data are co-located, but it is not a hard requirement. For example, it could work with applications that require only eventual consistency, where some federation-wide cluster periodically synchronizes the application state across all clusters. In these cases, allocation is done explicitly to one cluster, but leaves a safety hatch for running or migrating to other clusters under stress.

Strictly-decoupled

Some services have fault isolation or high availability requirements that force partitioning across clusters. There is no point running three replicas of a critical service if all replicas might end up scheduled to the same cluster, because that cluster just becomes an ad hoc **Single Point Of Failure (SPOF)**.

Uniformly-spread

Uniformly-spread is when an instance of a service, ReplicaSets, or pod must run on each cluster. It is similar to DaemonSet, but instead of ensuring there is one instance on each node, it's one per cluster. A good example is a Redis cache backed up by some external persistent storage. The pods in each cluster should have their own cluster-local Redis cache to avoid accessing the central storage that may be slower or become a bottleneck. On the other hand, there is no need for more than one Redis service per cluster (it could be distributed across several pods in the same cluster).

Cross-cluster scheduling

Cross-cluster scheduling goes hand-in-hand with location affinity. When a new pod is created or an existing pod fails and a replacement needs to be scheduled, where should it go? The current cluster federation doesn't handle all the scenarios and options for location affinity we mentioned earlier. At this point, cluster federation handles the loosely-coupled (including weighted distribution) and strictly-coupled (by making sure the number of replicas matches the number of clusters) categories well. Anything else will require that you don't use cluster federation. You'll have to add your own custom federation layer that takes more specialized concerns into account and can accommodate more intricate scheduling use cases.

Federated data access

This is a tough problem. If you have a lot of data and pods running in multiple clusters (possibly on different continents) and need to access it quickly, then you have several unpleasant options:

- Replicate your data to each cluster (slow to replicate, expensive to transfer, expensive to store, and complicated to sync and deal with errors)
- Access the data remotely (slow to access, expensive on each access, can be a SPOF)
- Sophisticated hybrid solution with per-cluster caching of some of the hottest data (complicated, stale data, and you still need to transfer a lot of data)

Federated auto-scaling

There is currently no support for federated auto-calling. There are two dimensions of scaling that can be utilized, as well as a combination:

- Per cluster scaling
- Adding/removing clusters from the federation
- Hybrid approach

Consider the relatively simple scenario of a loosely coupled application running on three clusters with five pods in each cluster. At some point, 15 pods can't handle the load anymore. We need to add more capacity. We can increase the number of pods per cluster, but if we do it at the federation level than we will have six pods running in each cluster. We've increased the federation capacity by three pods, when only one pod is needed. Of course, if you have more clusters the problem gets worse. Another option is to pick a cluster and just change its capacity. This is possible with annotations, but now we're explicitly managing capacity across the federation. It can get complicated very quickly if we have lots of clusters running hundreds of services with dynamically changing requirements.

Adding a whole new cluster is even more complicated. Where should we add the new cluster? There is no requirement for extra availability that can guide the decision. It is just about extra capacity. Creating a new cluster also often requires complicated first time setup that may take days to approve various quotas on public cloud platforms. The hybrid approach increases the capacity of existing clusters in the federation until reaching some threshold and then starts adding new clusters. The benefit of this approach is that when you're getting closer to capacity limit per cluster you start preparing new clusters that will be ready to go when necessary. Other than that, it requires a lot effort and you pay in increased complexity for the flexibility and scalability.

Managing a Kubernetes cluster federation

Managing a Kubernetes cluster federation involves many activities above and beyond managing a single cluster. There are two ways to set up the federation. Then, you need to consider cascading resource deletion, load balancing across clusters, failover across clusters, federated service discovery, and federated discovery. Let's go over each one in detail.

Setting up cluster federation from the ground up

To set up a Kubernetes cluster federation we need to run the components of the control plane, which are as follows:

`etcd`

`federation-apiserver`

`federation-controller-manager`

One of the easiest way to do that is to use the all-in-one hyperkube image:

`https://github.com/kubernetes/kubernetes/tree/master/cluster/images/hyperkube.`

The federation API server and the federation controller manager can be run as pods in an existing Kubernetes cluster, but as discussed earlier it is better from a fault tolerance and high availability point of view to run them in their own cluster.

Initial setup

First, you must have Docker running and get a Kubernetes release that contains the scripts we will use in this guide. The current release is 1.5.3. You can download the latest available version instead:

```
> curl -L https://github.com/kubernetes/kubernetes/releases/download/
v1.5.3/kubernetes.tar.gz | tar xvzf -

> cd kubernetes
```

We need to create a directory for the federation config files and set the FEDERATION_ OUTPUT_ROOT environment variable to that directory. For easy clean up, it's best to create a new directory:

```
> export FEDERATION_OUTPUT_ROOT="${PWD}/output/federation"
> mkdir -p "${FEDERATION_OUTPUT_ROOT}"
```

Now, we can initialize the federation:

```
> federation/deploy/deploy.sh init
```

Using the official hyperkube image

As part of every Kubernetes release, official release images are pushed to gcr.io/ google_containers. To use the images in this repository, you can set the container image fields in the config files in ${FEDERATION_OUTPUT_ROOT} to point to the gcr. io/google_containers/hyperkube image, which includes both the federation-apiserver and federation-controller-manager binaries.

Running the federation control plane

We're ready to deploy the federation control plane by running the following command:

```
> federation/deploy/deploy.sh deploy_federation
```

The command will launch the control plane components as pods and create a service of type LoadBalancer for the federation API server and a persistent volume claim backed up by a dynamic persistent volume for etcd.

To verify everything was created correctly in the federation namespace, type the following:

```
> kubectl get deployments --namespace=federation
```

You should see this:

NAME	DESIRED	CURRENT	UP-TO-DATE	
federation-apiserver	1	1	1	federation-
controller-manager 1	1	1		

You can also check your kubeconfig file for new entries via Kubectl config view. Note that dynamic provisioning works only for AWS and GCE at the moment.

Registering Kubernetes clusters with federation

To register a cluster with the federation, we need a secret to talk to the cluster. Let's create the secret in the host Kubernetes cluster. Suppose kubeconfig of the target cluster is at |cluster-1|kubeconfig. You can run the following command to create the secret:

```
> kubectl create secret generic cluster-1 --namespace=federation
  --from-file=/cluster-1/kubeconfig
```

The configuration for the cluster looks the same as this:

```
apiVersion: federation/v1beta1
kind: Cluster
metadata:
  name: cluster1
spec:
  serverAddressByClientCIDRs:
  - clientCIDR: <client-cidr>
    serverAddress: <apiserver-address>
  secretRef:
    name: <secret-name>
```

We need to set <client-cidr>, <apiserver-address>, and <secret-name>. <secret-name> here is name of the secret that you just created. serverAddressByClientCIDRs contains the various server addresses that clients can use as per their CIDR. We can set the server's public IP address with CIDR 0.0.0.0/0, which all clients will match. In addition, if you want internal clients to use the server's clusterIP, you can set that as serverAddress. The client CIDR in that case will be a CIDR that only matches IPs of pods running in that cluster.

Let's register the cluster:

```
> kubectl create -f /cluster-1/cluster.yaml --context=federation-cluster
```

Let's see if the cluster has been registered properly:

```
> kubectl get clusters --context=federation-cluster
NAME        STATUS    VERSION    AGE
cluster-1   Ready                1m
```

Updating KubeDNS

The cluster is registered with the federation. It's time to update `kube-dns` so that your cluster can route federation service requests. As of Kubernetes 1.5 or later, it's done by passing the `--federations` flag to `kube-dns` via the `kube-dns` `ConfigMap`:

```
--federations=${FEDERATION_NAME}=${DNS_DOMAIN_NAME}
```

Here is what the `ConfigMap` looks:

```
apiVersion: v1
kind: ConfigMap
metadata:
  name: kube-dns
  namespace: kube-system
data:
  federations: <federation-name>=<federation-domain-name>
```

Replace the `federation-name` and the `federation-domain-name` with the correct values.

Shutting down the federation

If you want to shut down the federation, just run the following command:

```
federation/deploy/deploy.sh destroy_federation
```

Setting up cluster federation with Kubefed

Kubernetes 1.5 has a new command-line tool (still in alpha) called Kubefed to help you administrate your federated clusters. The job of Kubefed is to make it easy to deploy a new Kubernetes cluster federation control plane, and to add or remove clusters from an existing federation control plane.

Getting Kubefed

Kubefed is part of the Kubernetes client binaries. You can get them here:

```
https://github.com/kubernetes/kubernetes/blob/master/CHANGELOG.md
```

You'll get the latest Kubectl and Kubefed. Here are the instructions for downloading and installing on Linux for the `1.5.3` version:

```
curl -O https://storage.googleapis.com/kubernetes-release/release/v1.5.3/
kubernetes-client-linux-amd64.tar.gz

tar -xzvf kubernetes-client-linux-amd64.tar.gz

sudo cp kubernetes/client/bin/kubefed /usr/local/bin

sudo chmod +x /usr/local/bin/kubefed

sudo cp kubernetes/client/bin/kubectl /usr/local/bin

sudo chmod +x /usr/local/bin/kubectl
```

Make the necessary adjustments if you're using a different OS or want to install a different version.

Choosing a host cluster

The federation control plane can be its own dedicated cluster or hosted with an existing cluster. You need to make this decision. The host cluster hosts the components that make up your federation control plane. Ensure that you have a `kubeconfig` entry in your local `kubeconfig` that corresponds to the host cluster. To verify that you have the required `kubeconfig` entry, type the following:

```
> kubectl config get-contexts
```

You should see something like this:

```
CURRENT    NAME       CLUSTER    AUTHINFO   NAMESPACE
           cluster-1 cluster-1 cluster-1
```

The content name `cluster-1` will be provided later when deploying the federation control plane.

Deploying a federation control plane

It's time to start using Kubefed. The `kubefed init` command requires three arguments:

- The federation name
- Host cluster context
- A domain name suffix for your federated services

The following example command deploys a federation control plane with the name federation; a host cluster context, `cluster-1`; and the domain suffix `kubernetes-ftw.com`:

```
> kubefed init federation --host-cluster-context=cluster-1  --dns-zone-
name=" kubernetes-ftw.com"
```

The DNS suffix should be for a DNS domain you manage, of course.

`kubefed init` sets up the federation control plane in the host cluster and adds an entry for the federation API server in your local `kubeconfig`. In the alpha release of Kubernetes 1.5, it doesn't set the current context to the newly deployed federation. You'll have to do it yourself. Type the following command:

```
kubectl config use-context federation
```

Adding a cluster to a federation

Once the control plane has been deployed successfully, we should add some Kubernetes clusters to the federation. Kubefed provides the `join` command exactly for this purpose. The `kubefed join` command requires the following arguments:

- The name of the cluster to add
- Host cluster context

For example, to add a new cluster called `cluster-2` to the federation, type the following:

```
kubefed join cluster-2 --host-cluster-context=cluster-1
```

Naming rules and customization

The cluster name you supply to `kubefed join` must be a valid RFC 1035 label. RFC 1035 allows only letters, digits, and hyphens, and the label must start with a letter.

Furthermore, the federation control plane requires credentials of the joined clusters to operate on them. These credentials are obtained from the local `kubeconfig`. The `Kubefed join` command uses the cluster name specified as the argument to look for the cluster's context in the local `kubeconfig`. If it fails to find a matching context, it exits with an error.

This might cause issues in cases where context names for each cluster in the federation don't follow RFC 1035 label naming rules. In such cases, you can specify a cluster name that conforms to the RFC 1035 label naming rules and specify the cluster context using the `--cluster-context` flag. For example, if the context of the cluster you are joining is `cluster-3` (underscore is not allowed), you can join the cluster by running this:

```
kubefed join cluster-3 --host-cluster-context=cluster-1 --cluster-context=cluster-3
```

Secret name

Cluster credentials required by the federation control plane as described in the previous section are stored as a secret in the host cluster. The name of the secret is also derived from the cluster name.

However, the name of a `secret` object in Kubernetes should conform to the DNS subdomain name specification described in RFC 1123. If this isn't the case, you can pass the `secret` name to `kubefed join` using the `--secret-name` flag. For example, if the cluster name is `cluster-4` and the `secret name` is `4secret` (starting with a digit is not allowed), you can join the cluster by running this:

```
kubefed join cluster-4 --host-cluster-context=cluster-1 --secret-name=4secret
```

The `kubefed join` command automatically creates the secret for you.

Removing a cluster from a federation

To remove a cluster from a federation, run the `kubefed unjoin` command with the cluster name and the federation's host cluster context:

```
kubefed unjoin cluster-2 --host-cluster-context=cluster-1
```

Shutting down the federation

Proper cleanup of the federation control plane is not fully implemented in this alpha release of Kubefed. However, for the time being, deleting the federation system namespace should remove all the resources except the persistent storage volume dynamically provisioned for the federation control plane's `etcd`. You can `delete` the federation namespace by running the following command:

```
> kubectl delete ns federation-system
```

Cascading delete of resources

The Kubernetes cluster federation often manages a federated object in the control plane, as well as corresponding objects in each member Kubernetes cluster. A cascading delete of a federated object means that the corresponding objects in the member Kubernetes clusters will also be deleted.

This doesn't happen automatically. By default, only the federation control plane object is deleted. To activate cascading delete, you need to set the following option:

```
DeleteOptions.orphanDependents=false
```

The following federated objects support cascading delete:

- Deployment
- DaemonSets
- Ingress
- Namespaces
- ReplicaSets
- SecretsFor other objects, you'll have to go into each cluster and delete them explicitly.

Load balancing across multiple clusters

Dynamic load balancing across clusters is not trivial. The simplest solution is to just say that it is not Kubernetes' responsibility. Load balancing will be performed outside the Kubernetes cluster federation. But given the dynamic nature of Kubernetes, even an external load balancer will have to gather a lot of information about which services and backend pods are running on each cluster. An alternative solution is for the federation control plane to implement an L7 load balancer that serves as traffic director for the entire federation. In one of the simpler use cases, each service runs on a dedicated cluster and the load balancer simply routes all traffic to that cluster. In case of cluster failure, the service is migrated to a different cluster and the load balancer now routes all traffic to the new cluster. This provides a coarse fail-over and high availability solution at the cluster level.

The optimal solution will be able to support federated services and take into account additional factors, such as the following:

- Geo-location of client
- Resource utilization of each cluster
- Resource quotas and auto-scaling

The following diagram shows how an L7 load balancer on GCE distributes client requests to the closest cluster:

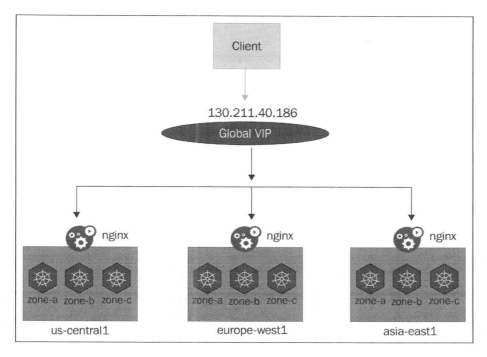

Failing over across multiple clusters

Federated failover is tricky. Suppose a cluster in the federation fails; one option is to just have other clusters pick up the slack. Now, the question is, how do you distribute the load across other clusters:

- Uniformly?
- Launch a new cluster?
- Pick an existing cluster as close as possible (maybe in the same region)?

Each of these solutions has subtle interactions with federated load balancing, geo-distributed high availability, cost management across different clusters, and security.

Now, the failed cluster comes back online. Should it gradually take over its original workload again? What if it comes back but with reduced capacity or sketchy networking? There are many combinations of failure modes that could make recovery complicated.

Federated service discovery

Federated service discovery is tightly coupled with federated load balancing. A pragmatic setup includes a global L7 load balancer that distributes requests to federated ingress objects in the federation clusters.

The benefit of this approach is that the control stays with the Kubernetes federation, which over time will able to work with more cluster types (currently just AWS and GCE) and understand cluster utilization and other constraints.

The alternative of having a dedicated lookup service and let clients connect directly to services on individual clusters loses all these benefits.

Federated migration

Federated migration is related to several topics we discussed, such as location affinity, federated scheduling, and high availability. At the core, federated migration means moving a whole application or some part of it from one cluster to another (and more generally from M clusters to N clusters). Federation migration can happen in response to various events, such as the following:

- A low capacity event in a cluster (or a cluster failure)
- A change of scheduling policy (we no longer use cloud provider X)
- A change of resource pricing (cloud provider Y dropped their prices - let's migrate there)
- A new cluster was added to or removed from the federation (let's rebalance the pods of the application)

Strictly-coupled applications can be trivially moved, in part or in whole, one pod at a time, to one or more clusters (within applicable policy constraints, for example `PrivateCloudOnly`).

For preferentially-coupled applications, the federation system must first locate a single cluster with sufficient capacity to accommodate the entire application, then reserve that capacity and incrementally move the application, one (or more) resource at a time, over to the new cluster within some bounded time period (and possibly within a predefined maintenance window).

Strictly-coupled applications (with the exception of those deemed completely immovable) require the federation system to do the following:

- Start up an entire replica application in the destination cluster
- Copy persistent data to the new application instance (possibly before starting pods)

- Switch user traffic across
- Tear down the original application instance

Running federated workloads

Federated workloads are workloads that are processed on multiple Kubernetes clusters at the same time. This is relatively easy to do for loosely-coupled and embarrassingly-distributed applications. However, if most of the processing can be done in parallel, often there is a join point at the end, or at least a central persistent store that needs to be queried and updated. It gets more complicated if multiple pods of the same service need to cooperate across clusters, or if a collection of services (each one of them may be federated) must work together and be synchronized to accomplish something.

Kubernetes federation supports federated services that provide a great foundation for such federated workloads.

Some key points for federated services are service discovery, cross cluster load-balancing, and availability zone fault tolerance.

Creating a federated service

A federated service creates a corresponding service in the federation's member clusters.

For example, to create a federated Nginx service (assuming you have the service configuration in `nginx.yaml`), type the following:

```
> kubectl --context=federation-cluster create -f nginx.yaml
```

You can verify a service was created in each cluster (for example, in `cluster-2`):

```
> kubectl --context=cluster-2 get services nginx
NAME      CLUSTER-IP      EXTERNAL-IP      PORT(S)    AGE
nginx     10.63.250.98    104.199.136.89   80/TCP     9m
```

All the created services in all the clusters will share the same namespace and service name, which makes sense since they are a single logical service.

The status of your federated service will automatically reflect the real-time status of the underlying Kubernetes services:

```
> kubectl --context=federation-cluster describe services nginx
```

Name:	nginx
Namespace:	default
Labels:	run=nginx
Selector:	run=nginx
Type:	LoadBalancer
IP:	
LoadBalancer Ingress:	104.197.246.190, 130.211.57.243, 104.196.14.231, 104.199.136.89, ...
Port:	http 80/TCP
Endpoints:	<none>
Session Affinity:	None
No events.	

Adding backend pods

As of Kubernetes 1.5, we still need to add backend pods to each federation member cluster. This can be done with the kubectl run command. In a future release, the Kubernetes federation API server will be able to do it automatically. This will save one more step. Note that when you use the kubectl run command, Kubernetes automatically adds the run label to the pod based on the image name. In the following example that launches an Nginx backend pod on five Kubernetes clusters, the image name is nginx (ignoring the version), so the following label is added:

```
run=nginx
```

This is necessary because the service uses that label to identify its pods. If you use another label, you need to add it explicitly:

```
for C in cluster-1 \
          cluster-2 \
        cluster-3 \
        cluster-4 \
        cluster-5
do
  kubectl --context=$C run nginx --image=nginx:1.11.1-alpine --port=80
done
```

Verifying public DNS records

Once the preceding pods have successfully started and are listening for connections, Kubernetes will report them as healthy endpoints of the service in that cluster (via automatic health checks). The Kubernetes cluster federation will in turn consider each of these service shards to be healthy, and place them in service by automatically configuring corresponding public DNS records. You can use your preferred interface to your configured DNS provider to verify this. For example, if your federation is configured to use Google Cloud DNS and a managed DNS domain example.com:

```
> gcloud dns managed-zones describe example-dot-com
creationTime: '2017-03-08T18:18:39.229Z'
description: Example domain for Kubernetes Cluster Federation
dnsName: example.com.
id: '3229332181334243121'
kind: dns#managedZone
name: example-dot-com
nameServers:
- ns-cloud-a1.googledomains.com.
- ns-cloud-a2.googledomains.com.
- ns-cloud-a3.googledomains.com.
- ns-cloud-a4.googledomains.com.
```

Follow up with the following command to see the actual DNS records:

```
> gcloud dns record-sets list --zone example-dot-com
```

If your federation is configured to use aws route53 DNS service use the following commands:

```
> aws route53 list-hosted-zones
```

The use this command:

```
> aws route53 list-resource-record-sets --hosted-zone-id K9PBY0X1QTOVBX
```

You can, of course, use standard DNS tools such as nslookup or dig to verify DNS records were updated properly. You may have to wait a little for your changes to propagate. Alternatively, you can point directly to your DNS provider:

```
> dig @ns-cloud-e1.googledomains.com ...
```

However, I always prefer to observe DNS changes in the wild after they were properly propagated, so I can inform users that everything is ready to go.

Discovering a federated service

Kubernetes provides KubeDNS as a built-in core component. KubeDNS uses a cluster-local DNS server as well as naming conventions to compose well-qualified (by namespace) DNS names conventions. For example, `the-service` is resolved to the `the-service` service in the default `namespace`, while `the-service.the-namespace` is resolved to the service called `the-service` in the `the-namespace` namespace, which is separate from the default `the-service`. Pods can find and access internal services easily with KubeDNS. Kubernetes cluster federation extends the mechanism to multiple clusters. The basic concept is the same, but another level is added of a federation. The DNS name of a service now consists of `<service name>.<namespace name>.<federation name>`. This way, internal service access is still usable using the original `<service name>.<namepace name>` naming convention. However, clients that want to access a federated service use the federated name that will be forwarded eventually to one of the federation member clusters to handle the request.

This federation-qualified naming convention also helps prevent internal cluster traffic from reaching across to other clusters by mistake.

Using the preceding Nginx example service, and the federated service DNS name form just described, let's consider an example: a pod in a cluster in the cluster-1 availability zone needs to access the Nginx service. Rather than use the service's traditional cluster-local DNS name (`nginx.the-namespace`, which is automatically expanded to `nginx.the-namespace.svc.cluster.local`), it can now use the service's federated DNS name, which is `nginx.the-namespace.the-federation`. This will be automatically expanded and resolved to the closest healthy shard of the Nginx service, wherever in the world that may be. If a healthy shard exists in the local cluster, that service's cluster-local (typically `10.x.y.z`) IP address will be returned (by the cluster-local KubeDNS). This is almost exactly equivalent to non-federated service resolution (almost because KubeDNS actually returns both a CNAME and an A record for local federated services, but applications will be oblivious to this minor technical difference).

However, if the service doesn't exist in the local cluster (or doesn't have healthy backend pods) the DNS query is expanded automatically.

DNS expansion

If the service does not exist in the local cluster (or it exists but has no healthy backend pods), the DNS query is automatically expanded to find the external IP address closest to the requestor's availability zone. KubeDNS performs this automatically and returns the corresponding CNAME. That will get further resolved to the IP address of one of the service's backing pods.

You don't have to rely on automatic DNS expansion. You can also provide the CNAME of a service in a particular cluster directly or in a particular region. For example, on GCE/GKE you can specify nginx.the-namespace.svc.europe-west1.example. com. That will get resolved to a backing pod of the service in one of the clusters in Europe (assuming there are clusters and healthy backing pods there).

External clients can't utilize DNS expansion, but if they want to target some restricted subset of the federation (such as a particular region) then they can provide the service's fully qualified CNAME just as the example. Since those names tend to be long and cumbersome, a good practice is to add some static convenience CNAME records:

```
eu.nginx.example.com              CNAME nginx.the-namespace.the-federation.svc.
europe-west1.example.com.

us.nginx.example.com              CNAME nginx.the-namespace.the-federation.svc.
us-central1.example.com.

nginx.example.com                 CNAME nginx.the-namespace.the-federation.svc.
example.com.
```

The following diagram shows how a federated lookup works across multiple clusters:

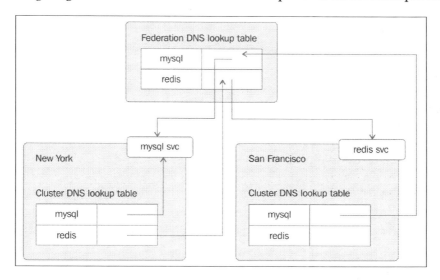

Handling failures of backend pods and whole clusters

Standard Kubernetes service cluster-IPs already ensure that non-responsive individual pod endpoints are automatically taken out of service with low latency (a few seconds). In addition, as alluded to in the previous section, the Kubernetes cluster federation system automatically monitors the health of clusters and the endpoints behind all of the shards of your federated service, taking shards in and out of service as required (for example, when all of the endpoints behind a service, or perhaps the entire cluster or availability zone, go down, or conversely recover from an outage). Due to the latency inherent in DNS caching (the cache timeout, or TTL for Federated Service DNS records is configured to three minutes, by default, but can be adjusted), it may take up to that long for all clients to completely fail over to an alternative cluster in the case of catastrophic failure. However, given the number of discrete IP addresses that can be returned for each regional service endpoint (see, for example, `us-central1`, which has three alternatives), many clients will fail over automatically to one of the alternative IPs in less time than that, given the appropriate configuration.

Troubleshooting

When things go south, you need to be able to figure out what's wrong and how to fix it. Here are a few common problems and how to diagnose/fix them.

Unable to connect to federation API server

Refer to the following solution:

- Verify the federation API server is running
- Verify the client (Kubectl) is configured correctly with proper API endpoints and credentials

Federated service is created successfully but no service is created in underlying clusters

- Verify the clusters are registered with federation
- Verify the federation API server was able to connect and authenticate against all clusters
- Check quotas are sufficient
- Check the logs for other problems:

```
Kubectl logs federation-controller-manager --namespace federation
```

Summary

In this chapter, we've covered the important topic of Kubernetes cluster federation. Cluster federation is still in the early stages, but it is already usable. There aren't a lot of deployments and the officially supported target platforms are currently AWS and GCE/GKE, but there is a lot of momentum behind cloud federation. It is a very important piece for building massively scalable systems on Kubernetes. We've discussed the motivation and use cases for Kubernetes cluster federation, the federation control plane components, and the federated Kubernetes objects. We also looked into the less supported aspects of federation such as custom scheduling, federated data access, and auto-scaling. We then looked at how to run multiple Kubernetes clusters, which includes setting up and Kubernetes cluster federation, adding and removing clusters to the federation along with load balancing, federated failover when something goes wrong, service discovery, and migration. Then, we dived into running federated workloads across multiple clusters with federated services and the various challenges associated with this scenario.

At this point, you should have a clear understanding of the current state of federation, what it takes to utilize the existing capabilities provided by Kubernetes, and what pieces you'll have to implement yourself to augment incomplete or immature features. Depending on your use case, you may decide that it's still too early or that you want to take the plunge. The developers working on Kubernetes federation are moving fast, so it's very likely that it will be much more mature and battle-tested by the time you need to make your decision.

In *Chapter 12, Customizing Kubernetes - API and Plugins*, we'll dig into Kubernetes internals and how to customize it. One of the best architectural principles of Kubernetes is that it is accessible through a full-fledged REST API. The Kubectl command-line tool is built on top the Kubernetes API and provides interactivity to the full spectrum of Kubernetes. However, programmatic API access you can leverage provides a lot of flexibility to enhance and extend Kubernetes. There are client libraries in many languages that allow you to leverage Kubernetes from the outside and integrate it into existing systems.

In addition to its REST API, Kubernetes is a very modular platform by design. Many aspects of its core operation can be customized and/or extended. In particular, you can add user-defined resources and integrate them with the Kubernetes object model and benefit from the management services of Kubernetes, storage in `etcd`, exposure through the API, and uniform access to built-in and custom objects.

We've already seen various aspects that are extremely extensible, such as networking and access control via CNI plugins and custom storage classes. However, Kubernetes goes even further and lets you customize the scheduler itself, which controls pod assignment to nodes.

12
Customizing Kubernetes - API and Plugins

In this chapter, we will dig deep into the guts of Kubernetes. We will start with the Kubernetes API and learn how to work with Kubernetes programmatically via direct access to the API, the Python client, and automating Kubectl. Then, we'll look into extending the Kubernetes API with third-party-resources. The last part is all about the various plugins Kubernetes supports. Many aspects of Kubernetes operation are modular and designed for extension. We will examine several types of plugin, such as custom schedulers, authorization, admission control, custom metrics, and volumes.

The covered topics are as follows:

- Working with the Kubernetes API
- Extending the Kubernetes API
- Writing Kubernetes plugins

Working with the Kubernetes API

The Kubernetes API is comprehensive and encompasses the entire functionality of Kubernetes. As you may expect, it is huge. But it is designed very well using best practices, and it is consistent. If you understand the basic principles, you can discover everything you need to know.

Understanding OpenAPI

OpenAPI allows API providers to define their operations and models, and enables developers to automate their tools and generate their favorite language's client to talk to that API server. Kubernetes has supported Swagger 1.2 (an older version of the OpenAPI spec) for a while, but the spec was incomplete and invalid, making it hard to generate tools/clients based on it.

In Kubernetes 1.4, alpha support was added for the OpenAPI spec (formerly known as Swagger 2.0 before it was donated to the OpenAPI Initiative) by upgrading the current models and operations. In Kubernetes 1.5, support for the OpenAPI spec has been completed by auto-generating the spec directly from Kubernetes source, which will keep the spec and documentation completely in sync with future changes in operations/models.

The new spec enables better API documentation and and an auto-generated Python client that we will explore later.

The spec is modular and divided by group version. This is future-proof. You can run multiple API servers that support different versions. Applications can transition gradually to newer versions.

The structure of spec is explained in detail in the OpenAPI spec definition. The Kubernetes team used the operation's tags to separate each group version and fill in as much information as possible about paths/operations and models. For a specific operation, all parameters, methods of call, and responses are documented. The result is impressive.

Setting up a proxy

To simplify access you can use Kubectl to set up a proxy:

```
kubectl proxy --port 8080
```

Now, you can access the API server on `http://localhost:8080` and it will reach the same Kubernetes API server that Kubectl is configured for.

Exploring the Kubernetes API directly

The Kubernetes API is highly discoverable. You can just browse to the URL of the API server at `http://localhost:8080` and get a nice JSON document that describes all the available operations under the paths key.

Here is a partial list due to space constraints:

```
{
  "paths": [
    "/api",
    "/api/v1",
    "/apis",
    "/apis/apps",
    "/apis/storage.k8s.io/v1beta1",

    .

    .

    .

    "/healthz",
    "/healthz/ping",
    "/logs",
    "/metrics",
    "/swaggerapi/",
    "/ui/",
    "/version"
  ]
}
```

You can drill down any one of the paths. For example, here is the response from /api/v1/namespaces/default endpoint:

```
{
  "kind": "Namespace",
  "apiVersion": "v1",
  "metadata": {
    "name": "default",
    "selfLink": "/api/v1/namespaces/default",
    "uid": "4eca8ced-0d90-11e7-b667-0242ac110023",
    "resourceVersion": "6",
    "creationTimestamp": "2017-03-20T17:11:50Z"
  },
  "spec": {
    "finalizers": [
      "kubernetes"
    ]
  },
```

```
"status": {
  "phase": "Active"
}
}
```

I discovered this endpoint by going first to /api, then discovered /api/v1, which told me there is /api/v1/namespaces that pointed me to /api/v1/namespaces/default.

Using Postman to explore the Kubernetes API

Postman (https://www.getpostman.com) is a very polished application for working with RESTful APIs. If you lean more to the GUI side, you may find it extremely useful.

The following screenshot shows the available endpoints under the batch v1 API group:

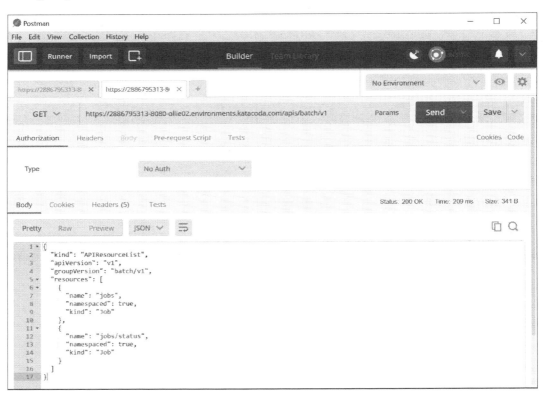

Postman has a lot of options and it organizes the information in a very pleasing way. Give it a try.

Filtering the output with httpie and jq

The output from the API can be too verbose sometimes. Often, you're interested just in one value out of a huge chunk of JSON response. For example, if you want to get the names of all running services you can hit the `/api/v1/services` endpoint. The response, however, includes a lot of additional information that is irrelevant. Here is a very partial subset of the output:

```
$ http http://localhost:8080/api/v1/services
{
    "apiVersion": "v1",
    "items": [
        {
            "metadata": {
                "creationTimestamp": "2017-03-21T15:16:09Z",
                "labels": {
                    "component": "apiserver",
                    "provider": "kubernetes"
                },
                "name": "kubernetes",
                ...
            },
            "spec": {
                ...
            },
            "status": {
                "loadBalancer": {}
            }
        },
        ...
    ],
    "kind": "ServiceList",
    "metadata": {
        "resourceVersion": "1076",
        "selfLink": "/api/v1/services"
    }
}
```

The complete output is 121 lines long! Let's see how to use `httpie` and `jq` to gain full control over the output and show only the names of the services. I prefer (https://httpie.org/) over cURL for interacting with REST APIs on the command-line. The `jq` (https://stedolan.github.io/jq/) command-line JSON processor is great for slicing and dicing JSON.

Examining the full output, you can see that the service names is in the metadata sections of each item in the items array. The `jq` expression that will select just the name is as follows:

```
.items[].metadata.name
```
```
Here is the full command and output:
$ http http://localhost:8080/api/v1/services | jq .items[].metadata.name
"kubernetes"
"kube-dns"
"kubernetes-dashboard"
```

Creating a pod via the Kubernetes API

The API can be used for creating, updating, and deleting resources too, given the following pod configuration file:

```
{
    "kind": "Pod",
    "apiVersion": "v1",
    "metadata":{
        "name": "nginx",
        "namespace": "default",
        "labels": {
            "name": "nginx"
        }
    },
    "spec": {
        "containers": [{
            "name": "nginx",
            "image": "nginx",
            "ports": [{"containerPort": 80}]
        }]
    }
}
```

The following command will create the pod via the API:

```
http POST http://localhost:8080/api/v1/namespaces/default/pods @nginx-
pod.json
```

To verify it worked, let's extract the name and status of the current pods. The endpoint is as follows:

```
/api/v1/namespaces/default/pods
```

The `jq` expression is as follows:

```
items[].metadata.name,.items[].status.phase
```

Here is the full command and output:

```
$ http http://localhost:8080/api/v1/namespaces/default/pods | jq
.items[].metadata.name,.items[].status.phase
"nginx"
"Running"
```

Accessing the Kubernetes API via the Python client

Exploring the API interactively using `httpie` and `jq` is great, but the real power of APIs comes when you consume and integrate them with other software. The Kubernetes incubator project provides a full-fledged and very well-documented Python `client` library. It is available at `https://github.com/kubernetes-incubator/client-python`.

First, make sure you have Python installed (either 2.7 or 3.5+) work. Then install the Kubernetes package:

```
pip install kubernetes
```

To start talking to a Kubernetes cluster, you need to connect to it. The Python client can read your Kubectl config:

```
>>> from kubernetes import client,config
>>> config.load_kube_config()
>>> v1 = client.CoreV1Api()
Or it can connect directly to an already running proxy:
>>> from kubernetes import client,config
>>> client.Configuration().host = 'http://localhost:8080>>> v1 = client.
CoreV1Api()
```

Note that the client module provides methods to get access to different group versions, such as `CoreV1API`.

Dissecting the CoreV1API group

Let's dive in and understand the `CoreV1API` group. The Python object has `459` public `attributes`!

```
>>> attributes = [x for x in dir(v1) if not x.startswith('__')]
>>> len(attributes)
459
```

Ignore the `attributes` that start with double underscores because those are special `class/instance` methods unrelated to Kubernetes.

Let's pick ten random methods and see what they look like:

```
>>> import random
>>> from pprint import pprint as pp
>>> pp(random.sample(attributes, 10))
['patch_namespaced_pod',
 'connect_options_node_proxy_with_path_with_http_info',
 'proxy_delete_namespaced_pod_with_path',
 'delete_namespace',
 'proxy_post_namespaced_pod_with_path_with_http_info',
 'proxy_post_namespaced_service',
 'list_namespaced_pod_with_http_info',
 'list_persistent_volume_claim_for_all_namespaces',
 'read_namespaced_pod_log_with_http_info',
 'create_node']
```

Very interesting. The `attributes` begin with a verb such as list, patch, or read. Many of them have a notion of a `namespace` and many have a `with_http_info` suffix. To understand better, let's count how many verbs exist and how many `attributes` use each verb (where the verb is the first token before the underscore):

```
>>> from collections import Counter
>>> verbs = [x.split('_')[0] for x in attributes]
>>> pp(dict(Counter(first_tokens)))
{'connect': 84,
 'create': 36,
```

```
'delete': 58,
'get': 2,
'list': 56,
'patch': 48,
'proxy': 72,
'read': 52,
'replace': 50}
```

We can drill further and look at the interactive help for a specific attribute:

```
>>> help(v1.create_node)
```

Help on method create_node in module kubernetes.client.apis.core_v1_api:

```
create_node(self, body, **kwargs) method of kubernetes.client.apis.core_
v1_api.CoreV1Api instance
    create a Node
    This method makes a synchronous HTTP request by default.
    To make an asynchronous HTTP request, please define a
    `callback` function to be invoked when receiving the response.
    >>> def callback_function(response):
    >>>     pprint(response)
    >>>
    >>> thread = api.create_node(body, callback=callback_function)

    :param callback function: The callback function
        for asynchronous request. (optional)
    :param V1Node body: (required)
    :param str pretty: If 'true', the output is pretty printed.
    :return: V1Node
            If the method is called asynchronously,
            returns the request thread.
```

You can poke around yourself and learn more about the API. Let's look at some common operations, such as listing, creating, watching, and deleting objects.

Listing objects

You can list different kinds of object. The method names start with `list_`. Here is an example listing all namespaces:

```
>>> for ns in v1.list_namespace().items:
...     print ns.metadata.name
...
default
kube-system
```

Creating objects

To create an object, you need to pass a body parameter to the create method. The body must be a Python dictionary that is equivalent to a YAML configuration file you would use with Kubectl. The easiest way to do it is to actually use a YAML and then use the Python YAML module (not part of the standard library and must be installed separately) to read the YAML file and load it into a dictionary. For example, to create an `nginx-deployment` with 3 replicas, we can use this YAML configuration file:

```yaml
apiVersion: extensions/v1beta1
kind: Deployment
metadata:
  name: nginx-deployment
spec:
  replicas: 3
  template:
    metadata:
      labels:
        app: nginx
    spec:
      containers:
      - name: nginx
        image: nginx:1.7.9
        ports:
        - containerPort: 80
```

To install the `yaml` Python module, type this command:

```
pip install yaml
```

Then the following Python program will create the deployment:

```python
from os import path
import yaml
from kubernetes import client, config


def main():
    # Configs can be set in Configuration class directly or using
    # helper utility. If no argument provided, the config will be
    # loaded from default location.
    config.load_kube_config()

    with open(path.join(path.dirname(__file__),
                        'nginx-deployment.yaml')) as f:
        dep = yaml.load(f)
        k8s_beta = client.ExtensionsV1beta1Api()
        status = k8s_beta.create_namespaced_deployment(
            body=dep, namespace="default").status
        print("Deployment created. status='{}'".format(status))


if __name__ == '__main__':
    main()
```

Note that we used the `ExtensionsV1Beta1Api` group here because deployments are still in beta.

Watching objects

Watching objects is an advanced capability. It is implemented using a separate watch module. Here is an example to watch for `10` namespace events and print them to the screen:

```python
from kubernetes import client, config, watch

# Configs can be set in Configuration class directly or using helper
utility
config.load_kube_config()
```

```
v1 = client.CoreV1Api()
count = 10
w = watch.Watch()
for event in w.stream(v1.list_namespace, _request_timeout=60):
    print('Event: {} {}".format(event['type'], event['object'].metadata.
name))
    count -= 1
    if cont = 0:
        w.stop()


print('Done.')
```

Invoking Kubectl programmatically

If you're not a Python developer and don't want to deal with the REST API directly, you have another option. Kubectl is used mostly as an interactive command-line tool, but nothing is stopping you from automating it and invoking it through scripts and programs. There are some benefits for using Kubectl as your Kubernetes API layer:

- Easy to find examples for any usage
- Easy to experiment on the command line to find the right combination of commands and arguments
- Kubectl supports output in JSON or YAML for quick parsing
- Authentication is built-in via Kubectl configuration

Using Python subprocess to run Kubectl

I'll use Python again, so you can compare using the official Python client versus rolling your own. Python has a module called subprocess that can run external processes such as Kubectl and capture the output. Here is a Python 3 example just running Kubectl on its own and displaying the beginning of the usage output:

```
>>> import subprocess
>>> out = subprocess.check_output('kubectl').decode('utf-8')
>>> print(out[:276])
```

Kubectl controls the Kubernetes cluster manager.

Find more information at https://github.com/kubernetes/kubernetes.

Basic commands (beginner):

- `create`: Create a resource by filename or stdin
- `expose`: Take a replication controller, service, deployment or pod

The `check_checkout()` function captures the output as a bytes array that needs to be decoded to `utf-8` to display it properly. We can generalize it a little bit and create a convenience function called `k` that accepts parameters it feeds to Kubectl, and then decodes the output and returns it:

```
from subprocess import check_output


def k(*args):
    out = check_output(['kubectl'] + list(args))
    return out.decode('utf-8')
```

Let's use it to list all the running pods in the default namespace:

```
>>> print(k('get', 'po'))
```

```
NAME                                   READY  STATUS    RESTARTS  AGE
nginx-deployment-4087004473-cc461      1/1    Running   0         21m
nginx-deployment-4087004473-hkd3w      1/1    Running   0         21m
nginx-deployment-4087004473-j3kfc      1/1    Running   0         21m
```

This is nice for display, but Kubectl already does that. The real power comes when you use the structured output options with the `-o` flag. Then the result can be converted automatically to a Python object. Here is a modified version of the `k()` function that accepts a boolean `use_json` keyword argument (default to False), and if `True` adds `-o json` and then parses the JSON output to a Python object (dictionary):

```
from subprocess import check_output
import json


def k(use_json=False, *args):
    cmd = ['kubectl']

    cmd += list(args)
    if use_json:
        cmd +=  ['-o', 'json']
    out = check_output(cmd)
```

```
if use_json:
    out = json.loads(out)
else:
    out = out.decode('utf-8')
return out
```

That returns a full-fledged API object, which can be navigated and drilled down just like when accessing the REST API directly or using the official Python client:

```
result = k(use_json=True, 'get', 'po')
for r in result['items']:
    print(r['metadata']['name'])
```

```
nginx-deployment-4087004473-cc461
nginx-deployment-4087004473-hkd3w
nginx-deployment-4087004473-j3kfc
```

Let's see how to delete the deployment and wait until all the pods are gone. The Kubectl delete command doesn't accept the -o json option (although it has -o name), so let's leave out use_json:

```
k('delete', 'deployment', 'nginx-deployment')
while len(k('get', 'po', use_json=True)['items']) > 0:
    print('.')
```

```
print('Done.')
```

```
Done.
```

Extending the Kubernetes API

Kubernetes is an extremely flexible and extensible platform. It even allows you to extend its own API with new types of resources called third-party-resources. What can you do with third-party-resources? Plenty. You can use them to manage through the Kubernetes API resources that live outside the Kubernetes cluster, but your pods communicate with. By adding those external resources as third-party-resources, you get a full picture of your system and you benefit from many Kubernetes API features such as the following:

- Custom CRUD REST endpoints
- Versioning

- Watches
- Automatic integration with generic Kubernetes tooling

Other use cases for third-party-resources are metadata for custom controllers and automation programs.

Let's dive in and see what third-party-resources are all about.

Understanding the structure of a third-party-resource

In order to play nice with the Kubernetes API server, third-party-resources must conform to some basic requirements. Similar to built-in API objects, they must have the following fields:

- `metadata`: Standard Kubernetes object metadata
- `kind`: The kind of resources described by this third-party-resource
- `description`: A free text description of the resource
- `versions`: A list of the versions of the resource

The kind field requires some explanation. Kubernetes uses `CamelCase` for resource types. The kind field must be of the form `<kind name>.<domain>`. The kind name should be all lowercase with hyphens between words. Kubernetes will transform it to a `CamelCase` resource kind. For example, awesome-resource will become `AwesomeResource`.

Beyond these fields, you can add any fields you want and store arbitrary JSON to create any structure you like.

Developing third-party-resources

It's important to distinguish between the third-party-resource that you define, which is not bound to a namespace, and the actual object that you create, which is always bound to a namespace. Currently, Kubernetes doesn't support namespace-less custom objects based on third-party-resources. Here is an example of a third-party-resource:

```
apiVersion: extensions/v1beta1
kind: ThirdPartyResource
metadata:
name: cron-tab.stable.example.com
```

```
description: A pod that runs on schedule
versions:
name: v1
```

It has all the required fields: `kind`, `metadata`, `description`, and `versions`. It also has `apiVersion` field to associate it with the `extensions/v1beta1` API group.

Let's create it:

```
$ k create -f 3rd-party-resource.yaml
thirdpartyresource "cron-tab.stable.example.com" created
```

Now, let's verify we can access it:

```
$ kubectl get thirdpartyresources
NAME                         DESCRIPTION                VERSION(S)
cron-tab.stable.example.com  A pod that runs on schedule v1
```

There is also a new API endpoint for managing this new resource:

`/apis/stable.example.com/v1/namespaces/<namespace>/crontabs/`

Let's use our Python code to access it:

```
>>> config.load_kube_config()
>>> print(k('get', 'thirdpartyresources'))
NAME                         DESCRIPTION                VERSION(S)
cron-tab.stable.example.com   A pod that runs on schedule  v1
```

Integrating third party resources

Once the `ThirdPartyResource` object has been created, you can create custom objects of that resource kind, in particular, `CronTab` in this case (`CronTab` becomes CamelCase `CronTab`). `CronTab` objects can contain arbitrary fields with arbitrary JSON. In the following example, `cronSpec` and image custom fields are set on the `CronTab` object. Also, the `stable.example.com` API group is derived from the `metadata.name` of the `ThirdPartyResource`:

```
apiVersion: stable.example.com/v1
kind: CronTab
metadata:
name: new-cron-object
cronSpec: * * * * /5
image: my-awesome-cron-image
```

Let's create it:

```
$ kubectl create -f crontab.yaml
crontab "new-cron-object" created
```

At this point, kubectl can operate on CronTab objects just like it works on built-in objects. Note that resource names are case-insensitive when using kubectl:

```
$ kubectl get crontab
NAME                    LABELS       DATA
new-cron-object         <none>       {"apiVersion":"stable.example.com/
v1","cronSpec":"...
```

We can also view the raw JSON data using the standard -o json flag.:

```
$ kubectl get crontab -o json
{
    "kind": "List",
    "apiVersion": "v1",
    "metadata": {},
    "items": [
        {
            "apiVersion": "stable.example.com/v1",
            "cronSpec": "* * * /5",
            "image": "my-awesome-cron-image",
            "kind": "CronTab",
            "metadata": {
                "creationTimestamp": "2016-09-29T04:59:00Z",
                "name": "new-cron-object",
                "namespace": "default",
                "resourceVersion": "12601503",
                "selfLink": "/apis/stable.example.com/v1/namespaces/
default/crontabs/new-cron-object",
                "uid": "6f65e7a3-8601-11e6-a23e-42010af0000c"
            }
        }
    ]
}
```

Writing Kubernetes plugins

In this section, we will dive into the guts of Kubernetes and learn to take advantage of its famous flexibility and extensibility. We will learn about different aspects that can be customized via plugins and how to implement such plugins and integrate them with Kubernetes.

Writing a custom scheduler plugin

Kubernetes defines itself as a container scheduling and management system. As such, the scheduler is the most important component of Kubernetes. Kubernetes comes with a default scheduler, but allows writing of additional schedulers. To write your own custom scheduler you need to understand what the scheduler does, how it is packaged, how to deploy your custom scheduler, and how to integrate your scheduler. The scheduler source code is available here:

```
https://github.com/kubernetes/kubernetes/blob/master/plugin/pkg/
scheduler.
```

In the rest of this section, we will dive deep into the source and examine data types, algorithms, and code.

Understanding the design of the Kubernetes scheduler

The job of the scheduler is to find a node for newly created or restarted pods, and create a binding in the API server and run it there. If the scheduler can't find a suitable node for the pod it will remain in pending state.

The scheduler

Most of the work of the scheduler is pretty generic – figure out which pods need to be scheduled, update their state, and run them on the selected node. The custom part is how to map pods to nodes. The Kubernetes team recognized the need for custom scheduling and the generic scheduler can be configured with different scheduling algorithms.

The main data type is the scheduler `struct` that contains a `Config` struct with lots of properties (this will soon be replaced by a configurator interface):

```
type Scheduler struct {
    config *Config
}
```

Here is the `Config struct`:

```
type Config struct {
    SchedulerCache schedulercache.Cache
    NodeLister     algorithm.NodeLister
    Algorithm      algorithm.ScheduleAlgorithm
    Binder         Binder
    PodConditionUpdater PodConditionUpdater
    NextPod func() *v1.Pod
    Error func(*v1.Pod, error)
    Recorder record.EventRecorder
    StopEverything chan struct{}
}
```

Most of these are interfaces, so you can configure the scheduler with custom functionality. In particular, the scheduler algorithm is relevant if you want to customize pod scheduling.

Registering an algorithm provider

The scheduler has the concept of an algorithm provider and an algorithm. Together, they let you use the substantial functionality of the built-in scheduler and just replace the core scheduling algorithm.

The algorithm provider lets you register new algorithm providers with the factory. There is already one custom provider registered called `ClusterAutoScalerProvider`. We will see later how the scheduler knows which algorithm provider to use. The key file is as follows:

`/plugin/pkg/scheduler/algorithmprovider/defaults/defaults.go`

Here is the relevant part of the `init()` function, which you should extend to include your algorithm provider in addition to the default and `autoscaler` providers:

```
func init() {
    ...
    // Registers algorithm providers. By default we use
    // 'DefaultProvider', but user can specify one to be used by
    //specifying flag.
    factory.RegisterAlgorithmProvider(factory.DefaultProvider,
                                defaultPredicates(),
                                defaultPriorities())
```

```
// Cluster autoscaler friendly scheduling algorithm.
factory.RegisterAlgorithmProvider(
    ClusterAutoscalerProvider,
    defaultPredicates(),
    copyAndReplace(defaultPriorities(),
                "LeastRequestedPriority",
                "MostRequestedPriority"))
    ...
```

In addition to registering the provider, you also need to register a fit predicate and a priority function, which are used to actually perform the scheduling.

You can use the factory's `RegisterFitPredicate()` and `RegisterPriorityFunction2()` functions.

Configuring the scheduler

The scheduler algorithm is provided as part of the configuration. Custom schedulers can implement the `ScheduleAlgorithm` interface:

```
type ScheduleAlgorithm interface {
    Schedule(*v1.Pod, NodeLister) (selectedMachine string,
                                    err error)
}
```

When you run the scheduler, you can provide the name of the custom scheduler or a custom algorithm provider as a command-line argument. If none are provided, the default algorithm provider will be used. The command-line arguments to the scheduler are `--algorithm-provider` and `--scheduler-name`.

Packaging the scheduler

The custom scheduler runs as a pod inside the same Kubernetes cluster it oversees. It needs to be packaged as a container image. Let's use a copy of the standard Kubernetes scheduler for demonstration purposes. We can build Kubernetes from source and build it to get a scheduler image:

```
git clone https://github.com/kubernetes/kubernetes.git
cd kubernetes
make
```

Then find the following Docker file:

```
FROM busybox
ADD ./_output/dockerized/bin/linux/amd64/kube-scheduler \
    /usr/local/bin/kube-scheduler
```

Use it to `build` a Docker image type:

```
docker build -t custom-kube-scheduler:1.0 .
```

Finally, push the image to a container registry. I'll use DockerHub here:

```
docker push g1g1/custom-kube-scheduler
```

You'll need to create an account on DockerHub and log in before pushing your image:

```
docker login
```

Deploying the custom scheduler

Now that the scheduler image is built and available in the registry, we need to create a Kubernetes deployment for it. The scheduler is of course critical, so we can use Kubernetes itself to ensure it is always running. The following YAML file defines a deployment with a single replica and a few other bells and whistles, such as liveness and readiness probes:

```
apiVersion: extensions/v1beta1
kind: Deployment
metadata:
  labels:
    component: scheduler
    tier: control-plane
  name: custom-scheduler
  namespace: kube-system
spec:
  replicas: 1
  template:
    metadata:
      labels:
        component: scheduler
        tier: control-plane
```

```
        version: second
  spec:
    containers:
    - command:
      - /usr/local/bin/kube-scheduler
      - --address=0.0.0.0
      - --leader-elect=false
      - --scheduler-name=custom-scheduler
      image: g1g1/custom-kube-scheduler:1.0
      livenessProbe:
        httpGet:
          path: /healthz
          port: 10251
        initialDelaySeconds: 15
      name: kube-second-scheduler
      readinessProbe:
        httpGet:
          path: /healthz
          port: 10251
      resources:
        requests:
          cpu: '0.1'
```

The name of the scheduler (custom-scheduler here) is important and must be unique. It will be used later to associate pods with the scheduler to schedule them. Note that the custom scheduler belongs in the kube-system namespace.

Running another custom scheduler in the cluster

Running another custom scheduler is as simple as creating the deployment. This is the beauty of this encapsulated approach. Kubernetes is going to run a second scheduler, which is a big deal, but Kubernetes is unaware of what's going on. It just deploys a pod like any other pod, except this pod happens to be a custom scheduler:

```
$ kubectl create -f custom-scheduler.yaml
```

Let's verify that the scheduler pod is running:

```
$ kubectl get pods --namespace=kube-system
NAME                         READY     STATUS     RESTARTS    AGE
....
custom-scheduler-1nf4s-4744f  1/1       Running    0           2m
...
```

Our custom scheduler is running.

Assigning pods to the custom scheduler

OK. The custom scheduler is running alongside the default scheduler. But how does Kubernetes choose which scheduler to use when a pod needs scheduling? The answer is that the pod decides and not Kubernetes. The pod spec has an optional scheduler name field. If it's missing, the default scheduler is used; otherwise the specified scheduler is used. This is the reason custom scheduler names must be unique. The name of the default scheduler is `default-scheduler` in case you want to be explicit in your pod spec. Here is a pod definition that will be scheduled using the default scheduler:

```
apiVersion: v1
kind: Pod
metadata:
  name: some-pod
  labels:
    name: some-pod
spec:
  containers:
  - name: some-container
    image: gcr.io/google_containers/pause:2.0
```

To have the `custom-scheduler` schedule this pod, change the pod spec to the following:

```
apiVersion: v1
kind: Pod
metadata:
  name: some-pod
  labels:
    name: some-pod
```

```
spec:
  schedulername: custom-scheduler
  containers:
  - name: some-container
    image: gcr.io/google_containers/pause:2.0
```

Verifying that the pods were scheduled using custom scheduler

There are two primary ways to verify pods get scheduled by the correct scheduler. First, you can create pods that need to be scheduled by the custom scheduler before deploying the custom scheduler. The pods will remain in the pending state. Then, deploy the custom scheduler and the pending pods will be scheduled and start running.

The other method is to check the event logs and look for scheduled events using this command:

```
$ kubectl get events
```

Writing an authorization plugin

Other implementations can be developed fairly easily. The API server calls the Authorizer interface:

```
type Authorizer interface {
  Authorize(a Attributes) error
}
```

It does this to determine whether or not to allow each API action.

An authorization plugin is a module that implements this interface. The authorization plugin code goes in `pkg/auth/authorizer/$MODULENAME`.

An authorization module can be completely implemented in go, or can call out to a remote authorization service. Authorization modules can implement their own caching to reduce the cost of repeated authorization calls with the same or similar arguments. developers should then consider the interaction between caching and revocation of permissions.

Writing an admission control plugin

Admission control plugins have a major role in making Kubernetes a flexible and adaptable platform. Every request to the API (after passing authentication and authorization) goes through a chain of configured admission control plugins. If any of the plugins reject it, then the entire request is rejected. But an admission control plugin can do much more than just give a thumbs-up or down. An admission control plugin can modify incoming requests, apply defaults, modify related resources, and more.

Many of Kubernetes' advanced features rely on admission control plugins. If you run an API server without any plugins you get a very diminished Kubernetes. For Kubernetes 1.4 and up, the following list of admission control plugins is recommended:

* NamespaceLifecycle
* LimitRanger
* ServiceAccount
* DefaultStorageClass
* ResourceQuota

You can write your own admission control plugin and it must be compiled into the API server process.

You tell the Kubernetes API server which admission control plugins to use via the --admission-control flag, which you can set to a comma-delimited list of admission control plugin names:

--admission-control=NamespaceLifecycle,LimitRanger,CustomAdmission

To browse through the API server code, check out https://github.com/kubernetes/apiserver.

The admission support is in /pkg/admission.

Implementing an admission control plugin

An admission control plugin must implement the admission.Interface interface (yes, it's a little confusing that the interface name is Interface):

```
type Interface interface {
  Admit(a Attributes) (err error)
  Handles(operation Operation) bool
}
```

The interface is pretty simple. The `Admit()` function accepts an `Attributes` interface and, based on those `Attributes`, make a decision if the request should be admitted or not. If it returns `nil`, the request id is admitted. Otherwise it is rejected.

The `Handles()` function returns the operations that the admission control plugin handles. If an admission controller doesn't support an operation, it is considered admitted (for this plugin).

The whole workflow of going through the chain of registered admission control plugins and determining if an operation is admitted is just a few lines:

```
func (admissionHandler chainAdmissionHandler) Admit(a Attributes) error {
    for _, handler := range admissionHandler {
        if !handler.Handles(a.GetOperation()) {
            continue
        }
        err := handler.Admit(a)
        if err != nil {
            return err
        }
    }
    return nil
}
```

Let's look at the simplest example – the `alwaysDeny` admission control plugin. It is designed for testing and will reject any request. You can find it here:

https://github.com/kubernetes/kubernetes/tree/master/plugin/pkg/admission/deny.

The `Admit()` function always returns a `non-nil` result and `Handles()` always returns `true`, so it handles every operation and `Admit()` rejects it:

```
type alwaysDeny struct{}

func (alwaysDeny) Admit(a admission.Attributes) (err error) {
  return admission.NewForbidden(a, errors.New("Admission control is
denying all modifications"))
}

func (alwaysDeny) Handles(operation admission.Operation) bool {
  return true
```

```
}
// NewAlwaysDeny creates an always deny admission handler
func NewAlwaysDeny() admission.Interface {
  return new(alwaysDeny)
}
```

Registering an admission control plugin

Every admission control plugin has its own `init()` function, which is called when the plugin is imported. In this method you should register your plugin, so it's available. Here is the `init()` function of the `AlwaysDeny` admission control plugin:

```
func init() {
    admission.RegisterPlugin(
        "AlwaysDeny",
        func(config io.Reader) (admission.Interface, error) {
            return NewAlwaysDeny(), nil
        })
}
```

It just calls the `RegisterPlugin()` function of the admission package, passing the name of the `plugin` and a `factory` function that accepts a configuration reader and returns a plugin instance.

Linking your custom admission control plugin

Go supports only static plugins. Every custom plugin must be linked into the API server executable in order to be imported and registered. The key file is here:

https://github.com/kubernetes/kubernetes/tree/master/cmd/kube-apiserver/app/plugins.go.

Here is part of the file. When you add your plugin, it will be imported later, which will invoke its `init()` function to register the plugin:

```
package app

import (
  // Cloud providers
  _ "k8s.io/kubernetes/pkg/cloudprovider/providers"
```

```
// Admission policies
_    "k8s.io/kubernetes/plugin/pkg/admission/admit"
_    "k8s.io/kubernetes/plugin/pkg/admission/alwayspullimages"
     ...
_    "k8s.io/kubernetes/plugin/pkg/admission/serviceaccount"
)
```

Another critical file is the build file at:

https://github.com/kubernetes/kubernetes/blob/master/cmd/kube-api-server/app/BUILD.

Here is a snippet that shows some admission plugins:

```
go_library(
    name = "go_default_library",
    srcs = [
        "plugins.go",
        "server.go",
    ],
    tags = ["automanaged"],
    deps = [
    
      .
      
      .
      
      .
      
          "//plugin/pkg/admission/admit:go_default_library",
        "//plugin/pkg/admission/deny:go_default_library",
"//plugin/pkg/admission/exec:go_default_library",
  "//plugin/pkg/admission/gc:go_default_library",
  
      .
      
      .
      
      .
```

You must add a line for your admission control plugin.

Writing a custom metrics plugin

Custom metrics are implemented as custom endpoints exposed by pods, and they extend the metrics exposed by cAdvisor.

Kubernetes 1.2 adds alpha support for scaling based on application-specific metrics such as **Queries Per Second (QPS)** or average request latency. The cluster must be started with the ENABLE_CUSTOM_METRICS environment variable set to true.

Further details are available here:

https://github.com/google/cadvisor/blob/master/docs/application_ metrics.md.

Configuring the pod for custom metrics

The pods to be scaled must have cAdvisor-specific custom (aka application) metrics endpoint configured. The configuration format is described here. Kubernetes expects the configuration to be placed in definition.json mounted via a config map in / etc/custom-metrics. A sample ConfigMap may look like this:

```
apiVersion: v1
kind: ConfigMap
metadata:
  name: cm-config
data:
  definition.json: "{\"endpoint\" : \"http://localhost:8080/metrics\"}"
```

Due to the way cAdvisor currently works, localhost refers to the node itself, not to the running pod. Thus, the appropriate container in the pod must ask for a node port:

```
    ports:
    - hostPort: 8080
      containerPort: 8080
```

Specifying a target metric value

Horizontal pod auto-scaling using custom metrics is configured via an annotation. The value in the annotation is interpreted as a target metric value averaged over all running pods:

```
    annotations:
      alpha/target.custom-metrics.podautoscaler.kubernetes.io:
'{"items":[{"name":"qps", "value": "10"}]}'
```

In this case, if there are four pods running and each of them reports the qps metric to be equal to 15, HPA will start two additional pods, so there will be six pods in total. If there are multiple metrics passed in the annotation or the CPU is configured as well, then HPA will use the biggest number of replicas that come from the calculations.

Even if the target CPU utilization is not specified, a default of 80% will be used. To calculate the number of desired replicas based only on custom metrics, the CPU utilization target should be set to a very large value (for example, 100,000%). Then CPU-related logic will want only one replica, leaving the decision about a higher replica count to custom metrics (and min/max limits).

Writing a volume plugin

Volume plugins are yet another type of plugin. This time it's a Kubelet plugin. If you want to support a new type of storage, you write your own volume plugin, link it with the Kubelet, and register it. There are two flavors: persistent and non-persistent. Persistent volumes require some extra work because you need to implement additional interfaces for persistence.

Implementing a volume plugin

Volume plugins are complicated entities. If you need to implement a new volume plugin you'll have to dig in deeper as there are many details to get right. We'll just go over the pieces and interfaces here. The main interfaces are defined here:

https://github.com/kubernetes/kubernetes/blob/master/pkg/volume/plugins.go.

Here is the bare-bones VolumePlugin interface (represent non-persistent volume):

```
type VolumePlugin interface {
  Init(host VolumeHost) error
  GetPluginName() string
  GetVolumeName(spec *Spec) (string, error)
  CanSupport(spec *Spec) bool
  RequiresRemount() bool
  NewMounter(spec *Spec,
             podRef *v1.Pod,
             opts VolumeOptions) (Mounter, error)
  NewUnmounter(name string,
               podUID types.UID) (Unmounter, error)
```

```
ConstructVolumeSpec(volumeName,

                        mountPath string) (*Spec, error)
SupportsMountOption() bool
SupportsBulkVolumeVerification() bool
}
```

The various interface functions accept or return several other interfaces and data types such as `Spec`, `Mounter` and `Unmounter`.

Here is the `Spec`, which is an internal representation of an API `Volume`:

```
type Spec struct {
    Volume              *v1.Volume
    PersistentVolume    *v1.PersistentVolume
    ReadOnly            bool
}
```

There are several other interfaces that derive from the `VolumePlugin` and bestow some extra properties on the volumes they represent. Here is a list of the available interfaces:

- `PersistentVolumePlugin`
- `RecyclableVolumePlugin`
- `DeletableVolumePlugin`
- `ProvisionableVolumePlugin`
- `AttachableVolumePlugin`

Registering a volume plugin

Registering a Kubelet volume plugin is a little different again. It is done by calling `ProbeVolumePlugins()` on each plugin, which returns a list of plugins that are appended together. Here is a snippet:

```
func ProbeVolumePlugins(pluginDir string) []volume.VolumePlugin {
    allPlugins := []volume.VolumePlugin{}

    allPlugins = append(allPlugins,
                        aws_ebs.ProbeVolumePlugins()...)
    allPlugins = append(allPlugins,
                        empty_dir.ProbeVolumePlugins()...)
    allPlugins = append(allPlugins,
```

```
                    gce_pd.ProbeVolumePlugins()...)
```
.

.

.

```
  return allPlugins
}
```

Check out the complete source code here:

`https://github.com/kubernetes/kubernetes/blob/master/cmd/kubelet/app/plugins.go`.

Here is an example of the `probeVolumePlugins()` function of the `aws_elb` volume plugin:

```
func ProbeVolumePlugins() []volume.VolumePlugin {
  return []volume.VolumePlugin{&awsElasticBlockStorePlugin{nil}}
}
```

In general, multiple plugins may be returned, and not just one.

Linking a volume plugin

A custom volume plugin must be linked into the Kubelet executable. You must add a line for your custom volume plugin in the deps section to the `build` file at `https://github.com/kubernetes/kubernetes/blob/master/cmd/kubelet/app/BUILD`.

Here is a snippet from the file that shows other volume plugins:

```
go_library(
    name = "go_default_library",
    srcs = [
        "auth.go",
        "bootstrap.go",
        "plugins.go",
        "server.go",
        "server_linux.go",
    ],
    tags = ["automanaged"],
    deps = [
        "//cmd/kubelet/app/options:go_default_library",
```

```
"//pkg/api:go_default_library",

    .

    .

    .

"//pkg/volume:go_default_library",
"//pkg/volume/aws_ebs:go_default_library",
"//pkg/volume/azure_dd:go_default_library",

    .

    .

    .
```

Summary

In this chapter, we covered three major topics: working with the Kubernetes API, extending the Kubernetes API, and writing Kubernetes plugins. The Kubernetes API supports the OpenAPI spec and is a great example of REST API design that follows all current best practices. It is very consistent, well organized, and well documented. Yet it is a big API and not easy to understand. You can access the API directly via REST over HTTP, using client libraries including the official Python client, and even by invoking Kubectl.

Extending the Kubernetes API involves defining your own third-party-resources. These are most effective when you combine them with additional custom plugins or when you query and update them externally.

Plugins are a foundation of Kubernetes design, and it was always meant to be extended by users to accommodate any needs. We looked at various plugins you can write and how to register and integrate them seamlessly with Kubernetes.

At this point, you should be well aware of all the major mechanisms to extend, customize, and control Kubernetes via API access, third-party-resources, and custom plugins. You are in a great position to take advantage of these capabilities to augment the existing functionality of Kubernetes and adapt it to your needs and your systems.

In *Chapter 13, Handling the Kubernetes Package Manager*, we'll look at Helm, the Kubernetes package manager, and its charts. As you may have realized, deploying and configuring complex systems on Kubernetes is far from simple. Helm allows grouping together a bunch of manifests into a chart, which can be installed as a single unit.

13

Handling the Kubernetes Package Manager

In this chapter, we are going to look into Helm, the Kubernetes package manager. Every successful and non-trivial platform must have a good packaging system. Helm was developed by Deis (acquired by Microsoft 04/2017) and later contributed to the Kubernetes project directly. We will start by understanding the motivation for Helm, its architecture, and its components. Then, we'll get hands-on and see how to use Helm and its charts within Kubernetes. That includes finding, installing, customizing, deleting, and managing charts. Last but not least, we'll cover how to create your own charts and handle versioning, dependencies, and templating.

The topics we will cover are as follows:

- Understanding Helm
- Using Helm
- Creating your own charts

Understanding Helm

Kubernetes provides many ways to organize and orchestrate your containers at runtime, but it lacks a higher-level organization of grouping sets of images together. This is where Helm comes in. In this section, we'll go over the motivation for Helm, its architecture and components, and discuss what has changed in the transition from Helm Classic to Helm.

The motivation for Helm

Helm provides support for several important use cases:

- Managing complexity
- Easy upgrades
- Simple sharing
- Safe rollbacks

Charts can describe even the most complex apps, provide repeatable application installation, and serve as a single point of authority. In-place upgrades and custom hooks allow for easy updates. It's simple to share charts that can be versioned and hosted on public or private servers. When you need to rollback recent upgrades, Helm provides a single command to rollback a cohesive set of changes to your infrastructure.

The Helm architecture

Helm is designed to perform the following:

- Create new charts from scratch
- Package charts into chart archive (`tgz`) files
- Interact with chart repositories where charts are stored
- Install and uninstall charts into an existing Kubernetes cluster
- Manage the release cycle of charts that have been installed with Helm

Helm uses a client-server architecture to achieve these goals

Helm components

Helm has a server component that runs on your Kubernetes cluster and a client component that you run on a local machine.

The Tiller server

The server is responsible for managing releases. It interacts with the Helm clients as well as the Kubernetes API server. Its main functions are as follows:

- Listening for incoming requests from the Helm client
- Combining a chart and configuration to build a release
- Installing charts into Kubernetes

- Tracking the subsequent release
- Upgrading and uninstalling charts by interacting with Kubernetes

The Helm client

You install the Helm client on your machine. It is responsible for the following:

- Local chart development
- Managing repositories
- Interacting with the Tiller server
- Sending charts to be installed
- Asking for information about releases
- Requesting upgrades or uninstallation of existing releases

Helm versus. Helm-classic

Helm was originally developed by Deis until version 0.70. Since then, the original Helm has been branded Helm-classic. The only reason to use Helm-classic is if you already have existing charts and you're not ready to upgrade. Helm classic is available here:

```
https://github.com/helm/helm-classic.git.
```

Using Helm

Helm is a rich package management system that lets you perform all the necessary steps to manage the applications installed on your cluster. Let's roll up our sleeves and get going.

Installing Helm

Installing Helm involves installing the client and the server. Helm is implemented in Go, and the same binary executable can serve as either client or server.

Installing the Helm client

You must have Kubectl configured properly to talk to your Kubernetes cluster because the Helm client uses the Kubectl configuration to talk to the Helm server (Tiller)

Helm provides binary releases for all platforms here:

https://github.com/kubernetes/helm/releases/latest.

For Windows, it is your only option.

For Mac OSX and Linux, you can install the client from a script:

```
$ curl https://raw.githubusercontent.com/kubernetes/helm/master/scripts/
get > get_helm.sh
$ chmod 700 get_helm.sh
$ ./get_helm.sh
```

On Mac OSX, you can also use Homebrew:

```
brew install kubernetes-helm
```

Installing the Tiller server

Tiller typically runs inside your cluster. For development, it is sometimes easier to run Tiller locally.

Installing Tiller in-cluster

The easiest way to install Tiller is from a machine where the Helm client is installed. Run the following command: `helm init`.

This will initialize both the client as well as the Tiller server on the remote Kubernetes cluster. When the installation is done, you will have a running Tiller pod in the `kube-system` namespace of your cluster:

```
$ kubectl get po --namespace=kube-system -l name=tiller
NAME                          READY  STATUS    RESTARTS   AGE
tiller-deploy-3210613906-2j5sh 1/1   Running   0          1m
```

You can also run `helm version` to check out both the client's and the server's version:

```
$ helm version
Client: &version.Version{SemVer:"v2.2.3", GitCommit:"1402a4d6ec9fb349e17b
912e32fe259ca21181e3", GitTreeState:"clean"}
Server: &version.Version{SemVer:"v2.2.3", GitCommit:"1402a4d6ec9fb349e17b
912e32fe259ca21181e3", GitTreeState:"clean"}
```

Installing Tiller locally

If you want to run Tiller locally, you need to build it first. This is supported on Linux and Mac OSX:

```
$ cd $GOPATH
$ mkdir -p src/k8s.io
$ cd src/k8s.io
$ git clone https://github.com/kubernetes/helm.git
$ cd helm
$ make bootstrap build
```

The bootstrap target will attempt to install dependencies, rebuild the vendor/ tree, and validate configuration.

The build target will compile Helm and place it in bin/helm. Tiller is also compiled, and is placed in bin/tiller.

Now you can just run bin/tiller. Tiller will connect to the Kubernetes cluster via your Kubectl configuration.

You need to tell the Helm client to connect to the local Tiller server. You can do it by setting an environment variable:

```
$ export HELM_HOST=localhost:44134
```

Or you can pass it as a command-line argument, --host localhost:44134.

Finding charts

In order to install useful applications and software with Helm, you need to find their charts first. This is where the helm search command comes in. Helm, by default, searches the official Kubernetes chart repository, which is called stable:

```
$ helm search
```

NAME	VERSION	DESCRIPTION
stable/chaoskube random pods in you...	0.5.0	Chaoskube periodically kills
stable/cockroachdb survivable, strongly...	0.2.2	CockroachDB is a scalable,
stable/dokuwiki compliant, simple to us...	0.1.3	DokuWiki is a standards-
stable/jenkins integration server. It s...	0.3.1	Open source continuous

```
stable/kapacitor               0.2.2   InfluxDB's native data processing
engine. It ca...

stable/kube-lego               0.1.8   Automatically requests
certificates from Let's ...

stable/kube-ops-view           0.2.0   Kubernetes Operational View -
read-only system ...

stable/kube2iam                0.2.1   Provide IAM credentials to pods
based on annota...
```

The official `repository` has a rich library of charts that represent all modern open source databases, monitoring systems, Kubernetes-specific helpers, and a slew of other offerings, such as a Minecraft server. You can search for specific charts. For example, let's search for charts that contain `kube` in their name or description:

```
$ helm search kube

NAME                     VERSION DESCRIPTION

stable/chaoskube         0.5.0   Chaoskube periodically kills random pods
in you...

stable/kube-lego         0.1.8   Automatically requests certificates from
Let's ...

stable/kube-ops-view     0.2.0   Kubernetes Operational View - read-only
system ...

stable/kube2iam          0.2.1   Provide IAM credentials to pods based on
annota...

stable/sumokube          0.1.1   Sumologic Log Collector

stable/etcd-operator     0.2.0   CoreOS etcd-operator Helm chart for
Kubernetes

stable/nginx-lego        0.2.1   Chart for nginx-ingress-controller and
kube-lego

stable/openvpn           1.0.1   A Helm chart to install an openvpn server
insid...

stable/spartakus         1.1.1   Collect information about Kubernetes
clusters t...

stable/traefik           1.1.2-h A Traefik based Kubernetes ingress
controller w...

Let's try another search:

$ helm search mysql

NAME            VERSION DESCRIPTION

stable/mysql    0.2.5   Fast, reliable, scalable, and easy to use open-
...

stable/mariadb  0.5.14  Fast, reliable, scalable, and easy to use open-
...
```

What happened? Why does `mariadb` show up in the results? The reason is that `mariadb` (which is a fork of MySQL) mentions MySQL in its description, even though you can't see it in the truncated output. To get the full description, use the `helm inspect` command:

```
$ helm inspect stable/mariadb
description: Fast, reliable, scalable, and easy to use open-source
relational database
   system. MariaDB Server is intended for mission-critical, heavy-load
production systems
   as well as for embedding into mass-deployed software.
engine: gotpl
home: https://mariadb.org
icon: https://bitnami.com/assets/stacks/mariadb/img/mariadb-stack-
220x234.png
keywords:
- mariadb
- mysql
- database
- sql
maintainers:
- email: containers@bitnami.com
   name: Bitnami
name: mariadb
sources:
- https://github.com/bitnami/bitnami-docker-mariadb
version: 0.5.14
```

Installing packages

OK. You've found the package of your dreams. Now, you probably want to install it on your Kubernetes cluster. When you install a package, Helm creates a release that you can use to keep track of the installation progress. Let's install MariaDB using the `helm install` command. Let's go over the output in detail. The first part of the output lists the name of the release - `alert-panda` in this case (you can choose your own with the `--name` flag), the namespace, and the deployment status:

```
$ helm install stable/mariadb
NAME:   alert-panda
LAST DEPLOYED: Sat Apr  1 18:39:47 2017
NAMESPACE: default
STATUS: DEPLOYED
```

The second part of the output lists all the resources created by this chart. Note that the resource names are all derived from the release name.

RESOURCES:

```
==> v1/PersistentVolumeClaim
NAME                 STATUS    VOLUME   CAPACITY   ACCESSMODES   AGE
alert-panda-mariadb  Pending                                     1s


==> v1/Service
NAME                 CLUSTER-IP      EXTERNAL-IP   PORT(S)    AGE
alert-panda-mariadb  10.3.245.245    <none>        3306/TCP   1s


==> extensions/v1beta1/Deployment
NAME                 DESIRED   CURRENT   UP-TO-DATE   AVAILABLE   AGE
alert-panda-mariadb  1         1         1            0           1s


==> v1/Secret
NAME                 TYPE      DATA   AGE
alert-panda-mariadb  Opaque    2      1s


==> v1/ConfigMap
NAME                 DATA   AGE
alert-panda-mariadb  1      1s
```

The last part is notes that provide easy to understand instructions on how to use `MariaDB` in the content of your Kubernetes cluster.

NOTES:

```
MariaDB can be accessed via port 3306 on the following DNS name from
within your cluster:
alert-panda-mariadb.default.svc.cluster.local
```

To connect to your database:

1. Run a pod that you can use as a client:

   ```
   kubectl run alert-panda-mariadb-client --rm --tty -i --image
   bitnami/mariadb --command -- bash
   ```

2. Connect using the `mysql cli`, then provide your password:

   ```
   $ mysql -h alert-panda-mariadb
   ```

Checking installation status

Helm doesn't wait for the installation to complete because it may take a while. The `helm status` command displays the latest information on a release in the same format as the output of the initial `helm install` command. In the output of the `install` command you can see that the persistent volume claim had a pending status. Let's check it out now:

```
$ helm status alert-panda | grep Persist -A 3
==> v1/PersistentVolumeClaim

NAME                   STATUS VOLUME       CAPACITY ACCESSMODES  AGE
alert-panda-mariadb    Bound  pvc-41...0156 8Gi          RWO      10m
```

Hooray! It is bound now, and there is a volume attached with 8 GB capacity.

Let's try to connect and verify `mariadb` is indeed accessible. Let's modify the suggested commands a little bit from the notes to connect. Instead of running `bash` and then running `mysql`, we can directly run the `mysql` command on the container:

```
$ kubectl run alert-panda-mariadb-client --rm --tty -i --image bitnami/
mariadb --command -- mysql -h al

ert-panda-mariadb
```

If you don't see a command prompt, try pressing *enter*.

```
MariaDB [(none)]> show databases;
+--------------------+
| Database           |
+--------------------+
| information_schema |
| mysql              |
| performance_schema |
+--------------------+
3 rows in set (0.00 sec)
```

Customizing a chart

Very often as a user, you want to customize or configure the charts you install. Helm fully supports customization via config files. To learn about possible customizations you can use the `helm inspect` command again, but this time focus on the values. Here is a partial output:

```
$ helm inspect values stable/mariadb
## Bitnami MariaDB image version
```

```
## ref: https://hub.docker.com/r/bitnami/mariadb/tags/
##
## Default: none
image: bitnami/mariadb:10.1.22-r1


## Specify an imagePullPolicy (Required)
## It's recommended to change this to 'Always' if the image tag is
'latest'
## ref: http://kubernetes.io/docs/user-guide/images/#updating-images
imagePullPolicy: IfNotPresent


## Specify password for root user
## ref: https://github.com/bitnami/bitnami-docker-mariadb/blob/master/
README.md#setting-the-root-password-on-first-run
##
# mariadbRootPassword:


## Create a database user
## ref: https://github.com/bitnami/bitnami-docker-mariadb/blob/master/
README.md#creating-a-database-user-on-first-run
##
# mariadbUser:
# mariadbPassword:


## Create a database
## ref: https://github.com/bitnami/bitnami-docker-mariadb/blob/master/
README.md#creating-a-database-on-first-run
##
# mariadbDatabase:
```

For example, if you want to set a `root` password and create a database when installing `mariadb`, you can create the following YAML file and save it as `mariadb-config.yaml`:

```
mariadbRootPassword: supersecret
mariadbDatabase: awesome_stuff
```

Then, run `helm` and pass it the `yaml` file:

```
helm install -f config.yaml stable/mariadb
```

You can also set individual values on the command line with `--set`. If both `--f` and `--set` try to set the same values, then `--set` takes precedence. For example, in this case the `root` password will be `evenbettersecret`:

```
helm install -f config.yaml --set mariadbRootPassword=evenbettersecret
stable/mariadb
```

You can specify multiple values using comma-separated lists: `--set a=1,b=2`.

Additional installation options

The `helm install` command can install from several sources:

- A `chart repository` (as we've seen)
- A local chart archive (`helm install foo-0.1.1.tgz`)
- An unpacked `chart` directory (`helm install path/to/foo`)
- A full URL (`helm install https://example.com/charts/foo-1.2.3.tgz`)

Upgrading and rolling back a release

You may want to upgrade a package you installed to the latest and greatest version. Helm provide the `upgrade` command, which operates intelligently and only updates things that have changed. For example, let's check the current values of our `mariadb` installation:

```
$ helm get values alert-panda

mariadbDatabase: awesome_stuff

mariadbRootPassword: evenbettersecret
```

Now, let's run, `upgrade`, and change the name of the database:

```
$ helm upgrade alert-panda --set mariadbDatabase=awesome_sauce stable/
mariadb
$ helm get values alert-panda

mariadbDatabase: awesome_sauce
```

Note that we've lost our `root` password. All the existing values are replaced when you upgrade. OK, let's roll back. The `helm history` command shows us all the available revisions we can roll back to:

```
$ helm history alert-panda

REVISION STATUS        CHART          DESCRIPTION

1        SUPERSEDED    mariadb-0.5.14  Install complete

2        SUPERSEDED    mariadb-0.5.14  Upgrade complete

3        SUPERSEDED    mariadb-0.5.14  Upgrade complete

4        DEPLOYED      mariadb-0.5.14  Upgrade complete
```

Let's roll back to revision 3:

```
$ helm rollback alert-panda 3
Rollback was a success! Happy Helming!
```

```
$ helm history alert-panda
REVISION STATUS        CHART          DESCRIPTION
1        SUPERSEDED    mariadb-0.5.14  Install complete
2        SUPERSEDED    mariadb-0.5.14  Upgrade complete
3        SUPERSEDED    mariadb-0.5.14  Upgrade complete
4        SUPERSEDED    mariadb-0.5.14  Upgrade complete
5        DEPLOYED      mariadb-0.5.14  Rollback to 3
```

Let's verify our changes were rolled back:

```
$ helm get values alert-panda
mariadbDatabase: awesome_stuff
mariadbRootPassword: evenbettersecret
```

Deleting a release

You can, of course, delete a release too using the `helm delete` command.

First, let's examine the list of releases. We have only `alert-panda`:

```
$ helm list
NAME           REVISION  STATUS    CHART           NAMESPACE
alert-panda    5         DEPLOYED  mariadb-0.5.14  default
Now, let's delete it:
```

```
$ helm delete alert-panda
So, no more releases:
$ helm list
```

But Helm keeps track of deleted releases too. You can see them using the `--all` flag:

```
$ helm list --all
NAME            REVISION  STATUS   CHART           NAMESPACE
alert-panda 5             DELETED  mariadb-0.5.14  default
```

Working with repositories

Helm stores charts in repositories that are simple HTTP servers. Any standard HTTP server can host a `Helm` repository. In the cloud, the Helm team verified that AWS S3 and Google Cloud storage can both serve as Helm repositories in web-enabled mode. Helm also comes bundled with a local package server for developer testing. It runs on the client machine, so it's inappropriate for sharing. In a small team, you may run the Helm package server on a shared machine on the local network accessible to all team members.

To use the local package server, type `helm serve`. Do it in a separate terminal window because it is blocking. Helm will start serving charts from `~/.helm/repository/local` by default. You can put your charts there and generate an index file with `helm index`.

The generated `index.yaml` file lists all the charts.

Note that Helm doesn't provide tools for uploading charts to remote repositories because that would require the remote server to understand Helm, to know where to put the chart, and how to update the `index.yaml` file.

On the client side the `helm repo` command lets you list, `add`, `remove`, `index`, and `update`:

```
$ helm repo
```

This command consists of multiple subcommands to interact with `chart` repositories.

It can be used to add, remove, list, and index chart repositories:

- Example usage:
    ```
    $ helm repo add [NAME] [REPO_URL]
    ```
- Usage:
    ```
    helm repo [command]
    ```

Available commands:

add	add a chart repository
index	generate an index file for a given a directory
list	list chart repositories
remove	remove a chart repository
update	update information on available charts

Managing charts with Helm

Helm provides several commands to manage charts.

It can create a new chart for you:

```
$ helm create cool-chart
Creating cool-chart
```

Helm will create the following files and directories under `cool-chart`:

```
-rw-r--r-- 1 Gigi 333 Apr  2 15:25 .helmignore
-rw-r--r-- 1 Gigi  88 Apr  2 15:25 Chart.yaml
drwxr-xr-x 1 Gigi   0 Apr  2 15:25 charts/
drwxr-xr-x 1 Gigi   0 Apr  2 15:25 templates/
-rw-r--r-- 1 Gigi 381 Apr  2 15:25 values.yaml
```

Once you have edited your chart, you can package it into a tar `gzipped` archive:

```
$ helm package cool-chart
```

Helm will create an archive called `cool-chart-0.1.0.tgz` and store both in the `local` directory and in the `local` repository.

You can also use `helm` to help you find issues with your chart's formatting or information:

```
$ helm lint cool-chart
$ helm lint cool-chart
==> Linting cool-chart
[INFO] Chart.yaml: icon is recommended

1 chart(s) linted, no failures
```

Taking advantage of starter packs

The `helm create` command takes an optional `--starter` flag that lets you specify a starter chart.

Starters are just regular charts located in `$HELM_HOME/starters`. As a chart developer, you may author charts that are specifically designed to be used as starters. Such charts should be designed with the following considerations in mind:

- The `Chart.yaml` will be overwritten by the generator
- Users will expect to modify such a chart's contents, so documentation should indicate how users can do so

Currently, the only way to add a chart to `$HELM_HOME/starters` is to manually copy it there. In your chart's documentation, you may want to explain that process.

Creating your own charts

A chart is a collection of files that describe a related set of Kubernetes resources. A single chart might be used to deploy something simple, such as a `memcached` pod, or something complex, such as a full web app stack with HTTP servers, databases, caches, and so on.

Charts are created as files laid out in a particular directory tree. Then they can be packaged into versioned archives to be deployed. The key file is `Chart.yaml`.

The Chart.yaml file

The `Chart.yaml` file is required for a chart. It requires a name and version fields:

- `Name`: The name of the chart (same as the directory name)
- `Version`: A `SemVer 2` version

It may also contain various optional fields:

- `description`: A single sentence description of this project keywords:

A list of keywords about this project:

- `home`: The URL of this project's home page
- `sources`: A list of URLs to source code for this project

- **Maintainers**:
    - ○ `name`: The maintainer's name (required for each maintainer)
    - ○ `email`: The maintainer's e-mail (optional for each maintainer)
- `engine`: The name of the template engine (defaults to `gotpl`)
- `icon`: A URL to an SVG or PNG image to be used as an icon
- `appVersion`: The version of the app that this contains
- `deprecated`: is this chart is deprecated? (boolean)

Versioning charts

The `version` field inside of the `Chart.yaml` is used by many of the Helm tools, including the CLI and the Tiller server. When generating a package, the `helm package` command will use the version that it finds in the `Chart.yaml` as a token in the package name. The system assumes that the version number in the chart package name matches the version number in the `Chart.yaml`. Failure to meet this assumption will cause an error.

The appVersion field

The `appVersion` field is not related to the version field. It is not used by Helm and serves as metadata or documentation for users that want to understand what they are deploying. Correctness is not enforced by Helm.

Deprecating charts

When managing charts in a `chart repository`, it is sometimes necessary to deprecate a chart. The optional deprecated field in `Chart.yaml` can be used to mark a chart as deprecated. If the latest version of a chart in the repository is marked as deprecated, then the chart as a whole is considered deprecated. The chart name can later be reused by publishing a newer version that is not marked as deprecated. The workflow for deprecating charts, as followed by the `kubernetes/` charts project, is as follows:

Update the chart's `Chart.yaml` to mark the chart as deprecated, bumping the version

- Release the new chart version in the `chart repository`
- Remove the chart from the `source repository` (for example, Git)

Chart metadata files

Charts contain various metadata files that describe the installation, configuration, usage, and license of a chart. A README for a chart should be formatted in markdown (README.md), and should generally contain the following:

- A description of the application or service the chart provides

- Any prerequisites or requirements to run the chart

- Descriptions of options in values.yaml and default values

- Any other information that may be relevant to the installation or configuration of the chart

The chart can also contain a short plain text templates/NOTES.txt file that will be printed out after installation, and when viewing the status of a release. This file is evaluated as a template, and can be used to display usage notes, next steps, or any other information relevant to a release of the chart. For example, instructions could be provided for connecting to a database, or accessing a web UI. Since this file is printed to STDOUT when running helm install or helm status, it is recommended to keep the content brief and point to the README for greater detail.

Managing chart dependencies

In Helm, a chart may depend on any number of other charts. These dependencies are expressed explicitly by copying the dependency charts into the charts/ sub-directory during installation.

A dependency can be either a chart archive (foo-1.2.3.tgz) or an unpacked chart directory. But its name cannot start with _ or .. Such files are ignored by the chart loader.

Managing dependencies with requirements.yaml

Instead of manually placing charts in the charts/ sub-directory, it is better to declare dependencies using a requirements.yaml file inside of your chart.

A requirements.yaml file is a simple file for listing the chart dependencies:

```
dependencies:
  - name: foo
    version: 1.2.3
    repository: http://example.com/charts
  - name: bar
```

```
version: 3.2.1
repository: http://another.example.com/charts
```

The name field is the name of the chart you want.

The version field is the version of the chart you want.

The repository field is the full URL to the chart repository. Note that you must also use helm repo add to add that repository locally.

Once you have a dependencies file, you can run the Helm dependency update and it will use your dependency file to download all of the specified charts into the charts sub-directory for you:

```
$ helm dep up foo-chart
Hang tight while we grab the latest from your chart repositories...
...Successfully got an update from the "local" chart repository
...Successfully got an update from the "stable" chart repository
...Successfully got an update from the "example" chart repository
...Successfully got an update from the "another" chart repository
Update Complete. Happy Helming!
Saving 2 charts
```

Downloading Foo from repo http://example.com/charts

Downloading Bar from repo http://another.example.com/charts

When the Helm dependency update retrieves charts, it will store them as chart archives in the charts/ directory. So for the preceding example, one would expect to see the following files in the charts directory:

```
charts/
  foo-1.2.3.tgz
  bar-3.2.1.tgz
```

Managing charts with requirements.yaml is a good way to easily keep charts updated, and also share requirements information throughout a team.

Utilizing special fields in requirements.yaml

In addition to the other fields, each requirements entry may contain the optional fields tags and condition.

All charts are loaded by default. If tags or condition fields are present, they will be evaluated and used to control loading for the charts they are applied to:

Condition - The `condition` field holds one or more YAML paths (delimited by commas). If this path exists in the top parent's values and resolves to a boolean value, the chart will be enabled or disabled based on that boolean value. Only the first valid path found in the list is evaluated, and if no paths exist then the condition has no effect.

Tags - The `tags` field is a YAML list of labels to associate with this chart. In the top parent's values, all charts with tags can be enabled or disabled by specifying the tag and a boolean value.

Here is an example `requirements.yaml` and `values.yaml` that make good use of conditions and tags to enable and disable the installation of dependencies. The `requirements.yaml` file defines two conditions for installing its dependencies based on the value of the `global enabled` field and the specific `sub-charts enabled` field:

```
# parentchart/requirements.yaml

dependencies:
    - name: subchart1
      repository: http://localhost:10191
      version: 0.1.0
      condition: subchart1.enabled, global.subchart1.enabled
      tags:
        - front-end
        - subchart1
    - name: subchart2
      repository: http://localhost:10191
      version: 0.1.0
      condition: subchart2.enabled,global.subchart2.enabled
      tags:
        - back-end
        - subchart2
```

The `values.yaml` file assigns values to some of the condition variables. The `subchart2` tag doesn't get a value, so it is considered enabled:

```
# parentchart/values.yaml
subchart1:
  enabled: true
tags:
  front-end: false
  back-end: true
```

You can set tag and conditions values from the command line too when installing a chart, and they'll take precedence over the `values.yaml` file:

```
helm install --set subchart2.enabled=false
```

The resolution of tags and conditions is as follows:

- Conditions (when set in values) always override tags. The first condition path that exists wins and subsequent ones for that chart are ignored.
- Tags are evaluated as if any of the chart's tags are `true` then enable the chart.
- Tags and condition values must be set in the top parent's values.
- The tags: key-in values must be a top-level key. Globals and nested tags tables are not currently supported

Using templates and values

Any non-trivial application will require configuration and adaptation to the specific use case. Helm charts are templates that use the Go template language to populate placeholders. Helm supports additional functions from the `Sprig` library and a few other specialized functions. The template files are stored in the `templates/` sub-directory of the chart. Helm will use the template engine to render all files in this directory and apply the provided value files.

Writing template files

Template files are just text files that follow the Go template language rules. They can generate Kubernetes configuration files. Here is the service template file from the Gitlab CE chart:

```
apiVersion: v1
kind: Service
metadata:
```

```
  name: {{ template "fullname" . }}
  labels:
    app: {{ template "fullname" . }}
    chart: "{{ .Chart.Name }}-{{ .Chart.Version }}"
    release: "{{ .Release.Name }}"
    heritage: "{{ .Release.Service }}"
spec:
  type: {{ .Values.serviceType }}
  ports:
  - name: ssh
    port: {{ .Values.sshPort | int }}
    targetPort: ssh
  - name: http
    port: {{ .Values.httpPort | int }}
    targetPort: http
  - name: https
    port: {{ .Values.httpsPort | int }}
    targetPort: https
  selector:
    app: {{ template "fullname" . }}
```

Using pipelines and functions

Helm allows rich and sophisticated syntax in the template files via the built-in Go template functions, sprig functions, and pipelines. Here is an example template that takes advantage of these capabilities. It uses the repeat, quote, and upper functions for the food and drink keys, and it uses pipelines to chain multiple functions together:

```
apiVersion: v1
kind: ConfigMap
metadata:
  name: {{ .Release.Name }}-configmap
data:
  greeting: "Hello World"
  drink: {{ .Values.favorite.drink | repeat 3 | quote }}
  food: {{ .Values.favorite.food | upper | quote }}
```

See if the values file has the following section:

```
favorite:
  drink: coffee
  food pizza
```

If it does, then the resulting chart would be as follows:

```
apiVersion: v1
kind: ConfigMap
metadata:
  name: cool-app-configmap
data:
  greeting: "Hello World"
  drink: "coffeecoffeecoffee"
  food: "PIZZA"
```

Embedding predefined values

Helm provides some predefined values you can use in your templates. In the Gitlab chart above the `Release.Name`, `Release.Service`, `Chart.Name`, and `Chart.Version` are examples of Helm predefined values. Other predefined values are as follows:

- `Release.Time`
- `Release.Namespace`
- `Release.IsUpgrade`
- `Release.IsInstall`
- `Release.Revision`
- `Chart`
- `Files`
- `Capabilities`

The Chart is the content of `Chart.yaml`. The files and capabilities predefined values are `map-like` objects that allow access via various functions. Note that unknown fields in `Chart.yaml` are ignored by the template engine and cannot be used to `pass` arbitrary structured data to templates.

Feeding values from a file

Here is part of the Gitlab CE default values file. The values from this file are used to populate multiple templates. For example, the serviceType, sshPort, httpPort, and httpsPort values are used in the preceding service template:

```
image: gitlab/gitlab-ce:9.0.0-ce.0
serviceType: LoadBalancer
sshPort: 22
httpPort: 80
httpsPort: 443


resources:
  requests:
    memory: 1Gi
    cpu: 500m
  limits:
    memory: 2Gi
    cpu: 1
```

You can provide your own YAML values files to override the defaults during the install command:

```
$ helm install --values=custom-values.yaml gitlab-ce
```

Scope, dependencies, and values

Value files can declare values for the top-level chart, as well as for any of the charts that are included in that chart's charts/ directory. For example, the gitlab-ce values.yaml file contains some default values for its dependency charts, postgresql and redis:

```
postgresql:
  imageTag: "9.6"
  cpu: 1000m
  memory: 1Gi
  postgresUser: gitlab
  postgresPassword: gitlab
  postgresDatabase: gitlab
  persistence:
    size: 10Gi
```

```
redis:
  redisPassword: "gitlab"
  resources:
    requests:
      memory: 1Gi

  persistence:
    size: 10Gi
```

The top-level chart has access to values of its dependent charts, but not vice versa. There is also a global value that is accessible to all charts. For example, you could add something like this:

```
global:
  app: cool-app
```

When a global is present, it will be replicated to each dependent chart's values as follows:

```
global:
  app: cool-app

postgresql:
  global:
    app: cool-app
  ...
redis:
  global:
    app: cool-app
  ...
```

Summary

In this chapter, we took a look at Helm, the Kubernetes package manager. Helm gives Kubernetes the ability to manage complicated software composed of many Kubernetes resources with inter-dependencies. It serves the same purpose as an OS package manager. It organizes packages and lets you search charts, install and upgrade charts, and share charts with collaborators. You can develop your charts and store them in repositories.

At this point, you should understand the important role that Helm serves in the Kubernetes ecosystem and community. You should be able to use it productively and even develop and share your own charts.

In *Chapter 14*, *The Future of Kubernetes*, we will look ahead to the future of Kubernetes and examine its roadmap and a few personal items from my wish list.

The Future of Kubernetes

In this chapter, we look at the future of Kubernetes from multiple angles. We'll start with the roadmap and forth coming product features, including diving into the design process of Kubernetes. Then we'll cover the momentum of Kubernetes since its inception, including dimensions such as community, ecosystem, and mindshare. A big part of Kubernetes' future will be determined by how it fares against its competition. Education will play a major role too as container orchestration is new, fast-moving, and not a well-understood domain. Then, we'll discuss a capability at the top of my wish list – dynamic plugins.

The covered topics are as follows:

- The road ahead
- Competition
- The Kubernetes momentum
- Education and training
- Dynamic plugins

The road ahead

Kubernetes is a large open source project. Let's look at some of the planned features and upcoming releases, as well the various special interest groups that focus on specific areas.

Kubernetes releases and milestones

Kubernetes has fairly regular releases. The current release as of April 2017 is 1.6.1. The next release 1.7 is about 22% done. Here are a couple of issues from the 1.7 releases to give you a taste of the work being done:

- WIP group the `KubeletConfiguration` parameters into substructures
- Mark Kubelet's `master-service-namespace` flag as deprecated
- Remove the `deprecated --babysit-daemons kubelet` flag
- Clean up the `pre-ControllerRef` compatibility logic
- Use `Watch()` for `VerifyControllerAttachedVolume` instead of a single poll

Minor releases are released every three months, and patch releases plug holes and issues until the next minor release. Here the release dates of the three most recent releases:

- 1.6.0 released on March 29, 2017, and 1.6.1 released on April, 2 2017
- 1.5.0 released on Dec 12, 2016, and 1.5.6 released on March, 29 2017
- 1.4.0 released on Sep 26, 2016, and 1.4.9 released on Feb 15, 2017

Another good way to look at what is coming is to look at the work being done on the alpha and beta releases. You can check the changelog here:

`https://github.com/kubernetes/kubernetes/blob/master/CHANGELOG.md`.

Here are some of the changes in the 1.7 alpha release:

- Juju: Enable GPU mode if GPU hardware detected
- Check the error before parsing the `apiversion`
- `get-kube-local.sh` checks pods with the `--namespace=kube-system` option
- Use `http2` in `kubeapi-load-balancer` to fix `kubectl exec` uses
- Support `status.hostIP` in downward API

Kubernetes special interest and working groups

As a large open source community project, most of the development work on Kubernetes takes place in multiple working groups. The complete list is here:

`https://github.com/kubernetes/community/blob/master/sig-list.md`.

The planning for future releases is done mostly within these SIG and working groups because Kubernetes is too big to handle it all centrally. SIGs meet regularly and discuss.

Competition

Kubernetes operates in one of the hottest technology areas of container orchestration. The future of Kubernetes must be considered as part of the whole market. As you will see, some of the possible competitors may also be partners that promote both their own offering as well as Kubernetes (or at least, Kubernetes can run on their platform).

The value of bundling

Container orchestration platforms such as Kubernetes compete directly and indirectly with larger and smaller scopes. For example, Kubernetes may be available on a particular Cloud platform, such as AWS, but may not be the `default/go-to` solution. On the other hand, Kubernetes is at the core of GKE on the Google Cloud platform. Developers who choose a higher level of abstraction, such as a Cloud platform or even PaaS, will more often than not go with the default solution. But some developers or organizations worry about vendor lock-in, or need to run on multiple Cloud platforms or a hybrid public/private. Kubernetes has a strong advantage here.

Docker Swarm

Docker is currently the de facto standard for containers (although CoreOS rkt is gathering steam) and often people say Docker when they mean containers. Docker wants to get a piece of the orchestration cake and released the Docker Swarm product. The main benefit of Docker Swarm is that it comes as part of the Docker installation and uses standard Docker APIs. So, the learning curve is not as steep and it's easier to get started. However, Docker Swarm is way behind Kubernetes in terms of capabilities and maturity. In addition, Docker's reputation is not great when it comes to high-quality engineering and security. Organizations and developers that are concerned with the stability of their systems may shy away from Docker Swarm. Docker is aware of the problem and is taking steps to address it. It released an Enterprise offering and also reworked Docker's internals as a set of independent components via the Moby project.

Mesos/Mesosphere

Mesosphere the company behind the open source Apache Mesos, and the DC/OS product is the incumbent that runs containers and big data in the Cloud. The technology is mature and Mesosphere evolves it, but they don't have the resources and momentum that Kubernetes has. I believe that Mesosphere will do very well because it is a big market, but it will not threaten Kubernetes as the number one container orchestration solution.

Cloud platforms

A large contingent of organizations and developers flock to public Cloud platforms to avoid the headaches of low-level management of their infrastructure. Those companies' primary motivation is often to move fast and focus on their core competency. As such, they'll often go with the default deployment solution offered by their Cloud provider, because the integration is the most seamless and streamlined.

AWS

Kubernetes runs very well on AWS via the official Kubernetes Kops project:

`https://github.com/kubernetes/kops`.

Some of Kops features are as follows:

- Automate the provisioning of Kubernetes clusters in AWS
- Deploy highly available Kubernetes masters
- The ability to generate Terraform configurations

However, Kops is not an official AWS solution. If you manage your infrastructure through the AWS console and APIs, the path of least resistance is to use AWS **Elastic Container Service (ECS)** – a `built-in` container orchestration solution that is not based on Kubernetes.

I'm just speculating here, but in my opinion it's unlikely that AWS will switch to Kubernetes as an underlying container orchestration platform because they have their own solution, tightly-integrated with other AWS services, such as load balancing, and they have the developers to maintain and evolve it. For companies that have made an explicit decision to run their application only on AWS it will probably make sense to use the `built-in AWS` container solution. However, as usual, when hybrid Cloud or avoiding vendor lock-in become decision factors, then Kubernetes shines again. Even Netflix, which used to be exclusively on AWS, now runs some workloads on other Cloud platforms.

Azure

Azure provides the Azure container service, and they don't pick favorites. You can choose if you want to use Kubernetes, Docker Swarm, or DC/OS. This is interesting because, initially, Azure was based on Mesosphere DC/OS and they added Kubernetes and Docker Swarm as orchestration options later. As Kubernetes pulls forward in capabilities, maturity, and mindshare, I believe it will become the number one orchestration option on Azure too.

Alibaba Cloud

The Alibaba Cloud is the Chinese AWS in more ways than one. Their APIs are intentionally very much like AWS APIs. Alibaba Cloud provides a container management service based on Docker Swarm. I've deployed some applications at a small scale on Alibaba Cloud, and they seem to be able to keep up with the changes in the field and quickly follow the big players. I'm not going to make any predictions on whether or not they'll adopt Kubernetes officially.

The Kubernetes momentum

Kubernetes has tremendous momentum behind it. The community is super strong. Users flock to Kubernetes as its mindshare increases, the technical press acknowledges its number one leadership position, the eco-system is sizzling, and a lot of big corporations and companies (in addition to Google) support it.

Community

The Kubernetes community is one of its greatest assets. Kubernetes recently joined the CNCF.

GitHub

Kubernetes is developed on GitHub and is one of the top projects on GitHub. It is in the top 0.01 percent in stars and number one in terms of activity.

More professionals list Kubernetes in their LinkedIn profile than any other comparable offering by a wide margin.

More than 1,000 contributors and 34,000 commits:

Conferences and meetups

Another indication of Kubernetes momentum is the number of conferences, meetups, and attendees. KubeCon is growing quickly and new Kubernetes meetups open up every day.

Mindshare

Kubernetes is getting a lot of attention and deployments. Large and small companies that get into the containers/DevOps/microservices arena adopt Kubernetes and the trend is clear. One interesting metric is the number of StackOverflow questions over time. The community steps in to answer questions and foster collaboration. The growth dwarfs its rivals and the trend is very clear:

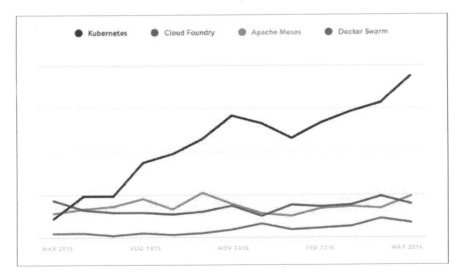

Ecosystem

The Kubernetes ecosystem is very impressive, from Cloud providers to PaaS platforms and startups that offer a streamlined environment.

Public Cloud providers

All the major Cloud providers support Kubernetes directly. Obviously, Google is leading the pack with GKE, which is the native container engine on the Google Cloud Platform. The Kops project, mentioned earlier, is a well supported, maintained, and documented solution on AWS. Azure offers Kubernetes as one of its backends to the Azure Container service.

OpenShift

OpenShift is RedHat's container application product that's built on top of the open source OpenShift origin, which is based on Kubernetes. OpenShift adds application lifecycle management and DevOps tooling on top of Kubernetes and contributes a lot to Kubernetes (such as autoscaling). This type of interaction is very healthy and encouraging.

OpenStack

OpenStack is the open source private Cloud platform and it is recently decided to standardize on Kubernetes as the underlying orchestration platform. This is a big deal because large enterprises that want to deploy across a mix of public and private Clouds will have a much better integration with Kubernetes Cloudfederation on one end and OpenStack as a private Cloud platform utilizing Kubernetes under the hood.

The latest OpenStack survey 2017 shows that Kubernetes is the most popular solution for container orchestration:

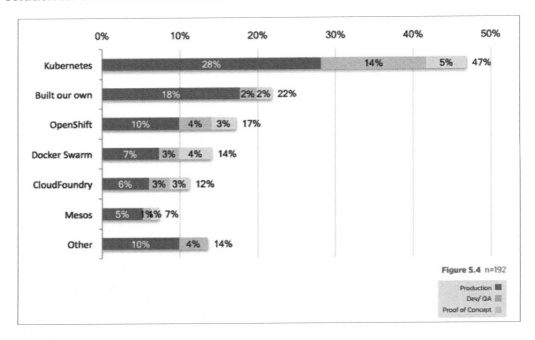

Figure 5.4 n=192

Other players

There are a number of other companies that use Kubernetes as a foundation, such as Rancher and Apprenda. A large number of startups develop add-ons and services that run inside the Kubernetes cluster. The future is bright.

Education and training

Education will be critical. As the early adopters of Kubernetes make way to the majority, it is very important to have the right resources for organizations and developers to pick up Kubernetes and be productive quickly. There are already some pretty good resources and in the future, I predict that the number and quality will just increase. Of course, the book you're reading right now is part of this drive.

The official Kubernetes documentation is getting better and better, but there is still a long way to go. The online tutorials are great for getting started.

Google has created a few Udacity courses on Kubernetes. Check them out here:

```
https://www.udacity.com/course/scalable-microservices-with-
kubernetes--ud615.
```

Another excellent resource is KataCoda, which provides a completely free Kubernetes playground, where you can get a private cluster within seconds, in addition to multiple hands-on tutorials on advanced topics:

```
https://www.katacoda.com/courses/kubernetes.
```

There are also a lot of paid training options for Kubernetes. As the popularity of Kubernetes grows even further, more and more options will be available.

Dynamic plugins

This one is not listed on any official roadmap. I plan to discuss it with the community, and if there is positive response, to start driving this effort forward.

Kubernetes is implemented using Go. Go is a great language that puts a lot of emphasis on simplicity. As such, one of its prominent features is the single executable binary. There is no separate runtime, and until Go 1.8 there were no dynamically loaded libraries. That approach is great in many situations. However, it is a hindrance for flexible and dynamically configured applications. Kubernetes is, of course, all about flexibility and plugins. But those plugins (with the exceptions of CNI plugins) must all be compiled into the Kubelet or the API server. CNI plugins are a different story and are deployed as separate executables, but that limits the interface for standard input and output. That works for CNI plugins because the API surface area is limited, but is not a good option for many more interactive plugins.

If, for some reason, the Go 1.8 dynamic plugins are inappropriate, another possible solution is to utilize the Go interface to C. By going through a C interface, it is possible to dynamically load Go plugins and have the best of both worlds: a stable Kubernetes platform where plugins that support well-defined interfaces can be loaded from carefully controlled directories without requiring the building and re-deployment of a whole Kubernetes API server or Kubelet. This is an important enabler as the Kubernetes usage moves into the mainstream, and as developers just want to deploy their applications and use third-party add-ons without building Kubernetes itself.

Summary

In this chapter, we looked at the future of Kubernetes, and it looks great! The technical foundation, the community, the broad support, and the momentum are all very impressive. Kubernetes is still young, but the pace of innovation and stabilization is very encouraging.

At this point, you should have a clear idea of where Kubernetes is right now and where it's going from here. You should be confident that Kubernetes is not just here to stay, but that it's going to be the leading container orchestration platform for many years to come and integrated with larger offering and environments.

Now it's up to you to use what you've learned and build amazing things with Kubernetes!

Index

66929049R00236

Made in the USA
Lexington, KY
28 August 2017